For: Patsy Kessinger Calloway

The Untold Story
&
New Information
From

Darrell's Perspective

A Confession, A Map, and A Cross

By: Tina M. Cummins

**Notes and Content
Contributions by: Darrell Kessinger**

Chapters:

True Crime Story - Character Guide:

1. **Patsy Kessinger-Calloway** – Mother of Alan, Tanya Cotrell and Shane Calloway; ex-wife of Larry Ray Calloway; missing person; murder victim.
2. **Darrell Kessinger** – Brother to the victim Patsy Kessinger-Calloway; military veteran; volunteer for the Jodi Powers Search and Rescue Technologies team; victim's advocate; contributor to the novels; personal investigator for his sister's case.
3. **Larry Ray Calloway** – Ex-husband of the victim, Patsy Kessinger Calloway; lover and eventual husband of Shirley Phelps Calloway; brother of Vernon Gene, Jimmy, Charlie, Mildred Calloway and Vicki Hoheimer; ex-brother-in-law of Debra Calloway; father of Tanya Cotrell and Larry Shane Calloway with Patsy, and four other children with Shirley Phelps Calloway; brother-in-law of Maryann Phelps; POI/Suspect.
4. **Vernon "Gene" Calloway** – Ex-Brother-in-law of Patsy Kessinger-Calloway; ex-husband of Debra Deese Calloway who stayed with him until his death; brother of Larry, Jimmy, Charlie, Mildred Calloway and Vicki Calloway Hoheimer; murder suspect (Deceased).
5. **Debra Calloway** Ex-wife and live-in lover of Vernon Gene Calloway until his death, sister-in-law of Patsy and Larry Calloway; murder suspect.
6. **Shirley Phelps Calloway** – child mistress and eventually 2nd wife of Larry Ray Calloway, sister of Maryann Phelps; daughter of Barbara Phelps.
7. **Jimmy Calloway** – Brother of Vernon Gene, Larry, Charlie, Mildred Calloway, and Vicki Hoheimer; eyewitness to Patsy's remains.
8. **Mildred Calloway Dunning, "Mill"** – Sister of Vernon Gene, Larry, Charlie, and Jimmy Calloway, and Vicki Calloway Hoheimer; witness.
9. **Vicki Calloway Hoheimer** – Sister of Vernon Gene, Larry, Charlie, Jimmy Calloway and Mildred Calloway.
10. **Tanya Cotrell** – Daughter of Patsy Calloway the victim, and Larry Calloway. Niece of Debra and Gene Calloway, the suspects of her mother's murder.
11. **Gary Fendel** – Ex-husband of Tanya Cotrell, witness.

12. **Shane Calloway** – Son of Patsy Calloway the victim, and son of Larry Calloway. nephew of Debra and Gene Calloway,
13. **Baby Boy Calloway**– First child of Larry Calloway and Shirley Phelps Calloway.
14. **Baby Girl Calloway**– Second child of Larry and Shirley Phelps Calloway.
15. **Ricky Calloway** – Son of Gene and Mary Calloway; Stepson of Debra Calloway; nephew of Patsy and Larry Calloway; witness.
16. **Angie Calloway** – Wife of Ricky Calloway.
17. **Maryann Phelps** – Sister of Shirley Calloway, witness, after the facts.
18. **Barbara Phelps** – Mother of Shirley Calloway; confrontation and fight with Patsy Calloway, the victim.
19. **Sharon Mattingly** – Friend of Barbara Phelps: confrontation and fight with Patsy Calloway, the victim, in May 1990.
20. **Detective Phillip Ballard** – Kentucky State Police 1st detective on the Patsy Calloway, missing person's case after the case was taken over by KSP; trial witness.
21. **Detective Bryan Whittaker** – Officer, Kentucky State Police, Post 16, Henderson, KY; Cold case detective; trial witness.
22. **Tim Coleman** – Prosecuting Attorney.
23. **Honorable Judge Ronnie Dortch** - Presiding judge over the murder trial and arson trials; Ronnie Dortch, who formerly served as the 38th Circuit Judge covering Butler, Edmonson, Ohio and Hancock counties.
24. **Andy Anderson** – Property owner, owner of media outlets around Ohio County, KY.
25. **Ben Anderson** – Property owner.
26. **Darrell Burton** – Property owner.
27. **Misty Gorby** – Witness for prosecution.
28. **Michael Hertzog** – Maintenance Supervisor, prosecution witness; employee at the nursing home
29. **Amy Hamilton** – niece of Gene Calloway, witness
30. **Employees at the Nursing and Rehab** – Cyndi Likens; Wanda Winkler; Phyllis Mudd; Patty D. Donald

Chapter One: Siblings

 Darrell Kessinger began a long and arduous journey to find out what happened to his missing sister, Patsy Calloway. It's taken him over 26 years to learn the true events surrounding her disappearance and murder. Patsy's untimely end gives the phrase "organized crime" new meaning. Her story is shared from Darrell's perspective.

Patsy Calloway

 One look at her face and you will see her soul. Patricia Ann Kessinger-Calloway (Patsy) was born on June 20th, 1954. She was a short-in-stature; thin; middle-aged woman; with short, black hair and a country smile. As a fun-loving, family woman who lived in the Midwest, Patsy was brimming with pride. She was the mother of three children, and a proud grandmother as well. Patsy's family and friends were her life. Her brother Darrell told me she had an obsession with Elvis Presley and thought he was the best thing next to sliced bread.   Taking care of her family and trying to make others happy was her whole world. Like many women who were born and raised in the hills, Patsy had her convictions, which were dictated by her beliefs in God; love; family; and the backwoods' tutorials of Kentucky.

I never knew Patsy, but judging only what I've heard, I'd say she was a very compassionate, and innocent woman. She could've been anyone's neighbor or friend. Her friends and co-workers described her as a gentle soul. Her brother Darrell said that she was very loving and kind, but equally, she was easily led. Darrell said she was a follower, because she trusted people too readily. She wasn't well-traveled, and so she spent her time, immersed in the traditions that the siblings grew up with. The most Patsy explored, was to visit her mom and other family members on trips to Arkansas. She didn't know much of the big world out there because Patsy grew up in a secluded region of Kentucky, away from world problems. The tiny town of Hartford, is just a smidge more than the dot on a map. It may be difficult for outsiders to understand that but each little town has its' own set of rules and Hartford is no exception.

Frequently, life in that isolated, country society is difficult. There's not much to do, so you live to work and take care of your family. You try to build a life with them, and the quintessential American dream. The pursuit of happiness doesn't mean you'll find it. Not every pastoral community is the quaint, picturesque image that we often see in our minds. We wish it could be as peaceful as those images portray. Sometimes, if you step outside of those small-town rules, it can land you in deep trouble. Darrell said, there's a sign that hangs on the entrance to town.

It reads, "**The Home of 2,000 Happy People and a Few Sore Heads.**" Today, the sign has been somewhat modified.

It's said that Patsy also had a stubborn streak about her. She could be outspoken at times or have no filter when something really bothered or angered her. The bottom line is, Patsy lived a straight life and tried to be a decent, hard-working woman. Putting up with nonsense, was not something she took lightly and she would speak out on things that upset her.

When it comes to having a family, many country girls from the hills get started young. Patsy Ann Kessinger married Larry Ray Calloway, when she was just a girl, at age 16. She had already had one child, a son Alan, previous to her marriage to Larry. Patsy stayed with Larry Ray Calloway for more than 20 years, even after they divorced. She believed in love and marriage to a fault, and parting only at death. In the Bible belt, divorce is looked down upon, even if the splitting parties have every good reason to leave their spouse.

The couple had two children together, Shane and Tanya. According to those who knew her, she treasured her family. She wanted nothing more, than her family; the simple, country life; and the house with the white picket fence. She wanted her and Larry to grow old together. That's what Patsy worked so hard to attain and thought she'd found. Still, everyone has their breaking point. Ultimately and most certainly, through no fault of her own, the marriage was doomed. You may agree with me that those mild, understanding, smiles can hide so much pain. By the time the end was near, it feels like everything inside of her mind was screaming for her to leave Larry and get out, but her heart hung on, as well as her Christian belief in marriage.

With no formal education or opportunity, her life and compassion led Patsy to a career as a medical assistant, in the local convalescent home. It was a small, local nursing facility that served the surrounding communities. She worked there for many years, with her friends and some family members, to help care for the elderly and disabled.

Patsy was described to me by her family as having very close relationships with her children and grandchildren. Her son Shane lived in a trailer with his girlfriend Marla, next door to his mom and dad. He saw his mom almost daily. Tanya said she spoke to her mother almost every day on the phone, even though she was grown; out of the house; and living in another state. She said her mom would call her, or vice versa, almost daily. Patsy was a medication aide/nursing assistant, and her daughter Tanya was following in her mother's footsteps. Now, working at a long-term care facility, Tanya wanted to share with her mom the new tasks she was learning on the job. Tanya said they'd talk about work, the grandkids, and all sorts of different things going on in their lives.

Her co-workers at the nursing home described Patsy as a hard-working, empathetic woman, who never forsook her duties on the job. They said she was very dedicated and was rarely late or rarely missed work. She took her job caring for the elderly and infirmed, very seriously. One of her nursing supervisors said it was rare for Patsy to ever leave work or miss work, and sometimes she would come in sick, even when she shouldn't.

Darrell Kessinger is Patsy's younger brother. He's retired from the U.S. Army and a war veteran. Darrell said that he and his sister were closer than close. They grew up together in Hartford with their siblings Sandra, Willard, and Theresa. Their parents divorced when he was a young boy and the two of them lived with their father and stepmother, along with the rest of the kids. Growing up in that environment was hard for them. They grew up very poor.

Darrell said he looked up to Patsy, his big sister, for support and guidance, but his stepmother was their primary caregiver. He said that Patsy was, for a long time, the "mother figure" in his life, and much more than a big sister. That's not to take anything away from their Mom Georgia, or their stepmom Phyllis. According to Darrell, he loved them both very deeply. However, Patsy was just a few years older than he was, and she often took care of him. With their mother Georgia not readily available, Patsy took on that role to her baby brother, so caring for people became her nature. It's who she was.

Patsy and Darrell grew up together as tight as siblings could be. Darrell said that every time Patsy would get excited or enthusiastic about something, she'd rub and twist her hands together in a wringing motion. She'd smile and shake a little bit, and then rub her hands back and forth.

Once grown, Patsy and her siblings talked on the phone when the opportunity presented, or visited each other in person. Darrell was a military lifer. For some time, he was away and deployed for the Army, in Operation Desert Storm, and stationed overseas.

Darrell, Patsy & Sandra
Old homestead, on Snow Hill

When the war ended in February 1991, Darrell was stationed in Mississippi with the Army Reserve. When he came back stateside to Mississippi, he'd spend time talking to Patsy on the phone, so they could catch up on everything in each other's lives.

Everyone that I've spoken to about Patsy said she was a very sweet, kind-hearted person. Ironically, her ex-husband Larry told me that he loved her. He said the very same things about Patsy. To my recollection of information I'd gathered, she'd get angry at her live-in ex-husband and threaten him, but those were empty words for the most part. She loved him and would do anything for him, even if that meant her demise, until finally, she'd had enough.

On **March 3rd, 1993**, Patsy Calloway, left her work at the Professional Care and Rehab Center in

Hartford KY, with her ex-brother-in-law, **Vernon Eugene Calloway**. According to eyewitnesses, she left the facility right around 10:30 a.m., give or take a few minutes. Normally, as stated by her co-workers, she'd never leave work unless there was a true emergency, because she took her job seriously. Since then, many reports have surfaced of Patsy being here or there, but none of them were credible and all were reported by her ex-husband Larry. She was 38-years-old at the time of her disappearance. No one has seen or heard from Patsy since that day. Her brother Darrell didn't learn of her disappearance until days later. No one had called him that day, or her mother.

Before she vanished, Patsy had revealed many things to Darrell on the phone, and so he had to find out what happened to her. Instantly he was suspicious and worried for her. He knew she wouldn't just up and leave and that something awful had to have happened to Patsy.

He and some family members, packed up and headed to Kentucky. It became Darrell's quest, or "mission in life," to find out the circumstances surrounding Patsy's disappearance and get justice for his sister. In his heart, he knew she was gone because he knew she would never abandon her family. Her love and bonds with all of them were stronger that steel. This is evidenced by her patterns of behavior with her husband Larry over the years. Patsy would never just "let go" of her children and grandchildren, or mother and siblings.

Calling My Brother

Going back a week prior to her disappearance, **February 26ᵗʰ, 1993**, Darrell spoke to his sister Patsy on the phone for the last time. This was a very intimate family call, to which the details would become paramount in the investigation. This phone call between the close siblings, was a true revelation of a chain of events, past and future. Patsy revealed all of her deepest secrets to Darrell.

For the purpose of her story, it's important that we remember the details of Darrell and Patsy's phone call. The siblings had a lot to catch up on, since they hadn't talked in a long time. Many things had happened to Patsy when he was gone for those few years for the Army and her circumstances had changed dramatically. First, they discussed Darrell being home, and the probability that he wouldn't return to the Middle East, ever again. Relieved, the conversation with Patsy turned into a discussion about Easter plans and Patsy buying dresses for her grand-daughter. Darrell said she was really excited about seeing her granddaughter Brooke, all dressed up for Easter. He said she was happy and the Easter dresses were hanging up in Patsy's closet, according to her. She couldn't wait to spend that time with her family.

Then, out of concern, Darrell asked Patsy about a fight she'd been in with some women, a couple of years earlier. He'd heard about this fist fight, from another family member. Darrell and Patsy discussed the assault. Darrell asked her if she'd had any more trouble out of Barbara Phelps or Sharon Mattingly, because they'd beat her up really badly. Patsy told her brother Darrell, the fight started over an affair her husband Larry had with a young girl. According to witnesses, while Larry was married to Patsy, he was sleeping with a teen mistress, Shirley Phelps. Even more shocking, Shirley was a friend to Patsy and Larry's daughter Tanya, and that's how Larry met the girl.

For years, Shirley would accompany them on various family outings like camping. According to Tanya and other witnesses, Larry was sleeping with Shirley at perhaps even as young as 12-13 years old, even though he was a middle-aged man and unbeknownst to Patsy. Patsy was clueless, that Larry was having sex with a child back then. Not to be a master of the obvious, but that's child molestation, even if it is consensual sex. Patsy was just a child when she married Larry, so it seems like a pattern had emerged from him.

This "affair" between Larry and Shirley went on for a few years, according to various witnesses, but still Patsy didn't know. During his marital affair, Larry had gotten the then-teenage mistress, Shirley, pregnant. Sadly, it's not that uncommon for a man to cheat on his wife and get another woman pregnant, but she was no fully grown woman. This "affair" continued without end. I have to ask myself, "How many young girls was Larry with?" He married Patsy at a very young age, and it appears he groomed and fathered a child with another underage girl. Was he not man enough to deal with grown women? Anyway...

Darrell was in Kuwait in 1990. That's when Patsy learned about the girl Shirley's, pregnancy and her messing with Larry. At this time, Shirley would've been

16 years old. She was seventeen in November 1990, when she delivered her first child that Larry fathered. Patsy relayed this notable event to Darrell on the phone, in February, 1993.

Back then, in May 1990, Patsy went after Shirley, to confront her and ask her about the affair and pregnancy. That's when the fight with Patsy ensued, against Shirley's mother Barbara Phelps, along with Barbara's best friend, Sharon Mattingly. So, Patsy was beaten by two grown women, who were defending the pregnant child, Shirley. This is an important fact that was discussed in this phone conversation Patsy had with her brother Darrell, about why all this drama started a few years earlier.

In May 1990, after the two women brutally assaulted Patsy, she left Kentucky that day. She was very distraught and went to her mother's house in Arkansas, to get away from her cheating husband. When family saw her beaten, they relayed the information to Darrell, which is the reason he questioned Patsy about the fight when he came home in '93. Witnesses said that Patsy showed up at her Mom's house, beaten to a bloody pulp.

At this point, Darrell wanted to know how Patsy handled all of this. He was shocked by the news. It had to be devastating for Patsy to learn that her husband got a teenaged girl pregnant, especially knowing the girl so well. She'd cared for Shirley in her home, on various occasions and on outings. So not only did she feel betrayed by her husband, but by Shirley, her daughter's friend, whom she'd been good to. On this phone call,

Patsy continued to discuss with Darrell, what followed that initial confrontation and assault.

Although angry and confused, Larry initially convinced Patsy to try to work it out with him, even though she was deeply hurt and ashamed of her husband. Patsy believed in the sanctity of marriage, and explained to her brother Darrell that she truly loved Larry. Larry claimed that he loved Patsy, not Shirley, but just made a mistake. Patsy didn't want her marriage to end and had been with him since she was a just child herself. She didn't know much about the affair, when it started, or how long it went on with Shirley. All she knew at that time, was that Larry got Shirley pregnant. She was explaining to Darrell her thought process. For most of us, that's shocking, but please remember, Patsy was just a teenager herself when she started seeing, and then married Larry. Back then, she didn't know any better.

Patsy struggled with her decision, but more than a year and a half after that fist fight, Patsy decided to finally end the marriage with Larry. She told Darrell that she had filed for this divorce on **March 3rd, 1992**, less than a year prior to this phone conversation with her brother. Keep that date in mind. The divorce was finalized on April 20th, 1992. However, Patsy chose to continue to live with Larry as man and wife in this tumultuous relationship... on the promise that Larry wouldn't see the young girl again. According to Patsy, Larry promised her the affair was over.

Catching Darrell up to the past events, we're now at the point where Patsy found out Shirley was pregnant for the second time! Simply put, even though he'd promised to stop seeing Shirley, Larry had continued the affair with his child-mistress. According to Patsy, Shirley was pregnant again. Larry told Patsy the affair was over, so Patsy was livid when she found out! She relayed this to Darrell in this specific **February 26th, 1993** telephone call, along with all the other information. She wasn't aware however, that the second child, had already been born, that prior October.

This information was very shocking for Darrell because Patsy and Larry had been together over twenty years. As if he wasn't stunned enough, Patsy shared another deep, dark secret with Darrell during that call. About a week after she made this phone call with Darrell, Patsy was gone. She disappeared on **March 3rd, 1993**, exactly one year to the day of her divorce filing from Larry. Learning this new dark secret and all of the other secrets, is partly why Darrell knew that Patsy didn't just get up and walk away from her life. Besides, she loved and adored her family! No. She wanted to be free from Larry Calloway for good, according to her own words. She was a fledgling bird that couldn't fly, no matter how desperately she wanted to. It was the final secret yet to come that clipped her wings, and stopped her mid-flight. What was this horrible secret she'd revealed to Darrell and how did it end up costing Patsy her life?

Chapter Two: More Calamities

In that same **February 26th, 1993** phone call with her brother Darrell, we have to go back in time again. The final secret to be revealed is that Patsy told Darrell, back in August 1991, the two Calloway brothers Larry and Gene, plotted to burn down her home for the insurance money. The payout was roughly $30,000. Patsy relayed this once vaulted, secret information to Darrell on the phone. This was the first time Darrell had ever heard about the arson. According to Patsy, Vernon "Gene" Calloway, Larry's brother, was promised $1000 to burn down Patsy's house.

The arson took place on **August 1st, 1991**, which is now a matter of court record. By 1993, Patsy was distraught, depressed, and extremely hurt over the affair and the arson. Yet still, she continued to live with her philandering husband, and according to her knowledge, Shirley was at that time, pregnant again. Since August 1991, prior to her disappearance, Patsy had used the arson information and threatened to turn Larry and his brother Gene in to police, if Larry continued to cheat on her, with his young mistress. She admitted to Darrell, that she'd held that arson over Larry's head, for a full year and a half.

I'm surmising that Larry tried to manipulate her into thinking that the teenager seduced him, and he was just being a dad to his new baby. I'm also wondering if Patsy didn't include threatening to turn Larry in for statutory rape, being that Shirley was just a child then. After all, Patsy wasn't a little girl anymore, but a middle-aged woman who could now, clearly see Larry's deceit and manipulation.

During the phone call with her brother Darrell, Patsy said she was absolutely leaving Larry for good. She said she was going to turn Larry and Gene in for the arson. She'd made up her mind. Darrell said he tried to talk Patsy out of going to the police. He told her he thought it was too dangerous. He said, "If it's over, it's over. Just let it go and walk away. That's dangerous! Just let it go!"

Darrell said that he tried his best to talk her out of going to the police. He said that Patsy was adamant about her plan and would not listen to him. She said to Darrell, "I don't care if I have to go to jail right along with them. I'm turning them in." Although she was unaware of the arson until it happened, Patsy was afraid she'd get in trouble for not calling it in to police in the first place. Darrell said he told her, "I don't see any good coming out of it," but he said, Patsy was very adamant about her intentions and was holding firm.

Darrell said that Patsy told him, "I don't care anymore. I'm still in love with Larry, and I have too much invested in our marriage and life together. If he doesn't stop seeing Shirley, I'm going to turn him in for the arson, even if it means, me going to jail." Darrell continued to plead with her not to do that, to no avail. He couldn't see how turning in the brothers would make Larry stay with Patsy. If anything, he felt it put her in extreme danger, but he couldn't get Patsy to understand his reasoning. She was emotionally wounded and very confused.

After discussing this for a while with Darrell, she eventually said, she was tired of Larry's nonsense and wanted to move on, because he wouldn't stop running around on her. She was still torn and heartbroken, but Patsy then said she wanted more out of life than a cheating husband. Darrell believes that the second pregnancy was the wake-up call for Patsy to leave him, because Larry was never going to change. She never got the chance to speak with the police. A week later, after they discussed it on the phone and she told Darrell of her plans, Patsy went missing.

I have to wonder about the arguments or conversations Patsy had with her then, live-in ex-husband Larry. The neighbors reported them having fierce arguments that week and hearing Larry screaming at her and threatening Patsy like never before. This was 1 ½ years after the arson had occurred, when Patsy went missing. That brings up other questions, but it definitely gives Larry motive for murder, as well as Larry's older brother, Gene.

In 1993, after learning that she was missing, and the fact she was still gone a week later, Darrell and his mother Georgia Ford and sister JoAnn, headed to Kentucky to try to find Patsy. Darrell suspected immediately that something sinister had happened. Once they arrived in Kentucky, Darrell set out to find what he could about the circumstances surrounding her disappearance.

Patsy and granddaughter Brooke

Darrell went to the police, only to find out that a missing person's report hadn't even been filed yet. This was more than a week after Patsy's disappearance! Why didn't Patsy's live-in ex-husband Larry, insist the police file a report? This alarmed me and set up red flags all over the place.

While in Kentucky, they started searching for Patsy. Every day and night, they were going out on searches. Darrell said that Larry would never go with him and his brother. He either stayed at the trailer and waited, or would call them after they left. Thinking back on this fact, he later found that very suspicious as well. Darrell said that Larry continuously called them and would tell him and his brother Willard Kessinger, that Patsy was seen in town, at a specific place. They'd drive there to see if it was her, but she'd never show up, or was never there in the first place. He said Larry had done this to them dozens of times, while they were searching for Patsy. He eventually found out that Gene, Larry's older brother, was the last person to see Patsy alive. But after Larry had lied to him so many times, he said that this is when he first knew for certain and started suspecting him of deeper involvement.

At first, he said he wanted to believe that Patsy walked away from her life, and told me Larry was trying to convince him of that the whole time they stayed in Kentucky. Darrell knew of the affair with Shirley, and that she'd had one baby with Larry because of the phone call with Patsy, but he said that Larry never mentioned a word about the other girl or his new child. Nor did Larry ever mention anything about the arson, or the second baby. Because of his suspicions, Darrell never questioned or said anything to Larry. He was also very confused and didn't want to believe that Larry would do something to hurt Patsy, even though he was a cheating husband and arsonist. Still, he suspected that he did.

After Patsy had vanished, Darrell kept a journal of what the various witnesses told him at that time. He went to Patsy's work and questioned some of her co-workers. He questioned her friends. He learned that no one at her workplace had been questioned by police yet! This shocked him, because by this time, it was weeks after her disappearance when he spoke to the nursing home workers. After going there, that's when Darrell learned that Patsy had left work with Gene Calloway, Larry's brother. This confused him even more because at that point, he was suspecting Larry of foul play.

He said that as soon as he'd leave Patsy's trailer to go to a meeting with police, Larry would stay at the trailer, but Gene would always show up to the secret meetings with the police. He said that Larry never went to the meetings with him. As a concerned live-in ex-husband, you'd think he'd insist on being a part of the meetings with police. At least, that was Darrell's thinking. That didn't happen, and that is a tell-tale sign to me, along with the fact that Larry didn't go with Darrell to search for Patsy, but once. That's not the normal behavior of a concerned person.

On his journey to Kentucky to find Patsy, Darrell conducted many interviews of Patsy's friends and co-workers. He spoke with family and the town's people. He met with police on various occasions. It was one of these occasions that would clinch in Darrell's mind, the person that caused Patsy's to vanish. Up until the moments prior, Darrell had suspicions that Larry Calloway was solely responsible for Patsy's disappearance.

Chapter Three: Confronting a Killer

How often in life does a person get the opportunity to confront their sister's murderer? Well, it happened, but from Darrell's perspective, he wished he'd done more. While at one of the secret police meetings, Gene Calloway was there. Darrell saw a bite mark on Gene's hand and he said, that's when he knew for certain, that Gene, Larry's brother, had killed Patsy. He said he instinctively knew it and wanted to kill him.

I asked Darrell about the bite mark. He said that Detective Phillip Ballard set up meetings with him and family to discuss Patsy's case. He told me that somehow, Gene Calloway would show up at every single meeting. At one of those meetings, Darrell said he saw the bite mark on Gene's hand and confronted him about it. Darrell's sister Theresa Kassinger and her husband Dustin were at that particular meeting. Darrell said that Dustin asked the detective, "Who is this Vernon Calloway that she was seen at the nursing home with? I heard he was over there that day." At that moment, Vernon "*Gene*" who was standing behind them said, "I am Vernon Calloway and I have a wife, and a girlfriend working there, and it's none of your fucking business." That's when Darrell jumped up off the counter and got in Gene's face and said, "If you had anything to do with the disappearance of Patsy, then that's my business!

He noticed the deep bite mark immediately on Gene's right had between the thumb and forefinger, because he had that hand up above his head, leaning against the wall. Darrell said he got in Gene Calloway's face and was screaming at him, "You've got a bite mark right there on your hand! Where did it come from? What did you do to my sister?!" Darrell said that's when Detective Ballard made Gene Calloway leave.

He said he asked Detective Ballard why he didn't arrest Gene. After Gene left, according to Darrell, Detective Ballard asked him, "Why do you think Gene's showing up to these meetings?" Darrell replied to the detective, "You're the detective, why don't you tell me? I'll tell you why he's here. He's here to cover his own tracks and make sure we're not onto him! You give me two weeks to cover up my tracks and I'll come here and commit any crime you want me to." According to Darrell, Detective Ballard replied, "I'm not gonna have you come down and criticize the way I handle an investigation. I'll lock you up!" Darrell said at that moment, he knew that Gene had done something to Patsy, because it was a clear bruised bite mark on his right hand and it was deep. He said he also felt like justice would never see the light of day, because of the way Ballard treated him after that. He later learned that Gene Calloway was left-handed.

Something was not right with that investigation or lack thereof. But why did the detective threaten Darrell and not Gene? Why wasn't Gene Calloway, named a suspect? Why was he allowed at those meetings? There has to be a reason. Why didn't the police go looking for Patsy for ten days? Why didn't they search Patsy's trailer? Darrell also goes on to say that the police never took pictures of the bite mark that was clearly visible on Gene's hand. In that moment, Darrell began to suspect police corruption. One can only speculate about this. I'm not saying it's true, but it's shocking and horrifying to say the very least.

The family meetings were supposed to be secret meetings. Darrell told me that only immediate family members were invited and those meetings included his sister and her husband only. Yet he said Vernon Gene Calloway showed up to every single meeting they had with Detective Ballard, and the detective never made him leave, until that specific confrontation. He said that he'd requested many times to have a new detective handle Patsy's case, but it didn't get shuffled off to another officer, until her case went cold. This is extremely suspicious to me or anyone looking at it. How would the murder suspect find out about secret meetings with a detective, if the only other person who knew about those meetings, was the detective? Someone had to leak it. The question is, who?

It wasn't until May 19th, 2016, that I found out that Darrell actually stayed in Patsy's trailer *with* Larry Calloway. I was like, "WOW!" Of course Larry was telling Gene about the meetings! At the time, Darrell didn't have the wherewithal to put all the puzzle pieces together, so he waffled between the two brothers guilt in his sister's case.

Darrell never considered at the time, the possibility of the two brothers working together. After all, who would do that? Most murders are only committed by a single person. Perhaps the police weren't going to tip their hand to Gene or Darrell for that matter, but Larry sure had reason to have Gene at the meetings. It didn't help that both brothers had worked for Detective Ballard in the past, in the tobacco fields. This left Darrell with the suspicion against the officer handling the case. He felt it was a huge conflict of interest. There are suspicious circumstances all around Patsy's disappearance. Because its small town America, it's not really suspicious that the men worked for Ballard at some point. Hartford is a town of two thousand people. However, it shouldn't be overlooked either.

Being that the police hadn't found Patsy, it was easy to keep Gene as a person of interest, instead of list him as a suspect. That's not an excuse for the detective. The rules of law change once someone is known as a "suspect." It's difficult to speculate and play armchair quarterback, but they didn't go looking for Patsy. They either knew of, or suspected Gene of foul play the whole time. It would be easier to just follow Gene or know where he was. I'm not making excuses for the way they handled her disappearance, and it is still suspicious to all of us for good reason. We'll get to that later. When Detective Ballard asked Darrell why he thought Gene was showing up at the meetings, perhaps he was trying to get Darrell to put two and two together, but I can't say for certain what the officer was thinking and didn't say. Darrell was in too much distress to add it all up.

Chapter Four: Darrell's Notes

(The following notes are from Darrell's personal files and journals that he'd kept initially, and over the years regarding Patsy's case.) Most of the notes were jotted down at the time, but some of them reflect the current situation as they are known today. I received these notes in December 2014, via email from Darrell. Some of the information is now

known to be fabricated, by people involved in the cover up of his sister's case. Much of the information is factual. We will discuss the information as it's laid out in various chapters.

1. _**1990 – October 17th**_ – *(Baby) Phelps is born to Larry and Shirley (Larry's mistress). Shirley's birthday is X/XX/1973. What's amazing about this story is, Larry would have been messing around with Shirley as far back as 1989. Larry was molesting Shirley at the age of 15 and perhaps even closer to 14 at the time of conception. This is a known fact, because it was mentioned in Phillip Ballard's affidavit, however, no rape charges were ever brought up against Larry Calloway at the time. Larry also fathered a 2nd child in 1992. I believe this was the straw that broke the camel's back and prompted Patsy to file for divorce on _March 3rd, 1992_. She disappears one year later on this exact same date. (DK)*

     Note: Shirley, was a juvenile at the time she conceived her 1st child with Larry and gave birth to, at age 17. Clearly, Darrell calculated the dates wrong. According to Tanya Cottrell (Larry and Patsy's oldest daughter) Shirley was one year older than her and was her close friend. She claims that Larry and Shirley were messing around when she was as young as 12-years-old. This would put Shirley's age at 12 or 13-years-old when she and this grown, middle-aged man started having sex. She stated that she witnessed them having sexual relations while they were on a camping trips. They were in a sleeping bag, in the same tent next to her, under the sleeping bag. This information was corroborated by other witnesses who knew them at that time. Seems many people around the town knew what was going on, but didn't care.

It makes me wonder how people can just let this man who is raping a child, just walk free! It's mind-boggling what some "accept" in country, backwoods society. Tanya was just a child herself and didn't know any better, but others certainly did. Tanya was also afraid to say anything because Larry was her father. What could she do? Nothing. Those facts put Patsy's daughter in a damn awful position!

In a recorded interview I did with Larry and Shirley Calloway in 2012, I questioned them about the affair. Larry claimed that Shirley was not a juvenile when they first started having sex. Shirley claimed that her first son was not Larry's, but in fact another man's child. Although I didn't believe there's any truth to that, they were willing to have Larry disclaim his son, because they were afraid Larry would be charged with statutory rape. They finally admitted this to me in a taped interview that I submitted to police.

In order to get Larry and Shirley to keep talking to me during the interview process, I had to reassure them over and over, that nobody was concerned with the affair they'd had, after they'd been married for so long and had four children together. Larry and Shirley knew they were being recorded at the time and agreed that they'd lied to cover up the fact that she was a juvenile when she got pregnant. Those taped conversations had been sent to KSP, post #16. I have to wonder if Larry and Shirley were trying to cover up motive for Patsy's disappearance as well. (TC)

2. _1990 - February 1993_ – _Darrell is activated for Federal service in Support of Operation Desert Storm. (DK)_

3. *1991 – May* – *Patsy is severely beaten up by Barbara Phelps and Sharon Mattingly because she was interfering in the relationship between Larry Calloway and Shirley Phelps. Barbara Phelps is the mother to Shirley. (DK)*

Note: Darrell said that he was in the service at the time and found out about the incident from other family members. It was actually May, 1990 when the assault occurred. He was off in military training at the time and getting ready to be deployed. (TC)

4. *1991 – June* – *Patsy, along with Tanya, Gary, Shane, and Marla, visit her mother in Atkins, Arkansas. (DK)*

Note: This was a vacation that Patsy took to visit her mother, along with her grown children and their significant others. It occurred during the last week of July, 1991, not June. Darrell's notes reflect the wrong month, as I had confirmed with other witnesses. (TC)

5. *1991 – June* – *Patsy receives 3 consecutive phone calls from Larry Calloway, telling her that he was going to have the house burned down. This has been confirmed by both my brother and my mother. (DK)*

Note: These calls took place while Patsy and others were still visiting her mother in Atkins, Arkansas, the day before the house was burned. One of these conversations was overheard by Mr. Gary Fendel, Larry and Patsy's future son-in-law. The call to Patsy from Larry, about him burning her house down, (or the arson on **August 1st, 1991**), is what prompted them to return to Hartford. When they got back to Kentucky, the

29

crime had been carried out, and the house was still smoldering. The other confirmation witnesses to the calls, are Georgia and Stephen Ford. (TC)

6. _1991 – June_ – _According to Patsy's brother, Steve Ford of Atkins, Arkansas, Patsy had packed enough clothes to stay for several days, and seemed unprepared to have to leave so urgently. According to Patsy's mother and brother, she left shortly back to Kentucky, after her last conversation with Larry. (DK)_

    Note: During an interview with Mr. Gary Fendel, (Tanya's, then-boyfriend) he told me that he'd overheard the argument, that Larry was planning on burning down their house. I later learned that the house was already burning by the time they left Arkansas to head back to Kentucky. (TC)

7. _1991 – June_ – _According to Patsy's brother Steve Ford, Patsy seemed shocked when she heard of Larry's plans, and she seemed clueless as to what was going to happen. (DK)_

    Note: I was told by Stephen Ford, Patsy's brother, that Patsy jumped up and grabbed her belongings to head back to Kentucky within minutes of speaking to Larry, because the house was already on fire. Patsy was in panic mode. This was the last conversation Patsy had with her then-husband Larry before heading back home. Steve said, "She grabbed everything she could and left Mom's house within five minutes." These conversations prove that Patsy was not aware of the plan in advance to burn her house. Before they left the house, the arson was already in progress. Her actions speak to the shock of the situation, not her knowledge of it before hand. Steve said she'd told Larry, "You're not going to burn down my house!" It was already too late. (TC)

8. *1991 – June* – *Gary Fendel, the boyfriend of Tanya, stated that the house was still smoldering when they arrived back in Hartford, KY, the following morning. (DK)*

   Note: Again, the arson actually took place on **August 1st, 1991**. Darrell wasn't aware of the factual date at the time, because he was in Kuwait when they burned the house. He'd written down what he'd inquired about to Patsy and other witnesses. Mr. Gary Fendel confirmed this during our interview. He stated to me, he told his girlfriend Tanya on the way back to Kentucky that, "They would have no home to go home to." He said he told her that, because he'd overheard the argument Patsy had with Larry.

   Commentary: The arson was probably that tell-tale warning from Larry to Patsy, to just stay at her mother's house or end up dead. It could've been her "out." Was the arson the starting point to getting rid of Patsy? It seems Larry's crimes were escalating. Why would Larry call Patsy, and tell her of his plans to have the house burned down for the insurance money? Was he hoping that Patsy would just stay at her mother's house with their daughter Tanya? Was it a warning? That's what I suspect. (TC)

9. *1991 – June – Arson* – *It is alleged that Larry Calloway agrees to pay his brother Gene Calloway, $1000 of the insurance money, for his part in burning down the house. (DK)*

31

Note: Darrell initially had the date of the arson wrong. After Patsy's disappearance in 1993, Larry Calloway turned himself into the police for the arson. The brothers were later indicted. Larry claimed he did this because he wanted to find Patsy.

Commentary: What did turning himself in to police for the arson, have anything to do with finding Patsy, other than to point the finger at his brother, Gene Calloway? Was Larry feeling guilty because he knew Patsy was dead over his actions? I don't think he feels remorse. I believe he knew he was caught. Darrell believes he did this because he already knew he was caught for the arson as well. Perhaps he did it to change law enforcement's focus. Darrell claims it had nothing to do with him wanting to find Patsy, and that Larry turned himself in, simply to get a shorter sentence. He said that evidence and items from the arson had turned up and Larry knew he was going to be prosecuted.

During one of my interviews with an investigator, I was told that items from the arson case appeared a full year or better, after Larry had turned himself in. I don't believe that. Some items may have turned up a year later, but Darrell claims items like jewelry showed up prior to Larry turning himself over to police, as told to him by certain family members. However, Larry was convicted in court for the arson because of his guilty plea and plea bargain agreement. His brother Gene was acquitted in 1996, three years after Patsy's disappearance, and five years after the arson. The brothers pitted themselves against one another during the arson trials. According to Darrell, it was a three-ring circus. It was hard pill to swallow for Darrell that Gene just walked free from everything, being that he suspected Gene of killing Patsy, over the arson.

The Divorce
Going back in time again:

10.   <u>1992 – March 3rd</u> – *Patsy files for divorce from Larry Calloway. Larry deeds the trailer and property over to Patsy on this same day. I believe this is also the day that the wheels go into motion to kill Patsy. (DK)*

Note: After learning of the birth of the 1st baby Larry and Shirley had together, Patsy filed for divorce on March 3rd, 1992. On the day she filed for divorce in '92, Larry deeded the remainder of the couple's shared property over to Patsy.

Commentary: Before they went to court for the divorce proceedings, did Patsy blackmail Larry for the remaining property over the affair with the young girl, or for the arson he and Gene committed? One could deduce that it was both. Larry didn't wait for a divorce hearing, he just signed the property over to her on the day she filed. We already know she was threatening him over the arson.

Let's talk about that situation. It was seven months after her house was burned that Patsy filed for divorce. How could she prove that an arson was even committed, even if they suspected it all along? The insurance monies were already paid out. It would be her word against Larry's. It would certainly make Gene fearful of incarceration, but Larry was smarter than that. The evidence was destroyed from weather after that long. It doesn't stand to reason that the arson was the only reason Patsy disappeared. Arson would be hard to prove, which is evidenced by the fact that Gene was eventually acquitted. Larry turned himself in and took a plea and the court admits if he hadn't done so, no charges would've ever been filed against the brothers.

Witnesses say that Larry and Shirley Phelps blew through the insurance money on furniture and other lavish stuff after Patsy's house burned. It was Patsy's house too! After that, Patsy got a loan for her trailer, in her name only. She didn't gamble or go on any lavish vacations, so we know she didn't reap the benefits of the insurance money.

We still don't know if Larry was truly living with Patsy at the time of her disappearance. During an interview that I did with him, Larry said he was staying with Shirley and Patsy both. He's lied about so many things. Did Patsy make him move out of the trailer before she vanished? She told Darrell she was absolutely done with him! Did he have a set of house keys, or did he get Patsy's keys when she disappeared? We don't know. The neighbors heard them fiercely arguing and Larry threatening her just before she disappeared. Darrell's last phone conversation with Patsy took place a week prior to that, so she could've already kicked him out of her trailer.

Darrell believes a plot to kill Patsy took place a full-year prior to her disappearance, on or around March 3rd, 1992, the day she filed for divorce. After she vanished, Darrell went to the county clerk's office and had all of Patsy's records printed out. She disappeared exactly one year later, to the day of her divorce filing. When he saw the records, that's how Darrell discovered that fact. He was stunned! He then turned the information over to police. He believes that Larry Calloway wanted revenge, for Patsy getting the remaining property and filing for divorce. I believe he wanted revenge for Patsy blackmailing him and getting the property, because for him, divorce wasn't good enough. Patsy was blackmailing him in order to make him stay put. She would always have those "secrets" over Larry's head, of the arson and child molestation. I believe he wanted Patsy dead.

Perhaps the plan started when Larry found out that Shirley was pregnant for the second time. Evidently, the relationship between them, had come to a boiling point. Any way you look at it, Larry had an enormous amount of motive for wanting Patsy gone. In domestic violence situations, it is usually the most dangerous time, when the victimized spouse decides to leave the relationship, and Patsy wasn't going to leave quietly. The toxicity of their relationship had reached its peak between Patsy and Larry. It makes the most sense that Larry specifically chose the anniversary of the divorce filing date, for her to disappear. That way, the brothers could point the finger at one another if anyone asked questions. This was no coincidence. She held his freedom in her decisions. Either way, the plot to be rid of her came together, long before she actually disappeared.

It was Patsy's habit to go to her mother's house in Arkansas when things were bad between her and Larry. She went to her Mom's when she was beaten up. She went to her Mom's to visit when her house was being burned down. She went on various other occasions when things were rough between her and

Larry. She always went home to her momma. But this time when things were at their worst with Larry, Patsy stayed in Kentucky at her own trailer. She didn't have to go home to Mom.

It makes sense that she would tell Larry to get out. It was *her* trailer that she got a loan for after the divorce, so he would have to go! He'd already paid Gene to burn their house prior to the divorce. He was on his way out the door and out of that relationship, but with her blackmailing him, he had motive to act.

According to different witnesses, Larry's brother Gene said, he'd cut Patsy's throat before going back to prison again. Everyone that I spoke with described Gene as a madman, with an evil streak and a horrible temper. Someone had to tell Gene that Patsy was making threats to turn them in. It was Larry no doubt. Who else would know? Since Larry turned himself in to police for the arson, one can easily see, that he was pointing the finger towards his brother, and trying to get a lesser sentence for the arson. Larry was tying up loose ends.

11. *1992 – April 20th – The divorce is finalized. (DK)*

Commentary: Although he continued to live with Patsy, that didn't stop Larry from wanting to be with Shirley, his young-lover/future bride. In one recorded interview I did with Larry, he claimed that he was in love with both women and didn't know what to do. Was that Larry's way of telling me he had no way out? Was that his excuse? Probably.

Darrell said during the arson trial, Charlie Calloway testified and pointed the finger at his brother Gene. That was the first time Charlie's name was ever brought up to me. Up to this point, Darrell had no clue that Charlie Calloway was involved in the arson, or how he was involved. Darrell called it a kangaroo court. He said the three brothers stood there pointing fingers at one another. He said, when he and his brother Willard walked out of that courtroom, they looked at each other and said, "What just happened? What was that?" He said they couldn't believe it.

In a nutshell, Larry got up there and said he'd paid Gene $1000 to burn the house down. Then when Gene got on the stand and they asked Gene "why do you think your brother would say that about you?" He replied, "Because he thinks I had something to do with the disappearance of his wife." Judge Ronnie Dortch intervened and said, "That won't be mentioned again in this trial." Charlie Calloway testified that Gene had bragged to him and was gritting his teeth saying, "He could burn it down and nobody would ever know how it was done." In our opinions, it's the same thing with how they set up Patsy's disappearance, so the individual brothers look guilty, leaving everyone scratching their heads. This also puts a cloud of suspicion over Charlie Calloway's head, regarding his position in Patsy's case. (TC)

12. 1992 – *Renee is born, this would be the 2nd of 4 children that Larry and Shirley have. (DK)*

Note: As stated before, Patsy was unaware at the time of her phone call with Darrell, of the birth of the 2nd child Larry fathered with Shirley. Patsy didn't find out about the pregnancy itself, until February, 1993, shortly before her disappearance. Up to this point, Larry Calloway claimed he was still living with Patsy and going on with his affair with the girl. In the recorded interview I did with Larry Ray Calloway, he admits this fact. He said that he was stringing both women along and lying to both of them. (TC)

What Happened to Patsy?

So what did actually happen to Patsy Calloway? The short, disheartening answer is that she was kidnapped, murdered, and her body has never been recovered. The long answer is a very twisted, unprecedented truth about a family, who plotted to kill an ex-family member. Never in history has a case like this been reported until now, with so many family members involved with the exception of organized crime. Darrell wasn't going to stop searching until he'd found the whole truth. On his trips to Kentucky, Darrell found out information, that proves a thick murder plot and premeditation in his sister's kidnapping and murder.

13. _1993 – February 22nd_ – _Larry and Shirley file for a marriage license in Davies County in Owensboro, Kentucky. (DK)_

Note: On **March 3rd, 1993**, Patricia Ann Kessinger Calloway, left her work at 10:38 a.m., never to be seen again. Her ex-brother-in-law Gene, showed up at Patsy's work. According to eye-witnesses that knew Gene, he was seen talking with Patsy and waving around a newspaper that contained a marriage license announcement for Larry Calloway and Shirley Phelps. An argument ensued between Gene and Patsy. Patsy told her boss that there is an emergency; she would explain later; and she had to leave. Vernon Gene Calloway was the last person to be seen with Patsy before her disappearance.

Darrell learned of this and other facts on his visit to Kentucky, when he was inquiring about the circumstances surrounding his sister's disappearance. He questioned everyone that knew anything about Patsy's disappearance; possible whereabouts; or ongoing things in her life. Darrell was the investigator, because up to that point, the police had done little to nothing. He even researched and gained access to the wedding announcement. I confirmed the actual filing date, nineteen years later.

Commentary: That marriage announcement was placed, only four days before Darrell and Patsy's last phone call. This further strengthens my theory that Larry is lying, and planning to be rid of Patsy. Even if Larry did overhear the conversation between Patsy and Darrell, that call certainly wasn't the catalyst for her murder. The fact that the newspaper announcement was placed days before the call, bolsters the opinion that her murder was planned prior to that call, but it doesn't mean Larry didn't overhear it. Perhaps this is what sparked the fierce arguments overheard by neighbors of Patsy and Larry.

By this time, Shirley was an adult. Shirley would've been almost 20 years old. If Larry *was* still living with Patsy and loved her like he claimed, why did he get a marriage license with another woman? Darrell said that one could only speculate that he was getting a lot of flak and pressure from both women.

My question is, "Why would Gene be carrying around a newspaper from another county that he didn't live in?" He lived in Ohio County. I now know, after interviewing many people, that Gene Calloway was nearly illiterate. This fact stuck out to me. He could barely write, but everyone I'd spoken to about this, claims that Gene was illiterate and could barely read anything. I doubt seriously that he'd just come across this newspaper by happenstance and see a marriage license announcement, regarding his brother Larry and Larry's mistress Shirley. That newspaper was from another county! No. That was planned in advance. Gene had to know that the announcement was going to be put in the paper. Someone had to give it to him and point it out to him to use as bait for Patsy.

Let's discuss this marriage license. Larry told me in a recorded interview, that his getting a marriage license meant "nothing," and that he'd gotten one with Shirley before. I believe that he's lying. The newspaper, nor the clerk's office had no record of them ever procuring one before that. If he wasn't planning on leaving Patsy, why get a marriage license and burn her house down prior? If he wasn't going to use the marriage license, why get it in the first place? Patsy had him trapped, because if he just left her, she would send him to prison. He claimed the license was to string Shirley along. If he was just stringing her along, why did he have four children with her and eventually marry her?

This strengthens my theory that filing for the marriage license was part of the murder plot. After all, Gene used this marriage announcement to lure Patsy out of her work. We'll delve into that facet later. It's too much of a coincidence that Larry and Shirley filed for the marriage license, right after Patsy found out that Shirley was pregnant for the second time. And Gene, this illiterate man, just happened to see it in the paper. He all of the sudden decides to use the announcement to lure Patsy out of the nursing home? I don't believe that for a second! The man could barely read or write according to his own family members! I can't see him buying an out-of-town newspaper, let alone, that specific one and just "finding" a wedding announcement. This was no serendipitous coincidence for Gene.

According to his ex-wife Mary, Patsy couldn't stand Gene and wouldn't leave with him normally on her own, under any circumstances, as also reported by her friends, family, and co-workers. Something set her off.

14. _1993 – February 22_nd – _Marriage license is never used according to the Clerk's Office in Owensboro, Kentucky. (DK)_

Commentary: Perhaps they didn't expect anyone to come looking for Patsy after her disappearance, or for anyone to poke into the case. Larry thought that Darrell was deployed at the time Patsy went missing. He'd just returned home. An official missing person's report wasn't completed until the day Darrell and his Mom showed up in Kentucky, 10 days after Patsy went missing! The puzzle is all starting to fit.

Note: Darrell said that Officer Elvis Doolin told him that they believed, that Patsy was just distraught and walking away from her life and problems with Larry, because that's the story the Calloway family was telling them.

15. *1993 – February 26th – Patsy and I talk on the phone (– I have submitted an affidavit to Bryan Whittaker with the context of this conversation.) At this time Patsy must not have been aware of Larry's intentions to marry Shirley, because it was never mentioned during the course of our conversation. (DK)*

Note: The submission of Darrell's affidavit to Detective Bryan Whittaker took place after the detective took over Patsy's case, and her case went cold. From the beginning, the other detectives refused to take Darrell's statements at all, according to him. They'd refused him or any information he had. They didn't want to hear about Darrell's phone call with his sister or the affairs of Larry Calloway. They felt it had no bearing on the case, according to Darrell.

Commentary: Detective Whittaker, KSP cold case detective, had to start from almost scratch when he took on Patsy's case, many years after her disappearance in 2002. He was the *only* one who would listen to Darrell, and even *they* butted heads a few times. Whittaker had to do most of the leg work that hadn't been done initially by police. It was clearly, a botched investigation from the beginning, but what Darrell wants to know is if it was botched on purpose by those officers who initially had the case. (TC)

16. *1993 – Week of March 3rd, 1993 – The wedding announcement is posted in the Messenger Inquirer out of Owensboro, Kentucky. (DK)*

Commentary: This marriage announcement was the incendiary device that got Patsy to leave the nursing home with Gene. From Larry's perspective, it certainly had nothing to do with the arson. She'd kept that secret for a year and a half, by the time of her disappearance. It may have been enough to convince Gene to do the dirty work for Larry. Gene also wanted to get rid of Patsy because of the looming thought of prison, but how did he know the marriage announcement would make her upset enough to leave work with him and go confront Larry? Larry's the one that put it in the paper. He knew his ex-wife and exactly what buttons to push.

I believe that Larry made Gene aware of what needed to be done with that announcement. Again, it stands to reason that the arson wasn't the only threat Patsy made to Larry. If Larry was going to marry Shirley, Patsy's accusations of statutory rape would be null and void. The courts wouldn't give a damn, and no way would Shirley testify against Larry. Of course Patsy in her anger and hurt, would care. She was desperately trying to keep her family together and she'd have nothing left to use to hold over Larry, except an arson that she may or may not be able to prove. So time was of the essence and she had to go to the police quickly, without haste. At this point, it seems a hurricane is coming.

Chapter Five: The Timeline

17. <u>**1993** – **March** 3rd</u> – *According to eyewitnesses, Gene Calloway takes the Messenger Inquirer with the marriage* *announcement to Patsy's workplace. Patsy goes outside and talks to Gene – Patsy comes back inside very upset and explains to her supervisor that she has an emergency at home, and she needs to leave, and she needs to leave right now, and that she would explain the next day. Patsy was reported leaving the nursing home at 10:30 a.m. that morning. This information is mentioned being reported by Dan McEnroe in the March 19th edition of the Messenger Inquirer. More to follow. (DK)* (Dan McEnroe was a local police officer.)

Note: Darrell said that he never met or talked to Officer Dan McEnroe. He said that the officer he spoke with at that time, regarding Patsy's case was Elvis Doolin and he's the *only* officer he spoke with at the Hartford, KY police department, before the Kentucky State Police took over the case.

Commentary: Our theory is: The brothers plotted the arson together so why not plan Patsy's murder together? The brothers were thick as thieves. It's never heard of in families to do this, with the exception of organized crime. I've been told that, "People don't commit murders together as a family." In light of the recent trials in Kentucky, I think they'd better rethink their position on that. If nothing else, those specific Calloway brothers were organized criminals, working in tandem, just as Darrell claimed they were. (TC)

18. 1993 – **March 3**rd – *Patsy is seen leaving the Professional Care Home with Gene Calloway in his black, 1978 Chevy Blazer. And her whereabouts are never known after this day. It is my belief that more was said than just Patsy looking at the wedding announcement in the newspaper. It is my belief that Gene must have said something to the effect that Larry was with Shirley at Patsy's house. Patsy clearly indicated that she had a problem at home. This would surely be enough to upset*

44

Patsy to the point that she was not thinking rationally. Patsy's prior comments give no indication other than she had an emergency at home and that is where she was headed. (DK)

19. _1993 – **March 3**[rd]_ – *Debbie Calloway is seen walking down highway 231 in the direction of Beaver Dam, Kentucky, dressed up like Patsy. At a later date this same wig is given to Gene's sister Vickie Hoheimer by Debbie Calloway to dispose of. This story was reported to the police by Vickie, according to her. Vickie also told me the same story that Debbie Calloway had given her the wig in a Walmart bag to dispose of, but later retracts this statement. (DK)*

    Note: Up to this point, **Debra Calloway's** name was never mentioned in regard to Patsy's disappearance. On the day Patsy went missing, Debra Calloway (Gene's then girlfriend) was seen dressed in a nurse's uniform, coat like Patsy's, and wig like Patsy's hair. She was walking south, toward Beaver Dam, KY. So Patsy was lured from the nursing home by Gene Calloway, while Gene's then girlfriend, Debbie, was out pretending to be Patsy! She was seen walking about 2:30 p.m., according to her ex-sister-in-law, Mildred Calloway Dunning. According to Darrell's conversation with Vicki Hoheimer, another Calloway sister, she was asked to dispose of the wig by Debbie, Gene's wife. This is confirmed, by Facebook texts sent back and forth between Darrell and Vicki, and I've obtained copies of them. Now she's changing her story.

    Commentary: Why would Vicki change her story? According to Darrell, Vicki is physically ill and wants no part of any of this. Why would Debra Calloway dress up like Patsy? Let's discuss this fact...

Just like the arson was pre-planned, I believe that the wedding announcement was strategically placed in the paper, because the plot to kill Patsy was already in motion. After all, Debra and Gene had to purchase a wig, uniform, and coat, in order for her to dress up like Patsy and go walking through Hartford to Beaver Dam, unless it was Patsy's stuff she was wearing, minus the wig.

If the wedding announcement wasn't part of the plan, why did they purchase the items for Debbie to dress up like Patsy? Other important details of that fateful day have emerged. So the idea that her murder was a spur of the moment act committed only by Gene Calloway and Debra, doesn't fit with what happened. It was a well-thought-out, pre-planned and carried out, kidnapping and murder. Question is, was Larry Calloway, Patsy's ex-husband, the mastermind? I believe he was. Darrell concurs and states that Larry was the mastermind behind the arson. He asks, "Why not the murder as well?" (TC)

At this moment in time and just because these things are coming to light, still doesn't convince me completely of my theories. More has to be known and information out there about Patsy's disappearance. The new information we have, points to more than three people involved in Patsy's disappearance now. It's a matter of the process of elimination... well, sort of. We'll get back to that.

Patsy's Car?   Darrell's Notes Continued...

20. _**1993** – **March 3**_rd _– Patsy's vehicle is discovered around 5:00 p.m. parked by the Community Center in downtown_

Hartford. There are several conflicting stories that have surfaced about the whereabouts of the keys and who found the vehicle. One story indicates that the keys were found in the ignition by Patsy's son and his wife Marla. Larry Calloway's story is they were found under the front seat, and he is the one that found the car. I was also told that the keys were never found until Gene later showed up, then they were discovered under the front seat. This was supposed to all taken place after Larry Calloway had searched the car and went to the police and was told to go back and look again and bring the car to the police station. It is very suspicious that it would be Patsy's husband that would find the car. The big question here – who drove the car there and parked it. According to Larry the seat had been scooted back. (DK)

Note: On the day Patsy Calloway left the nursing home with Gene, his brother Larry Calloway showed up at the police station to report Patsy as missing, shortly after noon that day. He said that Shirley's sister, Maryann Phelps, came to Shirley's apartment and told them Patsy left work with Gene. He told me in an interview that he'd been at Shirley's apartment all morning. He said that when Maryann came over there and told him Patsy had left with Gene, that he went by Patsy's work and didn't see her car. He said, he went straight to the police!

Commentary: Why would Larry go directly to the police to report her missing at 12:15 p.m. that day? This was according to Larry! If he didn't know in advance, that something was going to happen to Patsy, why would he go to the police at all? He didn't file a missing person's report. Larry said the police told him to go find Patsy's car. They said if he found the car, to bring it to them. As strange as that sounds, it's true. That said, we know Patsy left with Gene in his truck, so who would drive Patsy's car? Was it Debbie or Larry, or perhaps someone else?

The police told Larry, Patsy's ex-husband, if he finds the car, bring it to the station. I confirmed that with the lead detective! According to him, the police thought she may have just been angry at her husband and left to cool off. First of all, Larry was her ex-husband! Huge Red flags! She'd only left the nursing home with Gene at 10:38 a.m. that morning, so why would anyone assume she was missing!? According to what I was told, the police figured she'd gone somewhere for a few days and would return. I later found out, that was the agenda that the Calloway's were pushing to the police. (TC)

21. *1993 – March 3ʳᵈ – March 6ᵗʰ – This is the first story I was told – Gene takes Patsy's body upon Snow Hill and ask Jimmy Calloway (Gene's brother) to help him with something. When Gene opens up the hatch to his Chevy Blazer, Jimmy sees Patsy lifeless body in the back with her throat cut and says he wants no part of it. (DK)*

Note: Darrell told me, he later learned that Gene Calloway was up on Andy Anderson's farm a little more than a week prior to Patsy's disappearance. He was seen by a witness digging a hole and when asked what he was doing, he said he was digging for worms. Although the witness couldn't remember the precise location of the hole that was dug, they know the vicinity. During a search in May, 2016, Darrell learned that the person actually saw what appeared to be a gravesite. We have that witness's identity and statement, yet Patsy's remains have yet to be recovered. The farm is huge and has a partial forest on it; a large pond; and a river that runs around it. It has been searched many times.

Darrell said he'd checked the weather history for the weeks prior to her disappearance, and the temperatures were well below freezing. The ground would've been solid and very difficult to dig up. It would take some time and effort. The grave would've had to have been dug well in advance of Patsy's disappearance, because of the deep freeze that hit the area. Darrell stated that he was "stuck in Kentucky at the time because his radiator froze up." This again, goes to premeditation. Darrell said that it was the Superstorm of 1993, when the deep freeze hit KY.

22. *1993 – March 3rd – March 6th – This is another version of the same sequence of events. According to Jimmy Calloway he see's Gene and Debra Calloway cleaning out his Chevy Blazer at Hunter's trailer court. According to Jimmy, neither Gene nor Debbie are aware that he is he is there. Jimmy states that he sees a black trash bag in the back of Gene's Blazer, being curious Jimmy feels along the bag and describes what feels to be a shoulder and follows the bag down to the point where he feels what he believes to be a head. Jimmy states that he rips the trash bag open and he can see that it is Patsy inside. Jimmy describes seeing Patsy lying on her left side with one eye still open and that her windpipe had been cut. I have some suspicion about this story, how do you do all of this and never be noticed. (DK)*

Note: Years after Patsy's disappearance, in 2012, brothers Jimmy and Larry Calloway met up with Darrell Kessinger at the Hartford Community Center where Patsy's car was located. Jimmy Calloway admitted to seeing Patsy's body in the back of their brother Gene's 1978 Chevy Blazer, at Hunter's trailer court. Darrell's notes on the matter reflect that conversation in 2012, but he'd heard that Gene had cut Patsy's throat years earlier. Darrell met with Larry and Jimmy shortly before any arrests were made, and Jimmy confirmed seeing Patsy's lifeless body in the back of Gene's truck, but wouldn't go into much detail.

Note: The police had an eye-witness to the deceased body of Patsy, but nobody was arrested until 2012. Jimmy Calloway stated he told local police that he'd seen Patsy's body, from **the very first day Patsy went missing to Hartford police officer Dan McEnroe**. According to him, the police ignored his report, just like they ignored Darrell's reports of his phone call with Patsy. Jimmy Calloway said they just didn't believe him. I think something more sinister is going on in Hartford P.D.

Commentary: This still amazes me. If he told police this the first day Patsy went missing, why then, was there no arrest made? Why didn't anyone go to Gene's house which was blocks away and say "Hey, we've got a report of a body in the back of your truck?" This fact leaves many questions about the police who handled this matter initially. There was no record of Larry Calloway ever going to the police that day. There was no record of Jimmy Calloway going to police that day. Apparently the file on Patsy was merely backtracking and retracing done by the cold case officer. No missing person's report was filed until Darrell came to town. From what I know now, there was no record of Larry Calloway showing up at the Hartford PD, even though the police confirmed that he showed up three times on the day Patsy disappeared. Seems like a lot of information was never taken seriously, written down, or recorded on Patsy's case with law enforcement. This is reprehensible!

In the first novel I wrote about Patsy's case, **An Arson, A Wig, and A Murder**, I discuss how we came to the conclusion that Jimmy saw Patsy's body in the back of the truck on the day she was murdered, even before he admitted it to the court. After weighing all the facts, I believe Jimmy Calloway, especially, because Darrell had that confrontation with Gene Calloway in front of Detective Ballard, over the bite mark on Gene's hand. Jimmy isn't going to turn his own brother into police for murder, unless it's true!

Gene was in fact, the original suspect after Whittaker took over the case, and Phillip Ballard, the original KSP detective, did allow Gene to attend the secret meetings, even though he wasn't supposed to be there. Jimmy Calloway is known to be a little slow and has a speech impediment. Both Darrell and I were told that Jimmy's testimony wouldn't hold up in court. Was it because of his mental status? I can't say for the sake of certainty.

You have this man, Larry Calloway, come into the police department and report his "supposed" live-in ex-wife missing, around noon. Then, you have the brother go to police on the very same day, reporting that he saw Patsy's body in the back of his brother's truck with her throat cut. The police officers didn't feel the need to investigate? They claim that they thought Patsy just walked away from her life with Larry? I'm calling **BULLSHIT!**

Currently, certain officers would like to shut me up, leaving me to fear for my safety. Yet they don't want anyone to question their actions surrounding this kidnapping and murder investigation? I'm not buying it. I'm not pointing my finger at the detectives who investigated and helped with prosecuting the case, but those who handled it or should I say didn't handle it, initially. The cold case detective Brian Whittaker did his job well, especially considering it took nineteen years to prosecute this case and so many people covered it up. It appears to us that he was one of the few officers who wanted it solved. (TC)

Timeline:

May 1990, After Patsy learns that her husband Larry is cheating on her, she's confronts Shirley Phelps. She's physically assaulted by Barbara Phelps and Sharon Mattingly for confronting Shirley who was pregnant. This fact helps establish the affair between Larry Calloway and Shirley Phelps.

November 1990, Nicholas was born to Shirley Phelps and Larry Calloway. This was the first child the two had together, despite the fact that Larry was married to and living with his wife Patsy.

July 31st, 1991, Gary Fendel (Tanya's boyfriend) stated he overheard an argument between Patsy and Larry, in which Patsy tells Larry not to burn down her house.

August 1st, 1991, Two brothers Calloway committed the arson plot, and Vernon Gene Calloway burned down Patsy's house, according to their pre-arranged plan, while she was visiting with her mother in Arkansas.

August 1991, Patsy begins threatening Larry over the arson to keep him from leaving her for the other woman/girl, Shirley.

March 3rd, 1992, Fed up with his cheating, Patsy filed for divorce from Larry Ray Calloway. The same day she filed for divorce, he deeded the remainder of their property over to Patsy, which was a probable payoff to keep silent about the arson.

April 20ᵗʰ, 1992, Divorce between Larry and Patsy Kessinger Calloway was finalized, yet they continued to live together as man and wife.

October, 1992, Ruby Renee Calloway was born.

At this time, Patsy and Larry were still living together although he was seeing the young girl, Shirley, who'd had two of his children. Patsy was unaware of the birth of the 2ⁿᵈ child.

February 1993, Patsy learns of the 2ⁿᵈ pregnancy of Shirley Phelps. Unbeknownst to her, the child, Ruby was already born. This is when she decides to leave Larry Ray Calloway for good, and turn the brother's in to police for the arson.

February 22ⁿᵈ, 1993, Larry and Shirley file for a marriage license in Davies County, KY. The plot had already been planned by this time to kill Patsy.

February 26, 1993, Darrell speaks with Patsy for the last time, and she tells him of her plans to turn over the arson to police and be done with Larry for good. A neighbor of Patsy's overheard Larry Calloway making threats to her that same week.

February 28ᵗʰ – March 6ᵗʰ, 1993, Marriage announcement for Larry Ray Calloway and Shirley Phelps runs in the Messenger Inquirer. He was still living with Patsy at the time, but we're not sure if she threw him out of her house or not.

March 3ʳᵈ, 1993, Vernon "Gene" Calloway shows up at the nursing home in Hartford where Patsy Calloway worked. He showed Patsy a newspaper, The Messenger Inquirer, which contained a marriage license announcement for Larry Calloway and Shirley Phelps. She and Gene got into a confrontation. Patsy disappears after she was seen leaving work with Gene Calloway, her ex-husband's older brother at 10:30a.m, according to witnesses. Patsy was murdered and had her throat cut by Gene Calloway. Around 2:30pm Debra Deese Calloway, Gene's girlfriend at the time, was seen walking toward Beaver Dam, KY. She was disguised as Patsy according to Mildred Calloway. She did this in order to facilitate Patsy's kidnapping and murder and make it look like Patsy walked away from her life.

March 3ʳᵈ, 1993, Just after Patsy left the nursing home, Maryann Phelps left as well, to tell Larry and Shirley that Patsy left work with Gene. She told Darrell she did this, because she thought Patsy was going to beat up Shirley Phelps, her pregnant sister. As it turns out, the pregnancy was a lie that was fabricated. Shirley had already given birth to the 2ⁿᵈ child with Larry.

March 3rd, 1993, 12:15 p.m. Larry leaves the apartment after learning the news, and goes by the nursing home (according to him) and then directly to the police. According to police, he did show up at the station around noon and twice thereafter.

March 3rd, 1993, Sometime that day, Larry spoke with Mildred and Jimmy, his siblings, and discussed Patsy's murder and the wig.

March 3rd, 1993, Larry goes to police three times that day, for his "missing" ex-wife Patsy. Soon after, he makes up a missing poster that is directly deceitful. Larry already knew that Patsy was seen leaving work with Gene, yet the poster reflects her walking down route 231 from Hartford to Beaver Dam.

March 3rd, 1993, Around 5:30 p.m., Larry mysteriously finds the keys in the floorboard, after the 2nd time he visited Patsy's car.

March 13th, 1993, Darrell Kessinger heads to Kentucky for answers and discovers that much of an investigation hadn't even begun in his sister's disappearance. We and others believe that this may have be intentional to some degree. The official missing person's report was filed on March 13th, 1993, the day that Darrell Kessinger arrived in Hartford, KY. It was later changed to reflect the actual day of her disappearance and murder. Darrell has a copy of the original report.

June 10th, 1993, Larry and Gene Calloway were indicted for the August 1st, 1991, arson. The grand jury had convened the week prior, after Larry had turned himself in to police for the arson.

Chapter Six: Muddy Waters

Darrell's notes Continued:

23. *1993 – March 3rd – March 6th – Gene and Debra Calloway get stuck at 3a.m. in what was then known as the Mud College Bottoms. According to Darrell Burton, Gene Calloway had walked up to his house and ask if he would pull them out. As strange as it may seem, Vickie Hoheimer's daughter, Amy was spending the night with the Burtons. Amy would be the niece to Gene and Debbie, and according to Amy they both seem to be in shock when they see Amy. Amy also mentioned that she had seen 2 muddy shovels in the back of the truck. Darrell*

Burton questioned Gene as to why he was in the bottoms at such an hour, and Gene responded by saying they were dumping trash. This even eventually caused the KSP to have some suspicion and they later went out and dug up an old well. The JPRST along with Chris Williams and his dog bear, with the permission of the landowner John Lindley, would further search the property for clues. The Mud College Bottoms are now known as Johnson School Road. (DK)

Note: This last note, is information that Darrell had found out much later regarding the searches. It's noteworthy to state that this same property was searched for another missing young woman from the area, Heather Teague. Heather went missing in 1995. Heather's name was found among certain things relating to Gene Calloway, according to several different sources. That information is in the hands of the Kentucky State Police. Sarah Teague, Heather's mother, has fought relentlessly to obtain information about her daughter's case with KSP, with little to no avail. (TC)

24. 1993 *March 3ʳᵈ – March 6ᵗʰ* *– According to a May 5ᵗʰ affidavit submitted by Phillip Ballard, Gene Calloway removed all the carpet from his Chevy Blazer and burned it. This story does not match the story as told by Jimmy Calloway when he claims he seen the carpet in Gene's trash and he even touch it and got blood on his hand. So which is it, did Jimmy see it in the trash, and then Gene burned it later? (DK)*

Note: According to Darrell, Phillip Ballard was the lead investigator after Patsy's case was turned over to KSP, when Darrell and family came to town. After ten days, he started investigating and submitted that Gene and Debra cleaned out Gene's Chevy Blazer, including removing the carpets. In my interview with Larry Calloway, he admitted that his brother Jimmy said he saw Patsy's lifeless body in the back of Gene's truck, and her throat had been slit from ear to ear. He also admitted that his brother Jimmy witnessed Debra and Gene cleaning out Gene's truck that early afternoon. He said the carpets were removed and Debbie was in the front of the truck, wiping it down with hand sanitizer. This interview took place before any arrest was made in Patsy's case.

Commentary: It still leaves us with many unanswered questions re: Larry's possible involvement in the murder of his ex-wife Patsy, but he sure was ballsy for him to meet up with Darrell and Jimmy at the community center. (TC)

25. March 3rd – March 13th – *The rumor surfaces that Gene makes a trip to Florida. I have found nothing to indicate that this trip ever took place. I believe it was just another ploy to mislead the authorities so they would look elsewhere for answers. I had heard stories that Gene may have taken Patsy's body to either Florida or Louisiana and fed her to the alligators, again this I believe was a fabricated story and was one that they wanted everyone to believe. (DK)*

Commentary: This doesn't make sense. Nor does it match with eyewitness statement, that Gene had dug a hole or grave on Andy Anderson's property. Gene did in fact travel to Florida for vacation and work, much later on. Details of another woman's murder had surfaced in reference to Gene Calloway and that timeframe in Florida.

26. 1993 – March 18th – *Patsy is reported missing to the KSP by the Ohio County Sheriff's Office. It has been 15 days since Patsy's disappearance before it is reported and handed over to the KSP. I am not sure who dropped the ball on this one, this is a real head banger. She leaves her workplace with Gene Calloway on March 3rd, and is not reported missing by the Ohio*

56

County Sheriff until the 13ᵗʰ. What happened during those 10 days that Patsy was unaccounted for. And what happened within the 5 days between the time the Ohio County Sheriff declared Patsy missing and when she was reported to the KSP on the 18ᵗʰ. Why such a delay? And what was being done to find out what happened to Patsy? (DK)

   Commentary: What was the breakdown with the different police agencies involved and why did it happen as it did? In regard to Larry, he is so loving that he burned down Patsy's house and spent the insurance money. Again, Larry, her "loving, supposed" live-in, ex-husband, who is so dedicated to Patsy, doesn't report her missing to the police officially. Darrell had to make the official report. Larry did go to the police three times that day, within hours of Patsy leaving with his brother, but no report was ever filed regarding his claims, from what Darrell was told.

   I did verify with police that Larry showed up there three times, on the day Patsy disappeared. However, there is no record that I'm aware of, that him or Jimmy ever walking into that police station. Larry had two children by now, with the other child/woman mistress. He leads Darrell on these wild goose chases and fails to officially report his missing ex-wife. He filed for a marriage license to wed his mistress, according to him. But no one, including police seem to want to pursue anything further. They even sent the ex-husband after her car. (TC)

27. 1993 – March 3ʳᵈ – *Patsy's missing person poster is generated, indicating that she was last seen walking down highway 231 in the direction of Beaver Dam. Larry Calloway had the poster made up, just another ploy to mislead the authorities and family. Larry already knew that Patsy was last seen leaving the nursing home with Gene Calloway, so why* *would he say she was last seen walking down 231? It was my theory that the poster was made up before Patsy disappeared, and Mildred Calloway was part of the plan in place and new exactly how things would pan out. Larry knew that it would be Mildred that would report seeing Patsy, I believe coming up with Debbie and the disguise was just to add more confusion to the story, even though it was true. It just left too many unanswered questions and speculation. As things surfaced, it became easier to see that everything was carefully planned and calculated. Everyone needed to know where the other was and what they were doing to have an alibi. It was not difficult to figure out that it was Debbie Calloway dressed up like Patsy walking down 231 that day. (DK)*

Commentary: Let's discuss the missing posters drawn up by Larry. Larry Calloway stated he made up missing posters later, on the evening of **March 3rd, 1993**, according to him and other family members. According to Larry, he; daughter Tanya; and son Shane; went to the local library. Now I ask you, why would he make up a missing poster for someone who hadn't even been gone for 24 hours? This was Larry's live-in, ex-wife, according to him. He knew she'd left the nursing home with his brother Gene. So if he knew she was with Gene according to his own statements, and he believed she was just angry at him like the police said he tried to convince them of, why would he need to make a missing poster in the first place? He wouldn't, nor would he need to go to police. All he would have to do is go ask his brother Gene where Patsy went.

Why the two excuses? I don't know exactly what was said when Larry Calloway went to police that day, but I'm awestruck by their lack of response. There was also a second missing person's poster made up. Darrell is keeping the originals if ever it goes to trial.

In our interview, Larry told me he was staying with Patsy, but he was at Shirley's house that morning. Patsy found out that Shirley was pregnant again, according to her call with Darrell the week before. So if she's just upset over the pregnancy, she could be anywhere and angry. She had her own trailer and wasn't dependent on Larry, so she could've just told Larry to leave and go be with Shirley. Patsy was done with his ass! It doesn't stand to reason that Larry would make up missing posters within hours of Patsy's disappearance, on the very same day she went missing, unless he already knew something had happened to her.

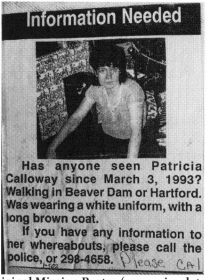

Original Missing Poster (never circulated)

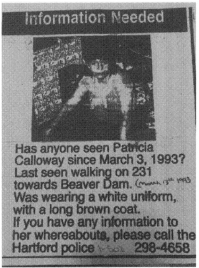

2nd **Missing Poster that was circulated.**

Why would he willfully mislead the public on
the missing posters, saying that Patsy was seen walking
from Hartford to Beaver Dam, after he already knew
she'd left the home with Gene? I believe he made a
mistake in his plot, or did it to throw off the dogs. In
the second poster, he says, "Last seen walking on 231
towards Beaver Dam." The poster is directly deceitful.
Obviously there are too many unanswered questions
about Larry's involvement.

Going back to those first hours after her leaving
with Gene, it stands to reason, that she could've just
gone off somewhere angry, like looking for Larry; or her
daughter's house; or even her mother's house in
Arkansas; like she'd done many times before when she
was upset. So why would Larry make up a missing
person's poster at all? Granted, they found her car, but
with no sign of foul play, other than Larry's claim that

the seat was scooted back. Patsy could've left with a friend to get away for a while.

Yet the first thing that comes to Larry is that Patsy is missing just an hour and a half later? No! He knew she'd left the nursing home with Gene, out of his own mouth! That's the route that Debra took dressed up as Patsy! How did Larry know what she was wearing for that matter? He claimed he was at Shirley's apartment until Maryann got there.

His sister Mildred initially told the police it was Debra dressed up like Patsy, then changed her story. She'd then discussed it with Larry! He KNEW that it was Debra walking that day, NOT PATSY! So he willfully, after discussing it with Mildred Calloway, put deceitful information on that 2nd missing poster, stating that Patsy was last seen walking on highway 231! This is direct evidence of Larry's involvement in Patsy's disappearance.

After Gene's death, Mildred finally admitted to police again, that it was Debra dressed up like Patsy. The missing posters were also part of the plot to mislead police and push the agenda that Patsy walked away from her life. If Larry had nothing to do with Patsy's kidnapping and murder, why would he automatically assume she was "missing within 1½ hours of her leaving work?" This is a person he wanted out of the way, who was blackmailing him and he needed an alibi. (TC)

28. 1993 – March 13th – *I go to Hartford along with my mother Georgia Ford. I stay nearly 1 month looking into Patsy's disappearance and discover nothing but blunders and negligence. It doesn't take me but a day to piece the puzzle* *together once I found out the circumstances behind her disappearance, I knew right away they had killed her. And at this time not a single official had questioned any of Patsy's co-workers, I was the first to ask questions about what happened on the day she was seen leaving with Gene Calloway. Again, who was responsible for the investigation or lack of investigation? And who dropped the ball once – again? (DK)*

Commentary: Darrell's anger was justified. The fact is, Larry showed up at the police station 1½ hours after she was seen leaving the nursing home with his brother Gene. It's interesting that the officer made a note of this, but never filed an official missing person's report until 10 days later, when Darrell and Patsy's family came to town. That note of Larry showing up has since disappeared as well, according to what Darrell was told by an investigator. I believe Larry was establishing an alibi. We just need him to admit in court that he went to police that day around noon. Common sense takes over from there.

No interviews took place until Darrell started poking around to find out what happened to Patsy. Perhaps the police thought she'd come home. They definitely failed to follow up. But that doesn't explain the fact that Jimmy Calloway told police about Patsy's deceased body in the back of Gene's truck and they did NOTHING! Again, Dan McEnroe was the officer he spoke with about it.

After all of this I still have to ask, "Where are Patsy's remains?" "Who took Patsy's car if she was with Gene?" Debra was dressed like Patsy, busy walking from Hartford to Beaver Dam on SR 231. She certainly wasn't driving, so someone had to take Patsy's car. After all, Patsy left with Gene, in his truck. (TC)

62

29. *1993 March 15ᵗʰ* – *We have our first meeting with Phillip Ballard. It is also at this time I learn that Phillip Ballard was the officer that had pulled my dad from his car when had his crippling car wreck. Phillip Ballard told me that he did not realize my dad had an older son. So initially we seemed to hit it off. For some unknown reason Gene Calloway showed up at the meeting, this particular meeting was at the sheriff's office. These meetings were supposed to be confidential and for immediate family members only, so how was Gene Calloway finding out about them, and who was tipping him on the meeting places and times? Gene Calloway would be the only Calloway family member to ever attend, even Larry was not invited. (DK)*

Note: At the time, Darrell was suspecting the police to tipping off Gene, because Gene Calloway had done some farmhand work for Phillip Ballard in the past, cutting tobacco. Also, Ballard allowed Gene to attend the private meetings, which is unprecedented.

Darrell said in 1993, he had received a call from Corinna Mullen's father Claude, who lived in Central City. Corinna was a young girl who went missing in 1987 and was murdered by a group of people, one named Billy Fields. Fields was a Lt. with the Central City Police Department, which is just 15 minutes from where Patsy lived. Mullen's father had warned Darrell that the corruption around that area was rampant and not to trust anyone. That's when Darrell had first started considering that there may be some corruption in his sister's case as well. That was shortly after they'd arrived in Kentucky.

It was during one of those first meetings, that Darrell Kessinger noticed the purple and green bruise

63

on Gene's right hand, between his thumb and index finger, shaped like a deep bite mark with teeth impressions. According to Darrell, the bite mark was still prevalent two weeks after Patsy's disappearance, but was turning green, yet this detective threatened to lock up Darrell instead of Gene. (TC)

30. *1993 - **March 16**th – This is when I find out that Debra Calloway did not work on the day of Patsy's disappearance, so this made it more evident that she was the one seen walking down 231 the day of Patsy went missing. Mary Calloway who was still Gene's wife at the time was working on the day Patsy disappeared. (DK)*

Note: Mary Calloway was Gene's soon-to-be ex-wife and close friend to Patsy Calloway. In March, 1993, Mary told Darrell that she didn't see Patsy that morning, but that Debbie Calloway didn't work that day or she'd have seen her, because they worked closely together. Also in March 1993, Wanda Winkler, Patsy's supervisor, confirmed that Debra Calloway didn't work that day. They checked her punch card. I wish they'd made a photo copy of it. Perhaps they did. Hmmm... (TC)

31. *1993 – **March 16**th – I find out on this day that Shirley Calloway's sister, Mary Ann Phelps (Felty) had left work shortly after Patsy left with Gene Calloway. Mary Ann's supervisor confirmed that Mary Ann did in fact leave, as was gone approximately 45 minutes to an hour. When Mary Ann returned according to her supervisor, she said she had gone to go check on her sister Shirley Phelps. Shirley Phelps is the woman that Larry was having an affair with. (DK)*

Note: *Maryann Phelps as it turns out, is also a key witness to this murder case. Please keep her name in mind. I will address her statements later. (TC)

32. *1993 - March 16th – I speak with Cindy Likens is the key witness that see's Patsy get into Gene Calloway's Chevy Blazer and leave with him on the day of her disappearance. Cindy Likens also informs me that the police had not yet questioned her. This is amazing, it is now 13 days after Patsy disappeared, and still no one has questioned Cindy. (DK)*

33. *1993 – March 16th – Bonnie Austin (Calloway) who is a co-worker of Patsy, and also a person I had known all my life. She and Patsy were best of friends, and Bonnie was very frustrated and felt that nothing was being done about Patsy's disappearance. Bonnie also believed that Gene and Debra Calloway were responsible for Patsy's disappearance. (DK)*

34. *1993 – March 16th – I speak with Hilda Young. Hilda provides information that Gene Calloway had visited Patsy on the morning of **March 3rd**. Hilda was also Patsy's neighbor, and via a telephone conversation with her, she stated that she had overheard Larry Calloway threaten Patsy on several occasions. (DK)*

Note: Darrell never eluded to what those threats from Larry entailed. When I asked him, he didn't know. I never got the opportunity to speak with Ms. Bonnie Austin Calloway or Hilda Young. Still, I have to wonder why Gene visited Patsy prior to her going in to work. (TC)

35. *1993 – March 16th – Angie Moseley provided information to Bonnie Austin via a phone conversation, that Gene Calloway had come to the Professional Care Home with the newspaper from the Messenger Inquirer which contained the **April 24^{th,} 1993** article written by Tracy McQueen, pertaining to the disappearance of Patsy. She states that Gene and Debbie got off into a corner and read the article together. I am sure Debbie*

65

had to read it to Gene, **because it is a known fact that Gene could not read nor write.** *(DK)*

Commentary: I was told that Gene was nearly illiterate and could write some, but barely, by his own brothers, Larry and Jimmy. First of all, he's a rough and tough outdoorsman. Most men of this type don't seek an out-of-town paper to read wedding announcements. However knowing that Patsy was missing, it makes perfect sense that Gene and Debbie would sneak off into a corner to find out information about Patsy's case, and that she'd read it to him, because she was in on it, and he was the last person to see Patsy alive. (TC)

36. <u>1993</u> – *March 16th – I am told by Ms. XXXX that her son XXXXX XXXXX had seen Gene out on Andy Anderson's farm digging for worms. At least that was his thoughts at the time. But I later have him contact me, letting me know he has something to tell me, but he goes to a retired state trooper, before I have the opportunity to talk with him. This information is later relayed to detective Whittaker, which prompts the initial search of Andy Anderson's farm. According to the retired trooper, it was an interview I had done with Jerry Wright that rattled XXXXX XXXXX to come forward. (DK)*

Commentary: In 2012, Nineteen years after Patsy went missing, I received a phone call from a friend, Shellee Hale. She asked me to speak to Darrell Kessinger, Patsy's brother, and work on Patsy's missing case. Patsy's case was considered cold and she thought I could help. She and I had worked on many missing person's cases together, and I was starting to branch out on my own. Shellee asked if I was busy, saying she'd like me to follow up and work on this particular case for our former website, MissingPersonsNews.com. I asked her to give him my number.

I followed up with Darrell and wrote an article on his sister's case for MissingPersonsNews.com. Although Detective Whittaker was actively working Patsy's case, we believe it was the article with the information that Darrell had collected over the years that prompted the arrests of the suspects. The article was called, "**An Arson, A Wig, and A Murder**." The title of the first book was inspired by the article of the same name.

On September 2nd, 2014, I spoke with Ruby Renee Calloway. She is the daughter of Shirley and Larry Calloway. She told me that when Patsy went missing, she was already a couple of months old. She is the one who confirmed the birthdates of the children for me. Up to that point, we had no idea what her birthdate was.

Darrell tried for nineteen years to put the pieces of his sister's disappearance together, with little to no help from law enforcement. He knew her ex-husband and ex-brother-in-law were involved, but he didn't know to what degree. He told me, "I always knew in my heart they killed her, but I couldn't figure out if Larry was involved or not. I didn't know if Gene did it or if Larry did it. Thinking back, I knew Gene was the one that actually killed her, but I suspected Larry was involved."

That's where I came in. I began to help Darrell in his quest for answers and justice. From the beginning of Patsy's disappearance, and 26 years later, Darrell is still searching for his sister. To no surprise, her missing person's case had gone cold with law enforcement and had changed hands several times over the years. Had he not followed up with his sister's case, I dare say she'd still be listed as a cold case. But, nothing was going to stop Darrell from pursuing the truth and justice for his sister Patsy. He relentlessly pursued her case.

Chapter Seven: The Arrests

In 2012, after a few months of chasing down leads, we discovered a lot of information regarding the investigation behind Patsy's disappearance, or lack thereof. Darrell had enlisted the help of a forensics investigator and a search and rescue team going out on searches. Because of his suspicions of Larry, Darrell wanted Patsy's trailer searched, because it had never been done before. Hard to believe right? It's true. That was a major complaint of Darrell's. He talked about how the police had search dogs go way out behind Patsy's house in the woods, but never inside her home. He was still trying to find answers and the location of his sister's remains. After so many years, Patsy's trailer still hadn't been investigated by police.

As I stated before, shortly after Patsy went missing, Darrell stayed, along with their mother and sister, in Patsy's trailer with Larry. They came up from Arkansas ten days after Patsy went missing. I spoke with Darrell on the phone about this. I asked him if he saw any blood in the trailer where Patsy and Larry lived. He said, "No, but I wasn't looking for it." The reason I brought up the question of the blood to Darrell in 2016, is that blood had been found in Patsy's trailer, some years after Patsy had vanished. It had been cleaned up before Darrell and family arrived in Hartford in 1993, but discovered later, by a forensics instructor.

Back in 2012, the Jodi Powers Search and Rescue Technologies; Tennessee K9 Search and Rescue; and Tracy Kane, former instructor at the Daymar College along with student volunteers; went to search Patsy's trailer. A lot of blood spatter was found after Aluminol had been sprayed in Patsy's trailer. There was blood spatter found in the living room on the wall; leading down the hallway to the bathroom; on the carpet and floors; and into the bathroom by the bathtub. Prior to and after the spraying, the students were kept at a distance. The reason they sprayed those spots is because a cadaver dog, "Bear" had hit on those spots for human blood or decomposition.

In 2012, Detective Whittaker was on the case and he became very angry at Darrell, for having those people there at Patsy's trailer and doing that. Again, all of this information was given in the article and the first novel. He was angry, because he thought Darrell had destroyed crucial evidence, but then further stated, the only thing the blood would prove is that Patsy is dead. Whittaker had made statements that he didn't intend to make any arrests at the time, because he didn't think Jimmy Calloway's testimony would hold up in court. Jimmy is a little slow. After learning all of this, I published the article anyway, which was shared on social media like wildfire.

In one of my interviews with Tanya, Patsy's daughter, she told me that her and her boyfriend moved into her mom's trailer after Patsy vanished. She'd began living there that summer, with her then boyfriend, Gary

Fendel. Tanya said they noticed a rancid smell from the trailer when the weather got warmer. Gary confirmed this information. They said it smelled like something or someone died in there. They said the odor emanated in the bathroom and by the back door. This is where the majority of the blood was later found, but not until 2012, when the search teams conducted their investigations. I published the article regarding Patsy's disappearance and forensic evidence on September 17th, 2012.

One month after my first article was published online, **An Arson, A Wig, and A Murder**, two arrests were made in the kidnapping and murder of Patsy Calloway. You can draw your own conclusions. Darrell was elated to get the news! He called me immediately and shared the information via Skype. He felt like finally, he would see *some* justice for his sister.

On **Wednesday, October 17th, 2012**, Vernon Gene Calloway and his wife Debra Deese Calloway, were both arrested and charged with four felonies: 1st degree Murder; Kidnapping; Tampering with Physical Evidence; and Intimidation of a Witness. This was nineteen years after Patsy disappeared. I was initially told that the prosecution would seek the death penalty. This wasn't true. Much of what happened prior to and after the couple's arrests is all covered in the first novel.

Photo, courtesy of Darrell Kessinger
Debra Calloway Lt, Vernon Gene Calloway Rt

While awaiting trial, both suspected murderers were let out of jail. That's appalling! Vernon Gene Calloway was released on $5000 house or property bond, and his wife Debra (Debbie) Calloway, was released on a $30 clerk filing fee. As difficult to believe as it is, that's true. Initially, bond was set at a half a million dollars each, but was later reduced by Judge Dortch. Due to medical hardship for Vernon Gene, his bond was reduced to $50,000 cash or property. Due to financial hardship for Debra, her bond was also reduced to $10,000 cash or property. A suspected criminal is only required to come up with 10% of the set amounts in order to be released. Kentucky gives them a $100/day reduction of bond, due to time served while incarcerated. This ultimately let the suspected murderers out of jail on a miniscule amount of cash/property.

You have to ask yourself, "How can a suspected murderer and an accomplice, be let out of jail on so little an amount?" Your guess is as good as mine. According to the law in this country, you're innocent until proven guilty, despite any evidence that was found. The couple was free to go, after they'd earned time served on their bond with the $100/day reduction law.

While that is unfathomable to most people, it's a loophole in the KY laws that can allow suspected murderers to go free. Still, the judge has to approve it. With the history of this couple and the reputation of Gene as a monster, we were left dumbfounded! That needs to change. In the future, we hope to make a change called **Patsy's Law**, which doesn't allow suspected murderers to benefit from the $100/day reduction law.

After the defendants were released from jail, Darrell and some family members and friends held a protest rally in Hartford, KY, regarding the defendants release from jail. This protest included Larry Ray Calloway, ex-husband of Patsy. When I asked Darrell about this, his response was, "I like to keep my friends close and enemies closer. This way I can watch him." I find Larry's sign horribly ironic.

Larry Calloway Lt, Darrell Kessinger Rt

While at the protest rallies, Debbie Calloway, Gene's wife or live-in ex-wife, pulled up in a car, even though she was supposed to be on house arrest. She threw rocks at Darrell, Patsy's brother, and was laughing and yelling at him that the charges would never stick. Even though she was on house arrest, she was out poking fun and taunting Tanya, Patsy's daughter, and Darrell, Patsy's brother. There were about ten witnesses to this incident. She was never re-arrested for the harassment or breaking her house arrest.

Darrell said the local officer, Sheriff Thompson, came down to the protest to offer his support. They reported the incident to him, and although he didn't see Debbie Calloway, it was now in the hands of state police. I'd written an article regarding the protest and the pair's release. These moments of Debra Calloway are noteworthy, in reference to the court case against her, but she was never prosecuted for the taunts or breaking house arrest.

Shortly after that, I received a call from Darrell, that he'd seen Gene Calloway out riding his lawn mower. It infuriated Darrell that this man was enjoying the day, while his sister had been left in a shallow grave somewhere. Knowing he was out riding his mower is also notable for later discussion. Keep that piece of information in mind.

There was a confession letter that was written years earlier and discovered while the pair were incarcerated. Just so you know, the letter was shown to Darrell as a courtesy before the trial. So even with a confession letter, Gene was wandering free. The judge never revoked his release. Darrell got a picture of the suspect on his mower and I wrote an article displaying Darrell's distain and anger regarding the situation, **"Confessed Murderer Leisurely Mows His Lawn."**

Before going to trial, Vernon Eugene "Gene" Calloway, confessed murderer, passed away in his home on July 11th, 2013. He was under hospice care. Being a military lifer, Darrell said to me, "It doesn't sit with me. As a soldier, it is engrained in us that no one gets left behind. I'm off fighting for our country and my sister is out there left in the woods somewhere." Darrell felt it was completely unfair that his sister died at the hands of Gene Calloway, but he got to die in hospice in his home, surrounded by family. And so, Darrell continues to pursue justice for Patsy and the location of his sister's remains, because he wants to give her a proper burial, where her family can visit and grieve.

What is so fascinating about Patsy's story is that a family was involved with the plot and cover-up of her kidnapping and murder. We've gotten more information now, but at that time we knew two brothers were pitted against each other to make the other look guilty, while a third person pretended to be Patsy walking away from her life. A case like this is unheard of. It left everyone that knew of the murder, asking the same question as Darrell Kessinger, "Was it her ex-husband or his brother and brother's wife?

After a few weeks had passed, nobody believed that Patsy just walked away. It is now Darrell's adamant belief that the brothers planned out Patsy's murder, a year before it was actually carried out, with Debra Calloway and others, going along for the ride. He believes this, because of the date of her disappearance.

In my opinion, all three were involved in the plot to kill Patsy and carried out their plan as they laid it out, but I believe the plot took place later than Darrell does. To date, we're unclear as how many people were actually involved in the plot and cover-up, but we now know more than three were involved, not including her ex-husband Larry. There is sworn testimony that suggests others were factually involved. This makes Patsy's case one of the most unprecedented and despicable murder cases in history. What else would be revealed to us at trial?

Chapter Eight: Debra's Trial Begins

It took another year after the death of Gene Calloway, for any justice to take place. On this day, justice would finally move forward. On August 4th, 2014, 9:17a.m., twenty-one years after Patsy's kidnapping and murder, Debra Calloway's trial began. The judge explained to the attendees that there has been a lot of publicity on the Patsy Calloway case. He wanted to make sure that seeing any news reports didn't influence the court members in any way.

During the initial phase of the trial, introductions were made. The judge, prosecutor, and defense attorney got the chance to question the potential jurors, to see if they could sit on the jury panel and be fair and impartial jury members. The judge made it clear that this was not a death penalty case, contrary to earlier reports. Although she was charged with pre-meditated 1st-degree murder, the maximum that Debra Calloway could receive was life in prison without parole.

Because of the defendant's age, one potential juror claimed that he couldn't see himself being responsible for sending an older woman to jail, for the rest of her life. I'm happy he spoke up, because believe it or not, many people feel the same way. I'd much rather a potential juror admit a problem with this, than get on the jury panel and set a murderer free, if they believed they were too old to go to jail. Another potential juror told the judge and relevant attorneys, that he wanted to know why it took so long for this case to be brought to trial. Darrell has asked the same questions many times.

The defense attorney asked questions to potential jurors in regard to prejudice and local media. He asked them about local radio programming and TV news, whether or not anyone had heard anything regarding this case. Once the questioning from both sides was finished, jury and alternates were selected.

Some jurors were released because of illness or doctor's appointments out of town. Another was released because he had tickets to a PGA event. The judge commented that he also had tickets for the same event and wouldn't be able to attend, because he would be doing his civic duty, serving the bench on this case. While this process was taking place, Debra Calloway could be seen giving heavy sighs. She sat with arms crossed in a defensive position in the defendant's box. She was visibly nervous, yet remained still. I found myself wondering if she'd testify or not. I didn't see how she could get out of it with the evidence they had against her. At 1:23p.m., the jury was called into court.

Opening Statements

In his opening statement, the prosecutor Tim Coleman led off by holding up a large photo of Patsy for everyone in the jury to see. He outlined his case against the defendant. He explained the difference between direct and circumstantial evidence. He made it clear that Patsy's case was a circumstantial case with some direct evidence. He explained that sometimes circumstantial cases are stronger than cases containing mainly direct evidence, because common sense can dictate a more reasonable verdict. He said that often, circumstantial evidence is better than direct evidence, because it's easier to come to reasonable conclusions than to try and unravel science. Scientific facts can become boring to a jury and they may tune out. He explained to the jury not to expect things like what they see on television, because those shows are fantasy and dangerous to the real judicial process in this country. I concur. Far too often, juries expect to see things like DNA or a smoking gun, which are not always readily available.

In his opening statement, the defense attorney claimed that it would be unreasonable to prosecute Debra Calloway because there was no body in this case. Patsy has never been found. He claimed that Patsy walking away from her life was a reasonable prospect, considering that her husband was cheating on her and she was unhappy, even though the trial took place twenty-one years after Patsy's disappearance. When discussing the circumstances or motive for Patsy's murder, he said "supposed arson." Had I been the prosecutor, I'd have moved to strike that. There was no supposed to it. It was an arson that took place in 1991, in which Gene was acquitted and Debra was never charged. It's now a matter of court record. He discussed Jimmy Calloway and eluded that Jimmy claimed he saw Patsy's body in Gene's truck, but didn't do anything with it "until it came time to save his own skin." That's simply NOT true.

He said in not so many words, that a jury would have reasonable doubt at the end of the trial. He announced, that Debra Calloway would testify on her own behalf. I knew that wouldn't be good for her cause, but would be a gift for the prosecution and for Darrell. I couldn't wait to hear what she'd come up with as her excuses, or lies for her behavior. I can't believe she actually thought she'd outsmart the prosecuting attorney. These people never cease to amaze me. Without her testimony and the evidence against her, the defense knew her ship had sunk.

Before witnesses were called, the defense attorney stated that he wanted to invoke the rule. What that means, the judge explained, is that all potential witnesses, would not be able to sit in the courtroom until they had completed their testimony and were released from testifying. In doing so, Patsy's children and her brother Darrell didn't see some of the trial.

Tanya Mae, Patsy and Larry's oldest daughter, was the first witness called to the stand. Once sworn, she said she learned about her mother going missing the same day, because her brother Shane had called her. She talked about her relationship with her mom Patsy, and how they talked almost daily, even though she lived in Indiana at the time. Tanya testified that she was in the same line of work as her mom and she was excited to tell Patsy the new things she'd gotten to do on a daily basis, at work, in nursing care. Contrary to the defenses claims, this helped to establish that Patsy wouldn't just walk away from her life without a trace. Tanya also stated that Patsy's bank accounts had no activity whatsoever after she disappeared. Her clothing and her personal belongings were still there at home, even though she'd gone missing.

Darrell Kessinger, Patsy's brother was next to testify. After general information, they discussed that on February 26th, 1993, he came back from Operation Desert Storm and Mississippi, where he had been deployed and out of town, for the army. He stated that was the last time he spoke with Patsy. They had a phone conversation in which Patsy made her intentions clear that she was going to turn over Larry and Gene Calloway to the police for the August 1st, 1991 arson. Darrell stated that he and Patsy had no contact after that phone conversation. Darrell discussed the close relationship he had with his sister. He said there is no way Patsy would just up and walk away from her life without contacting anyone. He stated on cross, questions were raised about Patsy's body being on Andy Anderson's farm, but an objection was called and that would be discussed later in the trial.

Next to take the stand was the Administrator at Patsy's work facility, Patty D. Donald. She stated that Patsy worked there for at least eleven years, because that's when she started working there, but Patsy worked there before her. She stated that Patsy was a good, very dependable, employee that always completed her work. She said Patsy was very compassionate with the residents and very helpful with the family members or co-workers.

She was asked if she happened to see Patsy that day, to which she agreed that she did. She stated that Patsy acted normal and didn't seem to be different than any other day. Ms. Donald said that Patsy was a medication aide and discussed Patsy's time punch card. The card showed that Patsy punched in at 5:88 a.m., military time. It showed that she punched out at 10:36 a.m. She said that she saw Patsy passing meds between 7–7:30 a.m. on the morning of her disappearance. The facility administrator then said she saw Patsy in the parking lot with Gene Calloway later on in the morning hours. She said she thought Patsy was having car trouble, because the hood of her car was up.

Commentary: This last bit of information establishes many things. First, the supposed car trouble could've been something that was part of the premeditated plot to kill Patsy, because her car was found parked at the Hartford Community Center later on, on the evening Patsy disappeared. Remember that Gene was at Patsy's trailer that morning before work, according to her neighbor Hilda Young. Patty Donald said that she and other nurses were in "care plans" when they saw Patsy Calloway in the parking lot with Gene, but she never saw Patsy after that.

Ms. Phyllis Mudd was next to testify. She was an LPN charge nurse at the facility where Patsy worked. As an employee, she worked closely with Patsy and said she knew her for approximately 6 years. She saw Patsy that morning. She said on that particular morning, Patsy acted normal and there didn't seem to be any problems. She said Patsy did a great job and was a wonderful worker.

Ms. Mudd stated that after Patsy came back from her lunch break, she said that Patsy was very nervous and pale. She testified that Patsy told her she had to leave. She said she asked Patsy why? She said Patsy told her, "I'll tell you later, and that's the last thing that she spoke to me." She was asked if she ever heard from her again and she replied, "No sir." On cross, the defense attorney asked her if she knew Gene Calloway. She said she didn't know him. She said she'd seen him a few times, but didn't know him. She also said when asked, that she didn't see him that particular day. She didn't have any information or knowledge about Patsy's car that day. She was then released.

Cyndi Likens, a charge nurse at the facility, said she worked there since 1986. She testified that she knew Patsy immediately since she started working there. She was asked if she recalled the events surrounding March 3rd, 1993, and she agreed she did. She was asked what time Patsy came to work. She about 5:30 a.m. She described Patsy as an above average performer of her duties. She stated that morning, an 11–7 nurse and Patsy had words, in which, she intervened. She stated that the problem was resolved immediately, and during the morning hours, Patsy's behavior seemed ordinary with a normal work attitude. She testified that later when the nursing staff was in a Care Plans meeting, she physically saw Patsy out of a room of windows they were in, in the parking lot, talking face to face with Gene. She said that Patsy had her coat draped over her arm her purse tucked under her arm. She said either Patsy or Gene was waving a newspaper around.

When asked about Gene's demeanor, she said he and Patsy were talking. She said it alarmed her, because she knew that Patsy didn't like Gene. She said it was unusual for a CMA to be in the parking lot during working hours. She said she didn't know that Patsy had clocked out and that's what alarmed her, because a CMA isn't supposed to be off the floor or out of the building unless they tell the charge nurse. She said that they can't leave the floor unless they come and get you. She said, "You're in charge of a lot of people, and it was very unusual that she would ever leave the floor." She said she saw Patsy get into Gene's truck and leave, but didn't see anyone else in the vehicle with them. She stated that after that moment, she never saw Patsy again.

Defense cross examination, Cyndi said she couldn't remember, but she didn't think she saw anyone else with Gene and Patsy. When asked what time they left, she said it was *before* her lunch break which was between the hours of 12–1 p.m., but she couldn't remember the exact time they left the premises. Then, there was a brief sidebar called, because an objection was called in regard to a question about a fight that had occurred between Patsy and the two women. The defense attorney was trying to establish that Patsy had others with motivation to cause her harm. The judge overruled the objection and questioning continued.

The defense attorney asked Cyndi again, about the fight that occurred sometime years earlier, between Patsy and Sharon Mattingly. He tried to say that the fight occurred in 1992, but Darrell and others strongly dispute this date, because the fight actually happened in May, 1990. She couldn't remember the incident, but claimed that Patsy had no problems with anyone at work as far as she knew, including Debra Calloway.

Chapter Nine: Hertzog & Gorby

After a court recess, Mr. Michael Hertzog, a maintenance supervisor at the facility, was called to the stand. He knew Patsy about four years prior to her employment at the nursing home. He testified that he saw Patsy early in the morning when she first started her shift. He said she seemed okay, like no problems were going on, but that changed about mid-morning. He said that Patsy was very vocal. He said that if she had something to say, she would say it regardless of who or what it was about. He was asked if he remembered Patsy ever talking about Vernon Gene Calloway or Larry Calloway, in regard to what she planned to do if something happened. He said, "No... not before that day. Do you want me to tell you what happened?" "Tell the jury what happened that day."

"She came into the break room cussing, saying." Objection! Hearsay. During the sidebar, the prosecution made the argument that this testimony was relevant in what Patsy had intended to do with information and was an exception to the hearsay law. Defense attorney disagreed, saying he didn't believe it was covered by any exception. Judges recollection stated that it would be covered by the exception rule of law. He noted the exception and overruled the objection.

"Okay, Mr. Hertzog go ahead and tell me. What did you hear Patsy say?" "Uh...She said uh, well she cussed, I don't. I don't cuss, so I'm not gonna repeat what she said, but she said um, my dirty SOB husband, has brought in this young girl and he wants to have her and Patsy, and you know to have a three, a threesome arrangement. You know and uh, she said, no way in H-E-L-L (he spelled out in letters using Patsy's word) was she gonna put up with that. And uh, she said uh...and she left the break room, and a little bit later on she, it was right around when she took her dinner break, and she said, uh... well I know how to put a stop to it. She said she was gonna turn them in for burning this house down and."

Prosecutor asked him, "Did she say who?" "She said her husband and Gene." Objection was renewed, then the prosecutor asked him to continue with what he heard Patsy say. Mr. Hertzog stumbled a bit to find the words, then he said, "Gene Calloway came into the break room, and she told him what she was going to do. "I'm gonna go to the courthouse and I'm gonna turn you in for burning that place down and collecting on that insurance!" "And um, he made some sort of threat and she said, "Over my dead body." And Gene said, "That can be arranged too." Well you said some kind of threat, did you hear exactly what she said? "No, she just threatened him with turning them in. You know, she said she was going straight to the courthouse." And that was in or around the breakroom, correct? "That was in the breakroom." What happened then? "She stormed out of the breakroom and Gene followed her." And did you see those two anymore? "No. I never saw her again." No further questions.

Defense asked him, "Were you, did you hear any other part of the conversation that you talked about here today?" "No sir. That was it." Defense had no further questions and the witness was released.

Now wait... Let's listen *very carefully* to Patsy's own words. "My son-of-a-bitch husband *brought* this young girl and he wants her and me to have a threesome arrangement." Brought her where? One could infer that Larry brought the young girl into the relationship, but why would she say the phrase like that? She already knew he had a child with Shirley, and one on the way, according to what she relayed to Darrell. If she was referring to Larry bringing someone into the relationship and having a threesome, why didn't she just say, "My son-of-a-bitch husband wants me to have a threesome with his girlfriend?"

Darrell has always maintained that Gene showing up with a newspaper containing a marriage announcement, wouldn't be enough to get Patsy to leave with him. Darrell is adamant that something else set her off. Patsy hated Gene with a passion and was afraid of him. A good possibility is that Larry came to the nursing facility first to bait Patsy, even though Larry wasn't seen by any employees. Just because nobody saw him at the facility doesn't mean he wasn't there before Gene came there. What about Larry's alibi? In my visuals, I saw the white car with two people in it at Patsy's trailer, while she was being murdered inside.

Larry was one, Debra was the other. This was covered in the first novel.

Again, someone had to drive Patsy's car after Gene left with her. Was it Larry? What <u>exactly</u> happened at that nursing facility? Why would Patsy ever leave the facility with someone who just told her they could arrange her death? Did Larry show up and an argument ensue? I had a recorded interview with Maryanne Phelps regarding some of this situation, which I forwarded to police. We'll discuss it in a later chapter.

The prosecution then calls Misty Gorby. She testified that she has a daughter, with Debra Calloway's son, William Embry. She stated that she was in a relationship with him around the time that Patsy went missing. She said that she'd see Debra on occasion, but only after her daughter was born and when her daughter was visiting with her grandmother. When asked, she said she didn't know Patsy, but heard about her disappearance. She heard about Patsy's disappearance from William, Debbie's son, and from the local newspaper.

The prosecutor asked Misty, "Did you ever have the opportunity to talk about Patsy's disappearance with the defendant?" She said "Yes." "What do you recall the defendant saying?" She replied that Debbie was adamant, that she did what she had to do and that it wasn't of her own free will. She was asked if she went to Debra's house on occasion to which she replied, "yes." She was asked, "Over at her house, did you ever see anything you thought was significant?" Misty said, "When I went to change my daughter in the bedroom, I seen a wig and a trench coat laying up on her dresser." "What color was the hair on the wig?" "It was like a darker brown," she replied.

The prosecutor was granted permission to approach the witness. She was handed a large printout picture of Patsy Calloway and asked if the hair on the wig was similar to the color of Patsy's hair in the photo, to which she replied, "Yes." The prosecutor asked her if she talked to the defendant about that wig. She said, "I don't really remember what I might have said, but I know it made her mad, and she threw the wig and the trench coat. And then William said we were getting the "F" out of there and we left."

She was then asked if at any time, "Did they discuss her walking there or anywhere after the disappearance of Patsy?" She said, "That she'd walked down the street, down Main Street, uh, and then when you get to where the light is, you can go right or left, and she went around the curve and got in the vehicle with Gene. But nothing specifically after that."

"Did she say anything about how she was dressed?" "No, not really." The prosecutor started to ask another question. There was an objection for leading the witness. The prosecutor rephrased his question. "Did she make any statements with regard to her appearance being similar to Patsy?" Misty said, "That she uh, that she had to uh...you know, do what she had to do, and she was, you know... walking down there with the wig. That they didn't um, you know, realize that Patsy was not around." "Where you still seeing William at that time?" "Yes." "Do you know where that conversation took place?" "It was at one of the get-togethers. I'm not familiar with the exact date." "But it was sometime, after the disappearance of..." "Yes." Prosecutor asks, "Was it before or after your daughter was born?" to which she replies, "after." "I think it would be like around '93/'94." No further questions.

Defense asked Misty if she was friends with Angie and Ricky Calloway and if she'd stayed with them last year. She said they used to be friends and they used to hang out when they were younger, but she didn't stay with them last year. Eventually she got around to telling the defense attorney that her and her daughter had spent a few nights there on different occasions. Then, the defense attorney asked her if she knew what the relationship was like between Angie and Debbie Calloway, to which she replied that it wasn't good. She stated that Angie didn't like Debbie coming over there all the time. He asked her if she knew why the relationship wasn't good, and that question was sustained as hearsay. No further questions at this time. She was released from her subpoena. They finished for the day.

Commentary: Darrell and I had *never* heard about the witness Misty, until the trial. Her testimony was shocking. She's at a family get together, according to her own words, yet they're discussing Patsy's disappearance openly. I'm curious to everyone that was privy to these conversations at the family gathering, who didn't come forward to tell the truth. Detective Brian Whittaker was on the case and had openly stated disgust, because there were witnesses out there who wouldn't tell him anything, yet they'd talk to me as a reporter. I concur with him on this. Apparently, everyone knew bits and pieces about Patsy's disappearance, but it took nineteen years before they'd come forward, with the exception of Jimmy Calloway and Mildred Calloway Dunning and originally Vicki Hoheimer. Officer Corey King showed the same distain for the lack of witnesses to come forth.

Note: After Michael Hertzog and Misty Gorby's testimonies, one could easily come to the conclusion that Larry Calloway may have also been at the nursing home that morning some time, just not seen. That could account for Patsy's demeanor and rage in the cafeteria at the nursing home. Again we question what other reason would make Patsy leave the nursing facility besides the marriage announcement and their testimony points to her comments about Larry wanting her to have a threesome with "This girl he brought."

Chapter Ten: Mildred Testifies

Next during the trial, Larry and Gene's sister Mildred, and old frail looking woman, was wheeled up in her wheelchair, to testify against her once sister-in-law, Debra Calloway. Mildred stated she was driving down route 231 at the time, and saw who she thought was Patsy. She pulled up and knew immediately that it was Debbie Calloway. She described her as wearing a dark brown wig, dark colored pants, and a tan coat like Patsy's. She said she couldn't remember if Debbie was carrying a purse or not. Mildred described an incident in which Gene told her in front of Debra, "You need to say it wasn't Debbie walking on the highway." She said after that, she never mentioned it until after Gene's passing. Mildred said she told the police initially what she'd seen, when it happened, but then changed her story because she loved her brother. She didn't want to see him go to jail for murder. She said that about two weeks before he passed away, Gene confessed to her that he'd killed Patsy. She said he told her that he choked Patsy to death and buried her about 2½ feet down, along with her purse. Mildred admitted that she'd lied about it being Debbie to police, because she loved her brother. She said, "He had a lot of meanness in him, but he had good too. He had a better soft streak than some people though. He had a temper and could be mean, but not as mean as others I know." She stated this while staring at her brother Larry, and then at Debra.

During Mildred's testimony, Debra Calloway adjusted her glasses in the direction of Mildred, clearly using her middle finger. She was flipping Mildred the bird. Then Mildred was questioned by the defense attorney about an incident that occurred at Walmart after Gene had passed on. The attorney claimed that Mildred only changed her story to say it was Debra, after she learned that Debbie was dating and living with another man. This prompted Mildred to confront Debbie Calloway in the courtroom. "You know that was you Debbie!" She screamed, "You couldn't even wait a year after my brother passed away and you was supposed to love him!" "I told the truth the first time and I told the truth this time and GOD knows I did!"

After Gene passed away and Debra started seeing and living with another man, Mildred no longer had a reason to keep quiet about the wig and seeing Debbie out walking on route 231. She may have ended her silence because she was angry at Debbie Calloway, but that doesn't change the fact that it was her initial account back in 1993, that it was Debra seen walking down that road. This is the same thing she told Darrell Kessinger back in 1993, after Patsy first went missing. It was the same information that Larry Calloway knew, in spite of making up that phony missing person's poster.

Mildred Calloway Dunning was still screaming at Debbie Calloway as they dismissed her as a witness and wheeled her out of the courtroom. Darrell maintains that he'd wished they didn't shut her up and let her stay there and talk and tell all. He believes that Mildred wanted to protect her brother Gene, because of her statements that Gene wasn't the real bad guy in not so many words, even though he killed Patsy. If you think about all of the evidence that's been ignored so far, look at who it points to as the mastermind. Mildred's anger at Debra was because she felt Debra turned her back on Gene, but that in no way meant she was going to protect Debra any longer. Mildred was done with Debra and went all in for the truth. They should've let her tell it!

Chapter Eleven:
Officer Phillip Ballard Testimony

Phillip Ballard is a retired officer with the Kentucky State Police (KSP), having 27 years of experience at that time. During that time he'd been on approximately 15 murder investigations in his career. He testified that initially, Steve White investigated Patsy's disappearance. Then, Patsy's case was turned over to him. He said that days had passed since Patsy first disappeared and the only thing he could do from that point was start back-tracking her steps. (This was the first time Darrell and I had ever heard the name **Steve White**.)

Mr. Ballard testified that the Hartford Police had impounded Patsy's automobile for the investigation. He said Detective White told him there was blood in the vehicle which was tested, but it latter turned out it was unrelated to Patsy. (Whose blood was it? Was it Gene's? Was it Larry's?) He said that the detective told him that Patsy's seat was out of position for her to be driving the vehicle. He said after ten or twelve days, he looked at the car. He said he conducted dozens of interviews after that, which lead him to Gene Calloway as the primary suspect. He said that Gene told him he was at the nursing facility to do some battery cable work on Patsy's car. *He said that Gene Calloway is the one who gave him the newspaper that contained the marriage announcement between Larry and Shirley.* According to Detective Ballard, the marriage license was obtained on February 25th, 1993, and was marked as states exhibit #17 – newspaper notice.

Commentary: I guess after Patsy didn't show up to claim her car, the police decided to impound her vehicle. The marriage license was actually obtained on February 22, 1993, but may have been filed in the clerk's office on the 25th. This means with certainty they had to start planning Patsy's murder as early as February 24th, 1993, but I'm sure it was earlier. I find it ironic and sickening that Gene would turn over the newspaper with the marriage announcement, to the lead detective on the case, thus pointing the finger at his brother

Larry. The question becomes, "When did he turn the newspaper over to Detective Ballard?" There is some dispute about that.

A key point to Phillip Ballard's testimony was that Gene's truck was cleaned up with no traces of dirt, blood or anything in the vehicle, after all of the interior carpet was removed. He stated that the interior of Gene and Debra's truck was wiped clean with some sort of chemical and they couldn't find a speck of dust or dirt. He said the truck lit up when sprayed with Aluminol, but it was sprayed with WD-40 or something because they found zero trace of blood, not even a drop. That's not surprising to us after the forensic investigator found all the blood at Patsy's trailer. Detective Whittaker believed that Patsy was murdered in Gene's truck, but we disagree.

Ballard stated that Mildred Calloway told him when he first started investigating, that she'd seen Debra Calloway walking Southbound on route 231, wearing a wig, dressed up like Patsy. This is a key point because Mildred testified that she changed her statement to police, *after* Gene spoke with her. She admitted to initially telling the truth to police, then lying, then telling the truth on the witness stand.

Detective Ballard was then questioned by the defense on another potential suspect that was reported by a police informant. He stated that this individual was a well-known police informant with zero credibility. He said the man the informant pinned with Patsy's disappearance, was in the penitentiary at the time of her disappearance. Therefore, there was no possibility that what the informant told him, had any truth to it. He was then questioned about the assault on Patsy by Barbara Phelps, Shirley's mother. It was the defense throwing any stones he could to take the blame off of his client. He was grasping at straws.

Finally, the prosecution's case was becoming clear, and there was no way Debra could talk her way out of what she'd done, unless a miracle would occur. It was time for Larry Calloway to take the stand to testify against Debra. I was particularly interested in what Larry had to say under oath. I knew some things that hadn't been made public yet and wanted to see if he'd turn on his probable, co-conspirator. I interviewed Larry in 2012 and was curious to see if his story would change or not under oath. It's been reported to Darrell and me, by Calloway family members, that Gene and Larry were great at faking illness and memory problems to get lesser sentences in their past trials. I wanted to see how "intact" Larry's memory is, and Debra's as well.

Chapter Twelve:
Larry Calloway Testifies

On August 5th, 2014, at the beginning of the trial day, the judge excused one of the jurors, whose relative was in very poor condition and not expected to make it. Then, Larry Calloway, Patsy's ex-husband, swaggered up to the stand. Larry is an older man with gray hair and broad shoulders. He's thin at the waist and had a tough, outdoor edge about him, even though he is/was older. He requested to have hearing equipment to help him and was given a set of headphones. He took an oath to tell the truth and nothing but the truth. I didn't expect much truth to come out of his mouth. I know from past experience, that criminals often mix lies with the truth. I anticipated what lies I could bust him on at this time. He had a very stern, angry demeanor.

Larry, who'd claimed to have memory problems due to a past stroke, had no trouble at all giving the past addresses that he and Patsy shared together as husband and wife. He was asked about Patsy's home in particular. He testified very "matter-of-fact" like, that he hired Gene to "burn it down." He said he was having trouble with some neighbors and he just wanted to move away. Prosecutor Tim Coleman asked him, "And what good would that do you?" He said, "Really, I didn't get to see them people no more, so I was doing pretty good." He was asked if he collected insurance money to which he replied, "Yes." He was asked, "When did you first decide to do that?" Larry replied, "Probably the day before." He was asked, "How did that come about?" He said, "Uh, Vernon and Debbie was up to my house and got to talking about it and I hired him to burn it down." "Was anyone there besides you, Debbie, and Vernon?" "No." Tim Coleman asked him, "And when you said you hired him, was he supposed to receive some compensation?" "Yes he was," Larry replied.

Larry was asked how he'd known Debbie at that time and how long Gene and Debra had been together. He said he'd known her ever since her and Vernon had been together and quite a few years. He was asked if he had personal knowledge of how Gene accomplished the fire. Larry replied, "No." He was then asked where Patsy was when the arson plan was formed and the fire

95

occurred, to which he replied, "She was in Arkansas at her mothers." He was asked if Patsy was aware of his plan. He said, "Yes she was." Tim Coleman asked Larry if Patsy had personal knowledge of it? Larry responded, "I had never told her who I hired." Tim Coleman then asks him, "Did she come to learn that at some point?" Larry said, "She'd never mentioned it."

Now, we already know he's lying, because according to many witnesses, Patsy had threatened to turn the brothers in over the arson many times. She fled back to Kentucky from Arkansas when she learned of the arson plan. The prosecutor asked, "Did she believe?" and he was interrupted. Larry says, "I'm sure she knew who it was." Then Coleman finished his question, "Did she have personal knowledge or believe that Vernon Calloway and Debbie were involved?" To which Larry responded, "Uh, I can't remember that." Yeah right Larry! Tim asked, "At any point prior to her disappearance, did she ever threaten you with regard, with that knowledge?" Larry replied, "No she did not."

His tactic changed. "Do you have personal knowledge of whether Vernon Calloway or Debbie Calloway were concerned about Patricia telling somebody?" He replied, "Not that I was aware of." Without delving into Patsy's knowledge and threats toward Larry, the prosecution continued. "Now, during I guess, at some point you became involved with Shirley Phelps is that a fair statement?" "That's true." "And were you involved with her prior to Patsy's disappearance?" "Yes I was." "And did that cause some trouble in your marriage with Patsy?" "Yes, we argued about it." "At some point, uh did that marriage end?"

"Yes it did." "When did it end?" "It was in." He hesitated, "It was in '92." "I can't... remember the day."

Commentary: Does he really think he can convince people he did remember the dates? After all, that was the anniversary of the day she filed for divorce when she disappeared! Come on! He trying to convince people that Patsy didn't threaten him over the arson, which we KNOW he's lying, according to multiple witnesses. He's still trying to cover his tracks!

"Uh, after the divorce, did you live with Patsy anymore?" "Yes I did." "When did that occur?" "I had never moved out." "Even after the divorce you didn't move out?" "No." "Why not?" "We was... I still loved her, I mean." "Uh, did you maintain a relationship with Shirley Phelps?" "Yes I did."

"At some point did you decide that you were going to become wed to Shirley Phelps?" "Yes. I did," Larry replied. "Did you inform Patsy of that?" "No I did not." "At some point did you and Shirley take a step to begin the process of becoming married?" "Uh, we got a marriage license, we had got a couple before that, and had never went through with it."

Note: To our knowledge, there is no record of them ever obtaining a marriage license prior to that one.

"Were you aware of that being reported in the newspaper?" "No, not at that time." Coleman asked, "Did you subsequently learn that it was in the paper?" "Yes." "Who told you that?" "I found out the day she went missing, that uh Gene had went to the nursing

97

home." "Who did you find that out from?" "I believe it was from Mr. Ballard." "So uh, on that day in question, was there some point on March 3rd, 1993, uh that you either became of concern or was made aware that Patsy was missing?" Larry replied, "Yes I did." "And uh, tell the jury about that. How did you either first become concerned or learn that she was missing?" **"I learned that she'd left the rest home. I was down at Shirley's and Shirley's sister had come down there on her dinner break, which I don't remember the times, and said that Vernon had came over there."** "Well, you can't really get into what Mary said," the prosecutor told him.

"At that point, did you become aware that Patsy was gone?" "I was aware that she'd left the rest home." "So what happened then?" "Well after all that, I went down at Mom's and figured if there was gonna be an argument, which was Hunter's Trailer Court, it'd be here in town. And, she never showed up. So around quittin time when she was supposed to be off work, I went by the nursing home. I didn't see a vehicle. So I left the nursing home so I went out to the... seems like I went out to the trailer. No one was out there. So I came back to town, and I went by the police station to tell them what was going on, and she was... didn't show up. And I started searching, Beaver Dam, Hartford, looking for the vehicle. First time I was lookin, I didn't find the vehicle. Later on that evening, me and my son had got together somehow in town. "Which son is this?" "That was Larry Shane Calloway. And we got to lookin, and the first time I had come past the community center here, I did not see a vehicle. I was by myself. The second time we come by here, it was about dark, the vehicle was parked beside the community center."

"What kind of vehicle was it?" "It was uh, Escort wagon. Anyway, I went back to the police station and told them I found the car." He was then interrupted by the prosecutor. He showed him a picture of Patsy's car and the witness identified it as identical and the approximate spot where he saw Patsy's car parked. "So you find this vehicle, you're with Shane, is that correct?" "Yes." "So what's the next step you took?" "We go up, back up to the police station." "And, do you remember who you talked to there?" Larry testified, "I'm not really sure. It was either Dan McEnroe or J.T. Boling. And I told them we found the car. Me and Shane did, and they asked me to bring the car up there, which we told them we couldn't find the keys. 'Cause we looked and there wadn't no key in it."

"Is there anything else about the vehicle you noticed that was significant when you looked at it?" "The seat was way back in it. Patsy was very short, always had to have the seat up, all the way. I couldn't even get in the car when she drove it, without scooting the seat back. And, the seat was back. I could not find the key in the floor. That was normally where someone would throw a key. So they told us, go back and search some more. We come back, still there was no key. And we seen Vernon and Debbie parked across the road on the corner, from the community center where the car was. So we walked over there and we told them we found the car... **'cause they said that they'd been searching too.** And uh, told them that we couldn't find the key to it, and they told us, did you look in the floor good? This is when we came back the second time."

"You see them, Debbie and Vernon. You mention you have no keys. What happened then?" "They told us to look." "Don't get into what you said. Just... after you talked to them, what happened?" "We went back over to the car, looked a little more and the key was back towards the seat, which we'd already searched the first time. So when we found the key, we went back up there to the police station. We told them that we found the keys; told them about Gene and Debbie settin across the road; and I was asked to bring the car up to where the old fire department is, police station. We take the car up there and park it and we give 'em the keys see, and we go back out lookin more. And when we got through lookin, we went home... wait and see if anyone would call or anything. And there was an anonymous call." The prosecution stopped them saying they can't get into any anonymous calls right now.

"Alright, when you talked to Gene, did you see anything that caused you some concern? Did he have any marks on him?" "Uh, not that, um you know, I didn't notice them at that time. We was down at Mom's. It was later on." "How much later we talking?" **"Week, I guess... two. And there, he was standing in the doorway as I was going out, and I noticed on one of his hands... don't remember which one, there was a bite mark right here, of teeth imprint."** (He's holding his left hand between the thumb and first finger.) Defense attorney, "Objection," which was sustained by the judge.

"You can't make a statement as to what it was, but what did it appear based on your observation?" "My observation." "What was it?" "It looked like a bite
100

mark." "Okay, from this point on, from that day, have you ever heard from your ex-wife Patsy Calloway?" "No I have not." "Uh, at a point after her disappearance there's uh, become an investigation with regard to the arson?" "Yes there was." "And, did you admit your role in that?" "Yes I did." "Did uh, over the years did you still continue to assist police in the crime and the time of what happened." "Yes I have." "Your brother Gene tried to say that Patsy had a walking problem. At times when she got angry, did she walk?" "Yes she has." "Uh has she ever walk and not come back?" "No."

"How would you describe her relationship with her children?" "Very good." "Would it be conceivable knowing Patsy, that she would not stay in contact with her children?" "No, that's very unusual... very." "How was her relationship with her brothers and sisters?" "Fine." "Is it conceivable knowing Patsy that she would not stay in contact with her family?" "She would stay in contact with someone." "No further questions."

<u>Chapter Thirteen: Larry's Cross</u>

"Was there an age difference between you and Shirley?" "Yes there was." "Uh, about how much?" "About twenty years." "Okay, uh how old was Shirley when you..." Prosecutor, "Objection." The judge sustained the objection, but I wish he'd have allowed Larry to answer that line of questioning. "Are you aware of uh, the relationship between Shirley and Patsy?" "Aware, what do you mean?" "Did they have a good relationship, a bad relationship?" "Nope uh, they were fine." "They were fine?" Defense attorney then goes on to question Larry about the fight between Patsy and Barbara Phelps and Shirley Mattingly. He asked Larry about the earlier assault, which was sustained. He then asked him about the outcome of the arson trials. "You're not telling us that you thought Debra was a part of burning down your house are you?" **"She was there when the deal was made, she was there when I paid him."** "You don't claim that she burned your house down?" "No." "That's all I've got of this witness.

Commentary: Now in my mind, it stands to reason that Debra was also there when the kidnapping and murder plot was taking place. She had to be, or why else would she dress up like Patsy and go walking through town?

Larry testified early on, that he found out about Gene, showing Patsy the marriage license in the newspaper, by Detective Phillip Ballard. He said he was made aware Patsy was with Gene, on the same day Patsy disappeared, and that Phillip Ballard was the one who told him about it, referring to the wedding announcement. Wait... "What?"! I find that odd, since *Phillip Ballard wasn't even assigned the case until 15 days after Patsy's disappearance!* Her case wasn't even turned into KSP until 15 days after she was gone. Phillip Ballard didn't receive the case immediately. He said the case went to Steve White of Hartford PD first, and he had to start from scratch. He didn't even do interviews until he got the information about Patsy's car, according to the detective. So either that was one flat out lie in court by Larry, or it did happen and Phillip Ballard was involved?

I don't know if this was a Freudian slip by Larry, but this strengthens my circumstantial argument that Larry knew the paper with the marriage license announcement would be used all along. **Larry admitted to knowing about it in court, on the day Patsy disappeared.** Whether or not detectives were involved, is still debatable and there's no proof of that. However, I believe it's a conflict of interest for Detective Ballard to even work the case, being that Gene and Larry had worked for him in the past as tobacco workers. I have no doubt that Larry knows more than he's telling, but in court, I don't trust his testimony.

Furthermore, Larry and Shirley are the ones who applied for the license and Gene could barely read. Why would Larry make that statement about Phillip Ballard in court? Why would the prosecutor ask this particular question, about how Larry learned of Gene, showing Patsy the announcement? Was he trying to bust Larry or get it on record that Ballard knew of Patsy's disappearance on that very day? Tim Coleman has sharp radar, but he completely missed the boat on that one... or did he? I want to know what the prosecutor knows. Just saying.

The prosecutor asked Larry how he learned about Patsy disappearing. Larry said that Maryann, Shirley's sister, came down to Shirley's apartment on her dinner break, "Which, I don't remember the times, and said that Vernon had came over there." An objection was called for hearsay which was overruled.

Larry stated that he was aware because of that, and that she left the rest home. (Larry told me that he was at Shirley's house with her and the kids that morning, as noted in our recorded interview in 2012. He testified to this in court.) Larry testified that he went to his mother's house, which was next to Gene's trailer at Hunter's trailer court, to stop an argument if one was going to occur. (Was this when he saw Jimmy?)

He said he waited there for hours and Patsy never showed up. (Wait. Hours? Prior record states he went from her work, looked briefly for her car and went to the police at noon.) He said he went by Patsy's work around quitting time and didn't see her vehicle. He said he left the nursing home and went out to their trailer, but no one was out there, so he came back to town and went by the police station and told them what was going on. (Suddenly, Larry is realizing his lies and must change his timeline.) He says, "She was – didn't show up – then I started searching, Beaver Dam, Hartford, looking for "the vehicle."

First Larry says, "She was" but then he stops himself realizing his mistake. She was what Larry? Any moron could see that Larry knew something about Patsy that day. Per my recorded interview with Larry, he stated he went to police around at noon that day. That's an hour and 10 minutes after she left her work with Gene. The police verified this. Why would he go immediately and report her missing, but then not file a missing person's report? The fact is, he knew who she was with and why she was gone. He needed to go to police there, to establish an alibi.

During his testimony, they talked about Patsy's car and how Larry "found it." It's interesting to me that Larry continually referred to Patsy's car as "the vehicle," thus disassociating himself with her car. He did the same thing when he disassociated with his children during our interview in 2012. Patsy was the woman he lived with and claimed to love, according to him. Normal speech calls for him to say, "Patsy's car." His story he testified to in court, was also a completely different story than the one he told me in our interview back in 2012.

So Larry is on the witness stand, lying through his teeth, clearly committing perjury. His typical pattern of behavior is to mix lies with the truth, and so far, nothing has changed. Of course he was going to throw Debra under the bus, because Gene was already dead and he couldn't care less about Debbie. He knew she couldn't turn on him without first admitting her part in Patsy's kidnapping and murder, and she was sitting there, facing life in prison, so obviously she wasn't going to open her mouth about Larry.

In testimony, Larry added that someone would "normally" throw the key in the floorboard. I believe this was his half-hearted attempt at covering up whatever occurred with Patsy's car, that he had first-hand knowledge of. Was he expecting the keys to be thrown in the floorboard? Normally, if someone is out walking, they would have their car keys with them. If someone isn't missing, they would keep their keys in their purse or pocket. At that time, only a little more than an hour after Patsy left work, Larry shouldn't have even known that Patsy was "missing." Yet he's already running to the police. He's already searching for her keys? Right!

I'm not buying Larry's version and if anyone else does, I have swampland in the Sahara for sale. He had to have a reason to look for the keys, especially with Shane seeing Gene and Debra across the street. Patsy was missing, so he had to get the keys in his possession somehow without raising suspicion. Perhaps that's where they'd planned on leaving the keys before her murder. Also, someone had to drive Patsy's car while Gene was committing murder and Debra was dressed up pretending to be Patsy.

Larry testified in court, that he was at Shirley's and also that he went to his mother's house at Hunter's Trailer Court, which is right next door to Gene's trailer. If there was a murder occurring in Gene's truck or at Gene and Debra's house, I find it hard to believe that Larry stayed there for hours (all day) until it was time for Patsy to get off of work at 2:30 p.m., yet knew NOTHING about the murder. If he already knew that Patsy left with Gene, why wouldn't he leave his mom's and go next door to Gene's house to look for Patsy? Bullshit!

On top of that, he told me a completely different story when I interviewed him in 2012, stating he'd went by the nursing home, then directly out to the trailer he and Patsy shared, then to police. He then said he went back out to the trailer. He said he waited out there for Patsy to come home, but she never did, and then he started calling people and looking. **Larry Calloway has no alibi**! Oh how I wish Debbie Calloway would just come clean with it all! But, she couldn't do that without implicating herself in Patsy's kidnapping and murder, and Larry knew it when he took the stand!

Note: (Much of the physical and direct evidence that we found was not introduced at trial. It was however discussed in the first book of this series.)

I also find it interesting that Larry stated he went to his mother's house to stop an argument. Is that what really happened? Did he stop his brother Jimmy from confronting their brother Gene about Patsy's body in his truck? Darrell's theory is that he did go to the nursing home that morning with or without Shirley, intending to start an argument with Patsy. Perhaps they or he were there, but just unseen. Patsy left with Gene, and so I'm assuming that Gene took her straight home to her trailer. Why would he kill Patsy in town, in a trailer next to his momma's house in the middle of the day, with many other trailers around? He wouldn't. Also, she drove to work fine, so it's some nonsense that was made up, about the battery cable. If she had a faulty battery cable, she wouldn't have made it to work driving her own car. Someone had to tamper with it. Her car was seen with the hood up. Was this to encourage Patsy to get in the truck with Gene? One could deduce that.

As far as blood evidence goes, we discussed that in the first novel. My theories make more sense, and with so much blood evidence in Patsy's trailer, I assume that Patsy was killed at her home. After all, the blood in that trailer was all over the place. It was on the living room wall; near and in the bathroom; and by the back door. There is still the possibility that it was someone else's blood in Patsy's trailer, but without a DNA sampling, I guess we'll never know. Since the blood information came out, the bathroom door was taken from Patsy's trailer by KSP. The wall panels were removed as well, but we have yet to learn anything of what the KSP found. Direct blood evidence was NOT introduced in the courtroom.

Larry is certainly telling partial truths about his involvement with Gene and Debra and the arson. He testified that about a week after Patsy's disappearance, he saw what appeared to be a bite mark on one of Gene's hand, but he couldn't remember which one. He certainly telling partial truths about the car and seeing Debra and Vernon Gene across the street from the car. He had to, because his and Patsy's own son, Shane, was with him at that time. After very little cross examination, Larry exits the witness stand, but is reserved in case of later testimony and has to wait outside of the courtroom. Larry said that he was only 20 years older than Shirley. Actually, he's 29 years older than his much younger wife. Just another lie out of his mouth in court.

Chapter Fourteen: Shirley & Shane Testimony

A much younger woman than her husband and partner Larry, Shirley Calloway is sworn in. She's a tall, thin brunette with long dark hair and dark circles under her eyes. She looks very tired and very hard. During questioning, she stated that Gene and Debra were always at hers' and Larry's house. She'd asked for a timeline in court of when this would occur, but admitted that they were at her house all the time. This is different than what she told me in our recorded interview in 2012.

In the interview then, she claimed that she was afraid of Gene and they only saw them in passing. She described an incident during our interview after Patsy's disappearance, in which she was on the phone with her mother, and Gene came in and it terrified her. At that time, she claimed she saw a very visible bite mark on his right hand between his thumb and forefinger. She said he had a look in his eyes that she'd never seen before in anyone and it terrified her. She said she stayed on the phone with her mother and just kept talking in order to wait for Gene to leave, even after her mother hung up the phone. She had to pretend to be still talking with her mom.

In court however, she claimed that Gene and Debra were at her house all the time. If she and Larry suspected Gene and Debra of killing Patsy, then why was the couple "*always*" at their house? Shirley goes on to testify, that on one occasion, she heard them discussing the arson in detail. She testified that Debbie dropped Gene off at the "colored" cemetery, went home, and went back later after the house burned down, to pick him up." Shirley claimed she didn't know about the arson of Patsy and Larry's house, until after Larry was convicted of it. She was never cross-examined on that, because that testimony would have no bearing on either side of the case. I find that hard to believe, considering that she was in a deep affair with him and had given birth to one of his children by this time.

According to Tanya and other witnesses, Larry and Shirley blew through the insurance money like it was water.

Commentary: So not only was Debra Calloway aware of the arson, she actively participated in burning down Patsy's house. It sickens me that there's still a "white" cemetery and a "colored" cemetery in Hartford, KY. It may be historic in nature, but that's a topic for another day. Anyway, Shirley's testimony still doesn't explain how Larry learned that Patsy was missing that day. She avoided perjury charges by not testifying on that information. Shirley was never asked about Larry being at her house that morning. Why not?

NEXT... It was Shane Calloway's turn on the witness stand. He testified that about 4:30 p.m., he became aware that his Mom was missing, because Vernon Gene Calloway came out to his mom's trailer and asked him where she was. (Wait, Larry said he waited at Patsy's trailer in court, then after her work went to police. So if Larry is telling the truth, why wouldn't he see Shane and tell Shane that his mother is missing? If Larry's testimony is true that he was at the house, Larry would've had to have seen him.) After he saw Gene, Shane said, he then went to looking. Why would Gene show up at Larry's pretending to look for his ex-sister-in-law? I think Gene went out there, not expecting to see Shane, but Larry. I believe Gene went to find Larry to see if he'd finished burying Patsy.

Shane testified that everybody went around looking, Debra, Gene... I find that particularly cold of Gene Calloway, that he would kill Patsy, then go out to

110

her house and ask her own son about her whereabouts. Then Gene and Debra would go to town and pretend to look for Patsy, knowing all along that they'd just murdered her. There's an old saying... A drug addict will help you search for your pills when the pills are in their pocket. I guess the same applies to murderers.

I'm sure that Shane never went inside Patsy's trailer and stayed in or near his own next door, because inside that trailer was a bloody scene, unless they'd cleaned it up by then. Patsy had only been murdered that morning by Gene. A cleanup had to take place sometime that day. If Gene fought with her in the living room, and then killed her in the bathroom, it would've been a lot easier to clean up the crime scene. This could also explain why there was "no blood found, not even a drop" in Gene's Chevy Blazer. In my opinion, Gene had Patsy at her trailer with Larry and they'd already bagged her up at this point in time. Detective Ballard never testified to what part of the truck "lit up" when sprayed with Aluminol.

Shane testified that once he learned his mom was missing, everybody went looking for her, Debra, Gene, everybody. He said that he ran into his father Larry, in town, not at Patsy's house. He stated that they found her car and looked in the car, but the key wasn't in it. He said they went somewhere, but couldn't say if it was the police station or not, because he couldn't remember. He said they went back to the car. He said that before dusk, when they returned to the car, they found the key in the floorboard, under the front seat. He said it was brighter, earlier in the day. He didn't see the key then, but when he returned, it was in plain sight, not under the seat. His testimony corroborated

111

what Larry had said on the stand as far as how they found the key, but that doesn't mean Larry didn't have the key and slipped it in the floor.

He said that it would be totally out of character for his mother to leave. He said they had a really good relationship and when asked if she'd just leave without saying a word, he replied, "Never." When asked by the defense attorney about his mother's feelings toward Larry, he said that his mom was very upset with him for having a child with another woman. It was obviously difficult testimony for Shane, Patsy and Larry's son. Nevertheless, it disagrees with his dad's testimony that Patsy and Shirley were fine with each other.

Chapter Fifteen:
Jimmy's Eyewitness Account

Prior to Jimmy Calloway's testimony, the prosecutor and defense attorney discussed at a sidebar, the charges Jimmy faced involving a plea agreement. Jimmy had been charged with Rape 1st degree and Burglary. The rape charge was dismissed, but he did plead guilty to amended Burglary and an Assault 2nd degree charge. His plea agreement had no bearing on his testimony, because he plead guilty prior to acquiring any agreement. However, his sentencing was delayed, pending the outcome of this particular trial over 30 times.

In other words, Jimmy Calloway was not going to be sentenced for his crimes until his testimony in this trial was completed, but the plea agreement was already reached before he even offered to testify. So the only bearing that had on Debra Calloway's case is the timeline of Jimmy's sentencing. This tells me that Detective Brian Whittaker was actively pursuing justice in Patsy's case for a long time, and not pushing it under the rug. In fact, he had questioned Jimmy Calloway in 2008 regarding Patsy's murder. He and the prosecutor were trying to plan arrest. They just had to get their ducks in a row and have witnesses come forward. I don't know if those arrests would've ever happened unless I'd written that news article in 2012, because I believe he wanted to go after Larry for his role in Patsy's kidnapping and murder. The way it all panned out, that didn't happen.

The defense was trying to say that Jimmy's plea agreement was the result of him agreeing to testify against Debra Calloway, and his now deceased brother Gene. That wasn't the circumstance at all, and so the judge didn't allow that into trial. Only that Jimmy's sentencing was delayed as they waited for this to come to trial. Prior to Debra's murder trial, I'd spoken with Larry and Jimmy Calloway about the rape charge against Jimmy. Jimmy said he slept with his then girlfriend, then robbed her. She got mad at him and accused him of rape, but he did admit to the burglary. Now he was about to take the stand at Debra's trial.

Jimmy Calloway required the assistance of headphones for his swearing in and testimony, just as his brother Larry did. He is a thin, small-statured man with white, curly hair and a thin, drawn-in face. He

113

speaks with a speech impediment where he can't say the letter "L" properly and it sounds like the letter r. His R's also sound like W. He also has a heavy southern draw in his speech. Yet when he talks, he is very sharply direct and to the point. Throughout his testimony, he seemed to still have some difficulty hearing, but after questions were repeated to him, he'd answer in a concise voice.

The prosecutor began to question Jimmy. When asked if he knew Debra Calloway, Jimmy replied, "She used to live with my brother, and after that murder, he used to live with his first wife, then he divorced her and married her," referring to Debra. Tim Coleman asks him, "That was after Patsy Calloway's disappearance and death?" To which he replied, "Uh Huh." He was asked if he remembered back in 1993 when Patsy Calloway was reported missing. He answered, "Yeah." He was asked if he remembered going over to Gene and Debra Calloway's house. He said, "Yeah, 'cause they was right next door to my trailer." (Jimmy Calloway lived with his mom.) He was asked if he went over there after Patsy was reported missing. He replied, "Before that." The prosecutor asks, "Before she went missing?" He said, "Yeah. I'm the one who found her in the back of that Blazer." Prosecutor, "That's what I'm trying to get to... when you did that."

"I came back from Charlie's market and I walk around, 'cause I used to pick up cans then. But I'm too old now. I can't hardly bend over. Well, coming into my brother's driveway, there's a... a, some carpet right in there by garbage can. Had a round spot on it like a plate you eat out of (as he makes a round circle motion with his right hand.) It was soppum up, soaking wet with

114

blood, and I a felt of it. And I walked up to the Blazer with the back hatch was open (as he points in the air like he sees the hatch), and the rest of it was shut. He's motioning with his hands as he sees the scene in his mind. There was two garbage bags on the right hand side, one on the left, and she was laying on the right hand side, 'cause I tore the "I almost cussed"... I, I tore the bags open, I seen her right eye, (as he points to his right eye) I seen her throat cut (as he makes a slicing motion across his throat.)"

"So, you're at Vernon Calloway's house, is that correct?" "Yeah."
"Okay. And, you come up and, did you see, uh, your brother and Debra on that day?" "Yeah."
"What were they doing?" "Well Debbie, she was cleaning the dash of the car with some kind of hand cleaner, that's all I seen that woman do." "And my brother was pulling carpet up under the seat on the driver's side."
"Did they see you?" "Huh... not that I walked up there."
"Okay, they didn't see you?" "No."
"Okay, uh why did you tear into the bag?" "Huh?"
"Why did you tear into the bag?" " 'Cause I felt this arm right here (as he grabs his left arm.) It felt like a person."
"And, when you tore into it, you told 'em, what was the first thing you saw?" "Eye."
"Who's eye?" "Patsy's."
"Did you know Patsy before then?" "Yeah."
"Was there any doubt in your mind who that was?" "Nope. That was Patsy Calloway."
"And what other injuries did you see on her?" "That's that's all I seen (and again, he takes his finger across his throat like her throat was cut)."
"Cut across the throat?" "Yeah."

"What did you do?" "Huh?" "What did you do then?" "I went home and got me some Scotch tape and taped it back." "I'm sorry, I couldn't understand. What did you say?" asks the prosecutor. Jimmy replies, "I went home to my trailer and got some Scotch tape, and taped it back."
"Why did you do that?" To which Jimmy answers directly, "Well, I don't want to get killed too!"
"Did you say anything to Vernon on that day?" "Nope. Not about that."
"Anything to Debbie?" "Huh... No. (As he shakes his head no.)"

"Did you tell anybody right away?" "I told Dan McElroy"
"What's that?" "I told Dan McEnroy."
"Dan McEnroe?" "Yeah."
"When did you tell him?" "I told him at uh, I seen the body and everything and he said that they told him, me that they didn't find enough blood in that Blazer on the dash, just one little tiny spot, and they didn't have that kinda test, that you know right there, that can uh, get whatever you wanna call it.'
"Did you tell anyone else?" "Huh?" "Did you tell anyone else?" "Nope." "Why not?" "Cause I was telling people. They didn't believe me so, I just said (and he motions his hands as if to say okay, I'm done.)" "So."
"You just kept it to yourself?" "Yep."

Commentary: Jimmy had told the detectives and others about Patsy on the very day she disappeared, but according to his own testimony, nobody believed him. This is the exact same thing he told Darrell in 2012.

After that, they discussed the crimes Jimmy was charged with. The prosecutor got it on record that he was charged with crimes and entered into a plea agreement, before he was asked if he had any information about Patsy's case. Jimmy basically said that after the plea agreement, he was asked if he knew anything about Patsy's case. He agreed to talk to them to get it off of his chest. His sentencing was held up until the completion of Debra Calloway's murder trial.

Then, Jimmy was asked if he ever discussed with Gene at any time, what he'd found in the back of Gene's vehicle. Jimmy said that they went fishing one day and he asked him. Eventually he relayed that Gene said it was "garbage." So this cold-blooded animal referred to Patsy's remains as garbage. It was clear that Jimmy Calloway had a speech impediment and perhaps was a little slow, but his testimony was extremely direct and you could tell that he was recalling what he saw in his mind as it happened that day. Of course the defense would try to discredit his testimony as hearsay and wanting to postpone his own sentencing, but it was obvious that Jimmy Calloway was telling the truth about his brother Gene and his wife Debra.

Commentary: With all of the witness statements, Patsy was murdered at the hands of Gene and Debra for certain at this point. That makes me wonder about my recorded conversation with Larry Calloway in 2012, in which Jimmy was told by Larry not to confront Gene. Was that the argument that Larry testified in court he was going to stop at Hunter's trailer court? (This again goes back to information in the first book, when I analyze Larry's speech.) Again, Larry knew about it, but his testimony in court didn't completely reflect that he was aware of Patsy's murder by Gene that day. He was still covering his tracks.

The defense attorney tried to make Jimmy look like a liar in court, but it was clear that he was telling the truth. They wanted it to seem like he withheld the information until it was useful for him to turn state's evidence, as a benefit to himself. That simply wasn't true. When he asked Jimmy Calloway about who he told about Patsy's body in the back of Gene's truck, he again said he told Dan McEnroe. The defense reply was "Well, we can't question him because he's not here anymore." Jimmy acknowledged that Dan McEnroe is now deceased. However, his testimony corroborates what Detective Ballard testified to, that the truck was missing the carpets and was cleaned out with some kind of chemical. How would Jimmy know that if he hadn't seen it happen as he stated? This also brings again into question why the cops didn't go to Gene's trailer that afternoon looking for Patsy, especially since Jimmy told Dan McEnroe that he'd seen her body in the back of Gene's truck. How shocking!

Chapter Sixteen:
Ricky Calloway

After Jimmy testified, Ricky Eugene Calloway took the stand. He stated that Vernon Eugene Calloway is his father. He confirmed that Mary Calloway is his mother and he knew the defendant, Debra Calloway.

When asked how he knew Debra, he stated that she was married to his dad after his mom and dad got divorced. The prosecutor begins, "Let's go back to 1993. Do you remember the day, March 3rd, 1993?" "Yes, my 3rd daughter was born." The daughters name was confirmed. When questioned, he stated that Stacy was his wife at that time. "And uh, do you remember, ah, is... birth is always a memorable thing. What time did you go to the hospital that day?" "We went at 4:30 – 5:00 that morning." He was asked if he knew the exact time his daughter was born. He said, he didn't remember.

"At some point, did you see your father, Vernon Calloway?" "Yes." "And was anybody with him?" "Yes." "Who was with him?" "Debbie." "And what time of the day was that?" "Um, uh, I know it was after lunch, but I don't know the exact time." "Um, and, what happened when they were there, anything?" "They waited around til the baby was born, and uh, he was the first one to hold the baby. And uh, it wasn't long after that, they left." "Do you recall, were they there more than an hour, about an hour?" "I'd say, probably about an hour." "And this was close to midday?" "Yes." "At some point, ah...thereafter, did your mother Mary show up?" "Yeah. After she got off of work." "What time would that have been?" "Uh, she got off at 3 o'clock." "Was that before or after Vernon and uh, Debbie left?" "I believe they were already gone."

"Did you subsequently learn or hear about uh, the fact that uh, Patsy Calloway was missing?" "Not until we got home and it all came out in the paper and we got to talk to the family, so." "Cause you were busy with the baby?" "Yeah." "Uh, let's go back to 2009. Uh, was there anything significant that happened in 2009?" "In 2009, he was in the hospital, and we were over there to see him. And he said wanted to talk to me and my sister..." "Objection." "Overruled." "And uh, said that he was gonna write a letter and draw a map and I was asking, what for? And he said the letter will explain everything and he told me, when I get it done, I'll call y'all, and have you come over to the house. Prosecutor asks, "At that time, did he ever mention it to you again?" "No."

"Alright. Let's skip on ahead a little bit more. Uh, at some point your father and your step-mom were charged in this case, is that correct?" "Yes." "Did you receive, you or your wife... who's your wife?" "Uh, Angie Calloway." "Did you or your wife receive a call from the defendant?" "Yes." "And, did the defendant ask you to do anything, uh, specifically?" "Yes. She said there was something buried back behind the house. She said she didn't know what it was. But uh, it was supposed to be back there were they cleaned a deer at. I tried to find it. I couldn't find it. And at the time I was on my way to work. And I told her, I said, I cannot find it. And she said well, and she remembered that there was a stone, or a cinder block or half a cinder block... something in this area. So we walked down about another 20 foot and we found a cinder block. Well, I chopped around in that area and I still couldn't find it. I had to go to work. I gave the shovel to my wife. I didn't make it halfway up the yard and she hollered at me and they had found the box. It was maybe an inch, inch and a half under the ground. And it was muddy, and it had black tape all the way around it. And I told her I said, take it over to the house and I said, and call the cops."

He asked the judge if he could approach the witness. He presented Commonwealth's exhibits #18-19. "Could you look and see what those photos depict?" "Yes." "Is that the box that you found in the back of..." "Well, when I seen it, it was all wrapped up in tape, but that is the size and the tin box that, the shape of it." "And what did you do with that box?" "Uh, left it taped... didn't try to open it. They took it over to my house, I lived across the road. And they called... called the police."

Police brought in a package that contained the mysterious tin box that Ricky and Angie had uncovered at the direction of Debra Calloway and sat it on the prosecutor's table. Then he states, "No further questions." The defense counsel conferred with his client. After the conference, the defense declined to question the witness and he was finally excused from testimony.

Commentary: Sometime after the murder of Patsy Calloway, Gene and Debra Calloway had the audacity to go to the hospital and visit their son and daughter-in-law. He in fact, held his granddaughter for the first time, shortly after he murdered his ex-sister-in-law and they worked to clean up the crime scenes. How could they look at the baby, knowing what they'd done to Patsy? That is an entirely new level of evil, without regard or conscience. More questions arose after Ricky's testimony, mainly, who disposed of Patsy's body. It was in the bed of the truck at Hunter's trailer court, according to Jimmy, early in the afternoon. They had to put her somewhere. Or someone else had to bury Patsy.

Commentary: Darrell said he talked to Stacy, Ricky Calloway's ex-wife. He said that Stacy told him that Gene asked his son Ricky Calloway to lie about the time that he was at the hospital that day. Darrell has repeatedly asked Stacy and others for the time of birth for their daughter, in an effort to establish an accurate timeline, but they have yet to give him that information. This information would've been easily obtained through the office of Vital Statistics by police. He's still wondering why this avenue wasn't approached.

Chapter Seventeen: Angie & Amy

Angela Calloway was sworn in. She's a pretty, taller, long, dark-haired woman with a medium build and a country look about her. She was dressed nicely with her hair and makeup done. She identified the defendant and acknowledged knowing Debra, as her step-mother-in-law. She stated that she was formerly married to Ricky Calloway for thirteen years. She spoke on the occasions that she'd seen the defendant over the years.

"During that time, did you ever have a discussion with the defendant, Debra Calloway, about a wig?" "Yes." "And, did she describe this wig to you?" "Yes." "And, how did she describe it?" "She said it was the same color as Patsy's, but it was just a little bit longer, but she curled it and made it shorter, so." "And what did, she tell you... who liked to see her wear the wig?" "Gene."

The prosecutor asks, "Now, did you have an opportunity, or did you have conversations with her after charges were brought in this case?" "Yes." "Uh, were you contact... you or your husband contacted by her, uh, concerning a box?" "Yes." "Uh, how did you first receive information about the location or the existence, and/or location of the box?" Angie replied, "She first tried to um...tell us, Rick and I, when we went to see her in jail. And then we got like three phone calls, from the jail to my cellphone, and she was describing where it was at." "And uh, tell us about the... did you ever receive correspondence as to the location of the box?" "Yes." "And in that correspondence, did they describe the area where you could find this...?" "Yeah, she drew a diagram."

Prosecutor continues, "So then, you said you had a telephone conversation, you said you had three calls, uh... let's talk about the final one. Do you know what date that was?" "No I don't." "Did you or your husband, or Ricky... were you married at that time?" "Yes." "Did you or your husband receive a phone call from the defendant?" "After we found the..." "No. Before you found the box?" "Yes." "And, what was she telling you during that conversation?" Angie replies, "She was tellin us, and she always referred to it as "X"... Uh, find X and give it to my attorney." "Now uh, during this conversation, who was initially on the phone with her?" "Which time?" "This last time when you found the box." "Rick was." "And um, was it on speaker phone, did you hear it, or was it just his part of the conversation?" "It was just his part of the conversation." "At some point, did you get onto the phone call as well?" "When she first called, I'd answered and she was trying to explain where it was at and I just said, here, tell Rick... 'cause I don't know what you're talking about. So then I just handed the phone to Rick."

"Did you or your husband try to go out during that phone call to try to find the location of what she was trying to get you to find?" "Yes sir." "And uh, kind of tell the jury... what was she, telling you, what was she trying to... to, what clues did she give you with regard to the location of that box?" Angie replied, "She said that there was a shade tree and a picnic table... it was down in the woods a little bit... where Gene and Rob, which is my son, skinned the last deer, and... and that there was a brick or block or something, and that's where it was at." "So did you follow her directions?" "Yes." "And, did you attempt to find this box?" "Yes." "How did you do that?" "Took a shovel and then we heard a clink. And it wasn't buried very deep so we brushed it off well, we saw what it was... and then, I called Detective Whittaker." "Did you find the picnic table?" "Yes." "That she was talking about... uh, did you find the cinder block?" "Yes." "And was it in the vicinity of that?" "Yes." "So her directions were accurate?" "Yes."

"And you mentioned... and what did you do with the box?" "I called Detective Whittaker." "And did you in fact give that to the..." "He sent two of his deputies and they came out there to get it." "Did you open it at all?" "No." "Did you ever look at the outside of the box and note that you were familiar with the box?" "Yeah, I was familiar with the box, but, and like I said I didn't open it, but when they opened it, I knew the box." "Were you there when they opened it?" "Yes." Prosecutor approached the witness and she identified photos of the box. "And uh, where exactly was it... and whose property was it found on?" "It was on her

124

property," replied Angie. "No further questions." The defense declined to question Angie Calloway and she was finally excused from court.

Once Angie Calloway was dismissed, the judge and attorneys met for a sidebar to discuss evidence that was in the locked box. This is the same box that Debra directed Angie and Ricky to find on her property. Inside the box was some paper that was discussed. There was a full version of this paper and a redacted version. The judge decided that both would be introduced, but at different times. In that way, the evidence wouldn't prejudice anyone as to its content of information. This letter would be marked as state's exhibits #20-21, both copies, to be introduced in whole and in part, on separate occasions. They discussed ways in which this particular evidence could be authenticated. They also agreed on how other evidence would be exhibited.

The judge and attorneys also discussed whether or not to admit into court, the civil judgment that Patsy Calloway is deceased. The defense argued that it wasn't proof that Patsy is deceased, only a civil judgment. The judge in fairness, decided to instruct the jury to give the document whatever weight they chose to give it, including none at all. It was up to the jury to determine the validity of whether or not Patsy is deceased.

Next, Amy Hamilton was called to the stand as a witness. She acknowledged that Vernon Gene Calloway is her uncle. She acknowledged that Debbie was the girlfriend of Gene at the time. She also stated that Patsy is her aunt. The prosecutor asked her if she remembered hearing about Patsy going missing in not so many words. She heard about it a few days later. "Where were you on that day?" "Um, I was at school... and then, um, after school, I was dating an older boy, which I later married. Um, we always met up as soon as school let out, and we would run around a little bit, through the night, before he'd take me home, etc...." "There was a day in particular, after school, when we left, um... we were driving from where the high school is. You make a left like you're going to Bob's IGA. Um, there was a lady walking on 231, which... at a glimpse, I thought was Patsy, so we had turned around, and was going back to pick her up. But as we went back by, um, it wasn't her. So we didn't even bother stopping, we went on."

"And, were you able to determine who it was?" "No." "And uh, later... did you think that was close in time to uh." "I think it was close and similar, cause I think it was a few days later, I heard she was missing." "Now were you, did you also around that same time period... uh, in '93, happen to see, uh your uncle Vernon Calloway and Debbie at another locations?" "Um, yes. It was at uh, Frank Burton's house. It was uh, my soon to be husband's "best friend." So we hung out there like all the time." She gave more info regarding her friendship and where she used to hang out.

"And on that evening, that night..." "It was like the middle of the night, um... we were there. I don't remember what we were doing. But, I just remember um, Gene coming up. I don't remember if Debbie was with him at that point or not. Um, he had gotten hung up by the river... and uh, he needed to know if they had a tractor to pull him out." "And did you in fact help

126

them get pulled out?" "Uh, yeah." "Frank Burton and my husband helped pull them out."

"At some point... you said you didn't see Debbie at the house, at some point did you see?" "Yeah, I rode down with them, you know." "And did you see the defendant?" "Yes." "Was it discussed, uh... did you ask her or did she tell you what they were doing?" "I don't remember which one I asked. I couldn't tell you if it was her or him. But I asked on of 'em, cause it was so late. I asked, "Hey, what are you'all doing down here this late?" You know, and... um, I got the response from one of 'em... getting rid of trash." Prosecutor asks, "Did you happen to see anything in the vehicle you thought was suspicious?" "We thought we'd seen muddy shovels. Uh, but they could... they were hung up in mud. You know, they could've been using that to get out." "Okay, no further questions."

Commentary: So Debra had various conversations with different people about the wig and how it pertained to Patsy's disappearance. She told one witness, "I did what I had to do." She also directed people to find X, or the "lock box." How did she know what was in the locked box? It was clear that she did know, because she wanted them to take it to detectives. This is some sort of plan I believe Gene and Debra and perhaps Larry, hashed out in advance before they were charged with kidnapping and murder. They knew we were getting closer to the truth every day.

After Amy testified, we get back to the whole "dumping trash" thing. According to Jimmy, when he got rid of Patsy, Gene referred to it as dumping trash.

Now here we are at the Burton's property and Amy states either Gene or Debbie told her they were dumping trash and they were stuck down by the river. This was just days after Patsy's disappearance. Were they getting rid of Patsy or the carpets and other evidence? We don't know, but it's damn suspicious for people to be out in the middle of the night, dumping trash anywhere. If it was just trash, why not leave it in their cans at the trailer court? The defense asked her if she was sure of the day that occurred. She said it would have to be a weekend for various reasons.

Darrell states that the property actually belonged to John Lindley, referred to as Mud College Bottoms where they also dug up a well in search of Heather Teague, another missing victim. Darrell said it was the same area that Vicki (Calloway) Hoheimer, Gene's sister, accompanied him and his brother Willard to go search. He said she was actually showed them different locations that she'd went and dug, and said Willard actually dug in those areas to look for Patsy's remains. Darrell said it seems awfully ironic that Vicki, Gene's sister, would have knowledge of Debbie and Gene being there, but now later retracts all her witness statements.

Chapter Eighteen: Sergeant Brian Whittaker

After placing an evidence package on the judge's bench, Whittaker, the once sergeant but now detective, was sworn in. He's a large, clean cut, middle-aged man.

He's a big man, with a downward mouth... almost a frown on his stern face, and a very serious look about him. He's got dark circles under his eyes. He's one of those people who is kind of difficult to figure out. Throughout the trial, he sat on the side of the prosecution with his hand over his mouth. It was like he wanted to speak, but couldn't allow himself to do that. It was interesting watching Whittaker, because when I knew someone was lying, he also knew and he'd get a look on his face that confirmed exactly what I was thinking. Now, taking the stand, I was eager to hear what he had to say. He'd served at that point for nineteen years with Kentucky State Police. After giving credentials about his narcotics and other work in the past, he is questioned about Patsy's case.

Prosecutor Tim Coleman asks, "When did you first become aware or made part of the investigation in the disappearance of Patsy Calloway?" "When Patsy came up missing in '93, I was actually still in the military, uh, stationed in Delaware. I was aware of the case, uh... her son Alan was a friend of mine. We went to school together. I was aware of it then. Of course I didn't join the state police until two years later, in '95. In 2001 when I switched over to investigations, being from Ohio County, that... of course that was one of the most recent cold cases that you could say that we still had on the file. Um, being Ohio county and assigned as an investigator, that basically came to assigned to me. I guess you could say Detective Ballard was uh, still around at that time, um, but he was in drug investigations at that point. Um, all leads had been exhausted as far as he was um... and then at that particular time and uh, it was always on my case file. I'd reviewed it a number of times. I read that case over and over. Um, so I knew it was there. I knew it was still open. I knew that most of the main characters, participants in the crime were still alive at that time. Um, and it just uh, like I said, it was personal to me because I was from here and I'd, I'd, I'd, always wanted to see that case get closed."

"Um, so you were checking on it at the time, was there a... at some point, uh... did something occur that was, kind of brought it to the front burner I guess?" "Yes. I was contacted by um, an attorney here um, a local attorney here... um advised at the time that one of her clients may have had information pertaining to the Calloway case here, that may be relevant... that she thought was important, that I needed to know about." "And who was that person?" "That was Jimmy Calloway." "And did you interview Mr. Calloway?" "Yes myself and Steve Manly interviewed him here at the courthouse one day... um, and heard the testimony that you heard today. Um, and to the fact of you know, that he did see Patsy's body in his brother's truck, that day... um, why he was there, what everybody else was doing, just as he testified today."

"Now at that point, had you had the opportunity to uh, go through Detective Ballard's report, uh and uh, possibly do any interviews in regard to this case, prior to talking to Jimmy?" "I'd reviewed the case, uh... was familiar with most of the case at that point. Uh, the case was kind of difficult to read back then, in '93 they were still handwriting the case, you know they were still doing that when I came on, but it... even as hard as it was, we reviewed the case and went through the case and had the gist of it... knew who was involved... we knew what search warrants were done; what evidence was taken; what evidence had been examined; what the results of that was."

"During um, that review of the case, were you aware of a search warrant being brought or to seize Vernon Calloway's vehicle?" "Yes, Detective Ballard had seized Gene's '78 Blazer, I believe it's what it was at the time, and had taken that to post to be examined by him and others. There was also some lab personnel to come in and examine it for any type of evidence, biological or otherwise. "Um, so when I heard Jimmy's testimony when, about um, Gene and Debbie cleaning the truck out, taking the carpet out, cleaning it, um... it rang a bell immediately, that that was obviously relevant and that it fit, um... the evidence we had on hand. I know it was fact that we'd taken the truck and examined it... the carpet was in fact, gone. Um, you know the seats were cleaned, the dash was cleaned... all of that stuff had been done. We knew that for a fact."

Prosecutor continues, "Was it uh, was there any... did Jimmy also discuss with you uh, this conversation that he had with Mr. Calloway in regard to the contents being garbage?" "He did. Um, he'd mentioned to me the fact, on a later date had a discussion with Gene and I believe Debbie was with him when this discussion was taking place... as far as what... where did the trash go that was in the back of the truck that day. Um, what'd you do with that trash, and he told that it was buried." "Objection." Judge, "Sustained." "Was that consistent with what Amy Hamilton had told you at some point." "Correct." "The trash part is the part that I keyed in on," replied Whittaker.

"Now uh, after you interviewed Mr. Calloway, um, what was uh, the next step in your investigation?" "Um, uh... I had been in contact with some of the people who were involved in this case, uh, Larry the ex-husband and Shirley his now wife and other members of the Calloway family. Um, at some point I received a phone call and this would've been after Jimmy initially made the statement that he made to me. Um, one thing about this family, it seems like once one member of the family knew about something, they all knew about it. So not long after this I get a phone call from Shirley saying that uh, and they're all in Florida at this point, they've got some family that lives around Saint Augustine area... Um, and I get a call saying well Gene and Debbie's on their way to Florida." "Objection." Judge, "Overruled."

"Did you take certain steps to uh, I guess gather information in Florida?" "Yes. Uh, not knowing the nature of the visit they were preparing to make to Florida, and knowing Jimmy just made the statement that he did just that was incriminating, that um... with the reputation that Gene had we, we thought maybe somebody's life could possibly be in danger at that time. Um, myself and a supervisor that I had at the time, um, basically within probably a few hours, uh left and traveled to Saint Augustine, Florida, and was there when Debbie and her then-husband arrived in Florida. Um, and at that time, I met basically the rest of the family that was all in Florida at that time."

The prosecutor continues, "Did you get a chance to interview those individuals at that time?" "Yes. I interviewed all of those, all the Calloway members I, um, Calloway family that was in Florida at that time. I just kind of... for me, we started all over. You know, I wasn't there in '93 when this started so we just sat down and discussed everything they knew. It was almost as if I was starting over, uh, making it fresh in my mind, um... and trying to figure out what we needed to do next."

Prosecutor continues... "So after that, uh... the investigation continued." "It did." "At some point, was the decision made to go to the grand jury?" "Yes sir." "And uh, as a result of that, after that, did you have the opportunity to interview the defendant?" "Uh, yes. After the indictment warrants came out they um, Debbie and Gene were both arrested at their home... transported to Ohio county jail at which time they were both interviewed on that day." "And what day was that interview?" He shuffled through his papers to find what day and responded, "Um, it was in October, 2012." "October 17th be about?" "That sounds correct. I don't have that date in front of me. That sounds right." "During that uh interview of Miss, uh, the defendant, was that tape recorded?" "Yes." "And did you have the opportunity to kind of go through the evidence that you had and determine what her statements would be with regard to that is that?" "Yes."

"Uh, during that interview did you discuss with her or did she indicate where she was on the day uh, Patsy Calloway went missing?" "She's always maintained that she was at work that day." "And where did she say she went to after that?" "Um and well, there's been a couple of different responses to that question. Um, at one point I was told she went to the hospital, uh where Ricky was having their child. Um, on another time, she told me she went home, then went out looking for Patsy. Um, I've gotten several different responses to the same question."

"With regard to the hospital, I'm gonna play a segment of that interview. He played a recording of a very emotionally charged Debbie stating she went to the hospital after work to see the baby. Some of the interview was inaudible, but you could clearly hear Debbie say she went straight to the hospital after work with her uniform on, that she didn't change and went straight from work. She was asked if Gene was there. She said she didn't remember if he was there if he come later on or if he stopped and picked her up. Debbie said, "I said I don't remember."

"Okay, she said she'd gone a couple of different ways in regard to the hospital and she couldn't remember, was that statement consistent to what Ricky Calloway testified to, today?" "Um, yes Ricky, you know he said that Gene was there at some point, that he held his child." "But he also heard, the jury heard that Gene left before Mary got there." "Right." "And Debbie wasn't there with Mary." "Correct." "It also, during that conversation did you ask her whether she thought Patsy was still alive?" "On numerous occasions with the defendant she ssszz, basically every interview I've done with her she's stated the fact that she doesn't believe Patsy's dead. It's come up every time." "We'll play a segment of that interview." Again, the audio played was difficult to understand, but you could hear Whittaker asking her if she believed Patsy was dead in not those words. Her reply was that she didn't know, but believes Patsy is still alive.

"During your conversations with the defendant did she try to support Gene Calloway's position that Patsy just walked off?" "Yes. She stated that she had heard about the fact that when uh, sometimes when Patsy would get upset she'd just go off walking." The prosecutor played the segment of that interview where Debbie tries to push Gene's agenda that Patsy left. Detective Whittaker spoke of Gene's theory and said that's the most ridiculous thing he'd ever heard, yet Debbie tried to give an example of a time when Patsy went out walking and she claimed Gene tried to give Patsy a ride. She said that Larry and Patsy would get to arguing and she'd seen her go off and walk and that she'd seen her do it more than once. "So she was in support of Mr. Calloway, is that a fair statement?" "Correct."

"Alright, uh... during that conversation, did you ask her whether or not she felt guilty about Patsy's disappearance?" "I did. Um, there's never been any remorse shown by the defendant towards any of this. Um, she's consistently lied about what her husband did." "Objection." Judge said, "Sustained." The prosecutor responds with, "Let's play a segment of that interview with part of that." You can hear Detective Whittaker ask Debbie, "You don't feel guilty for what happened to her?" A very emotionally charged Debbie responds with, "No. I don't feel guilty for what happened to her because I don't know what happened to her." That was quite disgusting to hear.

Chapter Nineteen: Locked Box, Prosecution Rests

Coleman continues with questioning Whittaker, "So after you had the opportunity, uh... during that discussion or a, interview with Miss Calloway... did she try to lead you toward the discovery of some information she thought would be helpful?" Whittaker responds, "She tried suggesting that there was possibly something buried in her back yard, that might have something to do with all this, but she didn't know what it was. Um, very vague, um... since we eventually figured out what it was, if it'd been me charged with murder I'd have told me exactly where it was at, but instead, I get all this... well maybe that's got something to do with it, I don't know. Um, but he buried something in the yard. I don't know exactly where it's at. I don't know anything. That's what I get. The we, we'll go try to figure out what that was, but she made no effort to uh, put no emphasis on it. She just kind of threw it out there like it was really not that important."

"So after that interview, did you have the opportunity or did you get informa... further information with regard to that?" Whittaker responds, "A few days later my wife and I were in, I think we were in Muhlenberg, County, and I get a call from uh, Angie Calloway, um, that they had un... at the direction of the defendant, had dug a lock box, or something covered in plastic up out of the yard, that felt like a box or something of the sort. It was still covered in plastic." "Did they provide that to you?" "Uh, since I was out-of-town, it was nine or ten at night... seems like, it was dark. I remember that. Um, I found a uniformed trooper that was working at the time, had him go pick it up. Um, I traveled to my residence. He then transported the evidence to my residence at that time." "Do you have that item with you today?" "I do."

"Go ahead and pull it out." Detective Whittaker reaches under the witness stand to retrieve a large evidence package. He's instructed by the prosecutor to go ahead and open it up. From the package, he retrieves a rusty, silver-colored box and sets it up on the witness stand. The prosecutor takes the item to have it entered as Commonwealth's exhibit #30. "Is that the item that you received?" "Yes sir." He handed the box back to Whittaker and he took it and set it up on the witness stand for everyone to view it.

"Did you open that item" "We did. I opened it there at my residence. Um, inside of the box was a single, white envelope. And um, at the time, you can see where it's rusty... at the time, the envelope rather, was stuck there to the bottom of the box. Um, worried that we may damage the evidence or the contents, I didn't know what was in it, it could've been hand-written, it could've been typed out... I didn't know what was in it. Um, so actually we left it until the following Monday. So this was uh, I guess this would've been a Thursday night when I got it, so the following morning, I transported it the following Monday to Frankfort, to the crime lab... at which time they opened it." "And where you there when that was opened?" "I was."

"Okay. Let me show you what's been marked as Commonwealth's #19 that was previously entered and introduced, and then #21. Look and see if those items were in the box." As he looks at the papers, Whittaker replies, "Yes sir. A letter upside-down, and right-side-up and an open box." "And also #21, is that the letter?" "Yes." So basically, the officer is handed two versions of the same letter that was found in the locked box. One is redacted, while the other is the same letter, but whole in its' content.

"Alright, on that first page, what does that letter say?" "It says uh, I kill Patsy, and Patsy is spelled wrong, but it's obvious that it's Patsy. That's what the intent was." "On the second page what does it say?" "Uh, at the top it says, Vernon Calloway, and there is directions to which we determined to be the location of the body, which says, "Go out to Andy Anderson's 2ⁿᵈ drive. Um, and then there's a makeshift map at the bottom of it. Do you want me to read that too? Uh, go up to the cross; go to the right; right of the 2ⁿᵈ stump; and then there's more, more map I guess you could say, very crude."

The confession letter copy was provided to Darrell Kessinger as a courtesy from someone within the investigation, after Debra's trial had commenced. He was also provided with maps in regard to the suspected location of his sister's remains. During the trial, the confession letter was presented to the jury to look at, as it was discussed between the prosecutor and detective. In looking at the letter, it is obvious to me that it's a fact, Gene Calloway could barely read, write, or spell for that matter. This goes again to my theory that someone had to provide him with the Messenger Enquirer, announcing the marriage license obtained between Shirley and Larry, that, Gene used as bait for Patsy. This confession letter further establishes the fact that Gene was illiterate.

Testimony continues: The defense objects, "Your honor, I'm making my contemporaneous objection." "Overruled." Prosecutor, "I'd like to focus this to the jury." "You may." He then shows the letter with the map to the jurors.

"Did you have a conversation with Miss Calloway after that?" "Um, after the... of course after we found the map, we went back and eventually we took pictures of the location, where it was recovered at, soil samples, in case that was ever an issue and uh... and eventually we went to the jail and re-interviewed the defendant, uh, in reference to the box and mail."

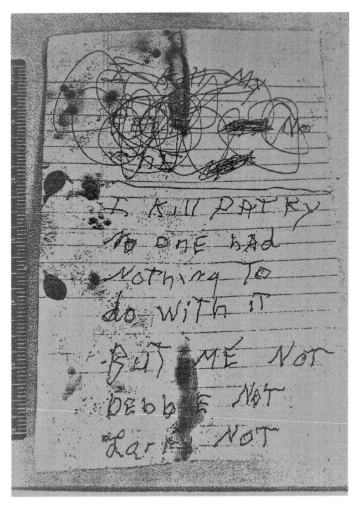

Gene Calloway's confession letter, Page 1.
Provided By: Darrell Kessinger

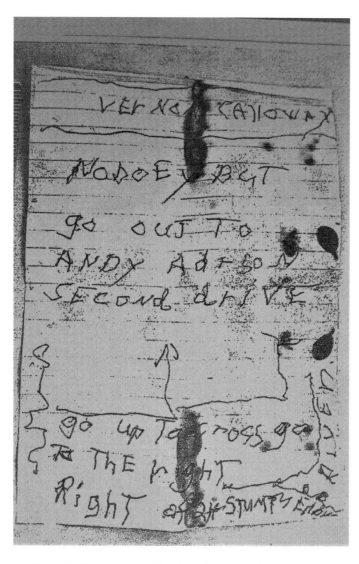

Gene Calloway's confession letter with map, Page 2.
Provided By: Darrell Kessinger

"During that 2nd interview did she admit that she knew what was in the box?" "She knew what was in the box, what was in the letter. Um, I don't know if I got a time when it was written it... she told me earlier that the box, she told me the box was put in there earlier that year, is what I got and this was October when we did the interview, so it'd been around the 1st of the year."

"Based on the information when you got this letter, did you make an attempt to locate the body of Patsy?" "We've made repeated attempts, um, on that property and other properties. So, as far as that goes, um, the map itself is very crude. Um, that particular farm is I believe 100 acres. Um, there's not 100 acres of woods on it anymore, cause I've tore a bunch of it down, you know in the last several years. Um, we've exhausted, um, and you know, we'll never quit looking, but at this point we've done, you know all we think we can do. We brought in cadaver dogs. We've used ground penetrating radar. Um, we've brought in the FBI and their search evidence recovery team has been out there assisting us. Um, you know, it's just a big area, and if we had somebody that could take us to the location, um... where the body's at, you know... I think we're kind of at a standstill at this point." "No further questions."

Defense cross of Detective Whittaker:

"Would it be fair to say you considered the uh, the statement of Jimmy Calloway to be a big break in the case?" "It was a starting point." The defense attorney asked, "I mean, there was... prior to the day that Jimmy Calloway made that statement to you all, was there any impending plan to formally charge anyone about Patsy's gone missing?" "No. Not at that point, but it was the first piece of new evidence that had been added to the case in several years." Right there, Whittaker admits that no charges were pending at that point and no plans for arrests were active.

Defense attorney continues, "And uh, you would agree with me that uh, Jimmy received something in return for that?" Whittaker responds, "He needed motivation to testify. Of course it was his brother he was testifying against too."

"Now um, I assume you talked to Amy Hamilton." "I have." "And, when you talked with Miss Hamilton did she tell you the information about the night at Frank Burton's?" "Yes." "And uh, was there some effort made to go out there?" "Yes." "What came of that?" "Uh, there was a well and of course when Amy took us out to the location, somewhere out again... we're talking about a large farm right along the river, um... she could point to the place where she believed them to be hung up that night. And again, we're talking at that time, sixteen/seventeen years have passed. So it's far from exact location. Um, the present landowner told us about a well that was in close proximity to where they were hung up that night. And we went out, um... really just based on you know, maybe a good working theory. We went out and dug that well up just to make sure. That'd have been a good spot, you know, as any I guess at the time."

"Did Miss Calloway tell you why or how she knew about the letter?" "I believe she said Gene had told her that if something were to ever happen, along those lines... um, that would keep her from going to

prison, or getting in trouble... that kind of thing."
Defense attorney asks, "Well, why would that be true?"
"Why would that be true?" "Yes sir." "Why would the
letter keep her out of prison?" "Yes sir." Prosecutor
objects. The judge admonished, "Only if you know of
your own personal knowledge of the letter itself as
presented to the jury." Whittaker asks, "The way the
letter is now, or it's?" "The redacted copy," the judge
instructs. "The redacted copy," the detective shrugs, I'm
kind of confused about the question then." "I'm asking
if you know of any reason, based off of your
investigation, uh, why that letter would keep her out of
trouble?" "Well it kind of keeps her out of trouble, then
it... I know according to Gene, it's written at the
defendant's behest. She told Gene to write the letter."
"Okay." "After he'd admitted to writing the letter." "Uh
hum." "Oh yeah, Debbie made me write that." "But,
you don't know of any other reason?" "Other than the
fact that... I mean it says that, in his writing, it says she
didn't do it. That's what you're getting at, I know what
you're going for." "Objection." "Sustained." "Your
honor, I think it's out there." "Sustained," the judge
scolds.

Commentary: So according to Detective
Whittaker, when he interviewed Gene Calloway, Gene
says that Debbie forced him to write the letter. Darrell
had heard this, but it wasn't confirmed until that day in
court by the detective.

Defense attorney Austin asks, "Okay. Based on
your investigation and your time with this case would
you, and how long now... what year did you get it?" "I
went over to investigations in 2002. I guess you could
say it's been in my case file ever since. I got actively

144

involved in it in probably 2008." "Okay, so you've been working it on a regular basis for about six years?" "Correct." "You form any opinion about what happened to Patsy?" "Well, I believe." Objection by the prosecutor. Judge says, "Let's stick with the evidence, rather than opinions."

"You've not uncovered anyone who claimed to see uh, Patsy being killed? Right?" "No." "You've not uncovered any witness who claimed to see Debra Calloway exert any type of force on uh, Patsy, uh Calloway, on March 3rd, 1993?" "No. She was never seen again, after she left with her husband (referring to the defendant)." "And, based on your interviews and your investigation, you're not aware of anybody that saw uh, Debra, in the presence of Gene and Patsy that day, are you?" "Just when Patsy was dead, but other than that, no." "You're talking about Jimmy's statement." "Yes sir. You asked about my investigation." "Yes sir." "And according to my investigation, she was seen cleaning the vehicle out containing the victim's body." "And uh, just to clarify, you're, what you're referring to is the statement by Jimmy?" "Of course." "Okay." "Part of the investigation," says Whittaker. "Alright. No other witnesses?" "No." "Okay."

Austin continues, "Where else have you all looked for her body?" "On Andy Andersen's farm, just as the map directs us to." "Okay, so there'd be Frank Burton's property, and search of Andy Andersen's property would be the two places you all looked?" "Frank Burton doesn't own it anymore, uh but." "The former owner, Frank Burton property?" "Yes." "Okay. Alright. I don't have any other questions of this witness."

Redirect: Prosecutor says, "Just to clarify something detective or sergeant... when you said when she said she left with her husband, you meant Patsy leaving with the defendant's husband, Vernon Calloway." "Gene Calloway, yes." "No further questions."

After Detective Whittaker and the jury was released, the prosecutor announced "close," meaning it was time for the defense to put on their case. Shortly thereafter when the courtroom was cleared of the jury, the attorneys approached the bench. The defense attorney moved to have the four counts against the defendant dismissed. Both attorneys gave their reasoning to why the case should be dismissed or tried, but the defense couldn't get around the facts in the case that Debra was seen with Patsy's body and she dressed up like Patsy. The defense attorney was however able to get the kidnapping charge out, because no evidence was produced at trial, which the prosecution conceded he was going to do that prior to trial anyway, but never got around to it. The rest of the charges stood. The court was called to recess.

Chapter Twenty: James Johnson

The defense called James Johnson. After being sworn, the witness was asked if he knew Gene Calloway, to which he acknowledged he did. He testified that Gene was a friend of his and he spent a lot of time around Gene toward the end of his life. He said, "I helped take care of him when he was bed passing." He

146

explained that Gene lived at home with Debra. He said he'd go to Gene and Debra's after work and help change him and they'd moved him from one bed to a hospital bed, and he'd helped them any way they could. He said he'd seen Gene 5 or 6 times a week. He was asked if he remembered the last month of Gene's life to which he replied, "Yes."

The defense asked about Gene's ability to communicate in the last weeks of his life. He said Gene didn't communicate much at all with him. He was asked if he saw Gene talk to other people, to which he replied, "No." He was asked if Gene was in full possession of his faculties at that point. He replied, "No." He was asked about the last two weeks of Gene's life, if there was any improvement in that, to which he replied, "No." He testified that he couldn't recall having any conversation with Gene at that time. He was asked to explain how Gene communicated at that point. He said he'd just moan and groan... just look at you. He was asked if he could remember, if Gene could complete a sentence in that time frame. He answered, "No." "Objection" called by the prosecution. A sidebar was called and the objection was eventually overruled. "That's all I have of this witness your honor."

The Prosecutor begins his cross-examination: He asked him basically similar questions about his relationship with Gene and how often he'd see him. He then asked how much time the witness spent at the home around Gene. He replied something to the effect of 2 or 3 hours at a time. The prosecutor then asked if he knew what Gene was like when he wasn't around him. He said, "No. I do not." "No further questions."

The witness was released from testimony. The court takes a brief recess.

The defense attorney was trying to undermine Mildred Calloway Dunning's testimony that Gene had confessed to killing Patsy on his deathbed. They wanted to make it look like Gene had no mental faculties at that point, which was completely fabricated by Debra Calloway. James Johnson later contacted Darrell Kessinger about his testimony and told Darrell that he lied under oath. He felt guilty, but said that Debra Calloway coerced him into saying that Gene wasn't fully aware of his life and surroundings or reality. He said that Debbie basically asked him to testify on his behalf and then told him exactly what to say under oath. Darrell has copies of the shared texts and emails between him and James Johnson. He said he'd asked Mr. Johnson why he did that and he said he replied, "Fear."

Darrell said that he took the tape and met up with James Johnson at MacDonald's in Hartford. He said they watched the video tape of the trial and he showed James that clearly you could see he was lying. And Darrell asked him if he'd be willing to go into the police department and make a statement and confess to the coercion. He said that James Johnson agreed. They then went together to Ohio County Sheriff's office. He agreed to do a statement. They talked to Detective Brian Whittaker and nothing ever came of it. Darrell never heard any more from Whittaker about the coercion and Johnson was never charged. Darrell said they weren't going to charge him anyway, but he's wondering why Debbie wasn't charged with coercion or

Tampering with a Witness in the Participation in the Legal Process.

We're going to leave this topic and tentative charges alone for now, but we will revisit this in later chapters.

Chapter Twenty-One: Debra Calloway Takes the Stand

The moment everyone has waited for is finally here. Debra Calloway is about to testify. Debbie is a small-in-stature, older looking woman, with a medium build. She's got a very short, feathered haircut, and she's wearing a purple, mauve colored blazer and pant suit, over a brown flowered blouse. As she walks to the stand, she has a very pronounced limp. Her facial expression is a frown that is worn and defiant. She speaks with a southern draw, but it's clear to understand her accent.

She's first questioned by her defense attorney. She state's her name and address for the record as she's focused on him. "Miss Calloway, did you know Vernon Eugene Calloway?" "Yes I did." How did you know him?" "I was married to him at one time." "Okay. Let's talk about that relationship. Um, do you recall approximately when you met Mr. Calloway?" "It was in uh, early 80's." "Okay. And, you had been married before, correct?" "Yes." "And, how long did you date one another?" "It was about 7 or 8 years before we got married." "When did you get married?" "It was August the 17th of '93." The defense continues: "Okay. So, you and Gene, did you call him Gene?" "Yes." "You and Gene, uh, got married about 5 months, 4½ months after Patsy was uh..." "Yes." "missing." "Yes." "Okay."

Commentary: I find it interesting that she and Gene got married just 5 months after Patsy's murder. Perhaps they were counting on spousal privilege laws, but those rules of law exclude criminal proceedings for crimes that occurred prior to marriage or if they're co-defendants.

"Did you know Patsy?" "Yes I did." "Okay. We'll come back to that. How long were you and Gene married?" "Uh, from '93 to 2002." "Okay. What happened in 2002?" "Um, we could not financially make, make it, and so we divorced and so our check wouldn't be cut." "Okay. And uh, what was the nature of your relationship with him after that point? Did you all part ways or what happened?" "No. I, we still lived together." "Okay. Uh, did you all ever remarry?" "No." "So at the time of his death, he was your ex-husband? Legally?" "Yes." "Okay."

"Uh, during the time of your marriage, uh, was... was it a happy marriage?" "No, not all the time." "Was Gene violent towards you?" "Yes he was." "Did he strike you?" "He did." "More than once?" "Yes." "On more than one occasion?" "Yes." "Uh, how long of a period did this abuse go on?" "It went on, uh, several years. Well, 'til before he got real sick." "Okay. Was he also a controlling person?" "Yes he was."

"Do you, uh, remember the... the events around the last day that anybody saw Patsy?" "Yes I do." "Okay. Well let's talk about that. Tell me what happened that day." "Is best I can remember, I got up, dressed and he took uh, he took me and his ex-wife to work." "Where'd you work?" "Professional Care Home in Hartford." "Okay." "And, I don't know what time of the morning it was. I was on my hall, going down the hall, taking care of my residents. And uh, Gene walked in and he seen me, and he said that Ricky and Stacey had had the baby and it was a little girl. And then he said he was gonna go around and tell Mary, and I went on doin my job. And, I'm assuming he went to the other hall where she was working and I never seen him no more 'til that afternoon." "Okay."

Austin continues, "Well let me ask you this. Uh, did you clock in that day at work?" "I'm assuming that I did." "Okay, uh... are you able, I mean... How clear is your recollection of that day, twenty-one years ago?" "Well, the only reason I remember is because of the baby being born." "Okay. Um, so you saw Gene. You knew that Gene was there at the nursing home." "Yes I did." "And then you didn't see Gene 'til when?" "Til that afternoon." "Okay. Uh, did you go to the hospital?" "I'm assuming that I did after work." "Okay. Uh, did you see Ricky there?" "I don't remember." "Okay. Was Patsy with Gene when you next saw him?" "I never seen either, I never seen either one of them, I see Patsy that morning, passing medication and... uh, then later... I would say 10:30, 11:00 o'clock when it was time to pass meds again, there was talk goin around that she wasn't there that she had left and hadn't come back." "Okay. Have you ever seen Patsy since then?" "No I have not." "Okay. Uh, did you have anything to do with Patsy, uh,

151

leaving that day?" "No I did not." "Did you have anything to do with... anything to do with... did you have anything to do with Patsy ever again?" "No I did not." "Okay. Did you kill Patsy?" "No I did not."

Defense attorney continues, "The uh, there's been talk about a arson." "Yes." "There was some discussion about something happening a year or two prior to Patsy going away." "Yes." "Uh, did... did you know, at that time, that, uh... there had been any kind of a scheme to burn down Larry Calloway's house?" "No I did not." "There was testimony earlier today, that you were at Larry's house, and this topic was brought up and this plan was made between Larry and Gene. Is that true?" "No I was not there at the time they discussed it." "Okay." "I knew nothing about it." "Okay, um... when was the first you ever heard about it, there uh, plan to... being any kind of a plan to intentionally burn down Larry's house?" "Not 'til after, way after the house was burnt down, the house had burnt down, and uh, Vernon and Larry were charged with the charges for arson." "Now, they weren't charged with that until after Patsy went away. Correct?" "That's correct." "So is it, are you telling us that, you did not know about this, this uh, alleged scheme." Prosecutor, "Objection." "Before?" "No I did not." Judge overruled stating, "I took that as preliminary. Continue." "Could you repeat your answer, I didn't hear that." "No I did not. I didn't know anything about it 'til afterwards." "Okay."

Commentary: This defense attorney keeps referring to the arson as "alleged." No. Larry plead guilty to the arson. Just because Gene wasn't convicted, doesn't mean it didn't happen. Fact is, the house was burned by arson. It's a matter of court record as fact.

"Now um, on the day that uh... Patsy was last seen, did, did you help Gene in some way with, with his vehicle?" "No I did not." "Were you involved at any point in cleaning or pulling out carpet or anything inside that, that vehicle after that?" "No I was not." "Did you see Jimmy... did you know Jimmy Calloway?" "Yes I did." "Did you see Jimmy Calloway that day?" "No sir. I did not." "What did you all do with your garbage typically at that time?" "It set in garbage cans, beside the building by our trailer, and the city picked it up once a week." "Okay."

"Um, do you know Amy Hamilton?" "Yes I do." "Did you know Amy Hamilton then?" "Yes I did." "Okay. And, do you recall a night where you... you and Gene were at Frank Burton's farm and ran into Amy?" "Yes I do." "What happened that... on that occasion? "We had went out there that afternoon. Uh, was riding around... and he went out that way... and he went through the field, because and, he was looking for signs of deer. It was during deer season and he always went out driving around and scouting around and seeing where deer were at... to see where they, more at than anything else to find deer, to see where they were located." (Deer season wasn't in March. Furthermore, Debbie testified "afternoon," but it was actually 3 a.m. when they were seen, according to Darrell's notes from '93, and Amy's testimony.)

"Did you all have any difficulty with your vehicle on that night?" "Yes we did. He got hung up in the mud." "What'd you do about it?" "I'm thinking that he tried, he tried to get out and he couldn't. Then we got

153

out of the vehicle and we remembered that there was a house up there. We got out and walked to the house. I knocked on the door, and Amy came to the door. And, then I reconi... I mean, I didn't know she was there 'til I knocked on the door, and she answered the door. And I told her that we had got up there, and were hung up in the mud and we couldn't get out. And Gene asked if they had anything to, a tractor or anything that they could come pull us out with." "And, and did you all eventually get free that night?" "Yes, they come up there and pulled it out." "Okay. Did Gene bury a body out there?" "No he did not, not that I know anything about." "Okay. Did you see Gene that whole... were you all together that whole time?" "Yes we were." (She said, "Not that I know anything about." Of course she'd deny it.)

"Okay. Um, do you know anything about um... carpet being removed from that uh, vehicle that a Gene had?" "Yes I do." "What happened?" "It, he took it to his son-in-law's car wash, because they had been fishin, and uh, one of them fell through a hole in the back bed of the truck. So he took it up there to his son-in-law and they took the carpet out, and fixed the hole in the bed of the truck. And then, I'm assuming that he put the carpet in it because I wasn't there. They put other carpet in it after they fixed the hole." "Okay. Do you know of any reason um, no... nevermind."

Commentary: Darrell had been told that Gene's daughter Linda and her husband Tim helped him clean the blood out of the truck at the detail shop, after the carpets were removed. He was told this in 1993, when he went to Kentucky. It's interesting that Debbie came up with the "hole-in-the-truck" story and said the

154

truck was fixed at the shop. I guess she had to, because she didn't know if they had any witnesses to rebut her testimony about the detail shop, and cleaning the truck out. However, her testimony doesn't explain why the carpet was removed from the front of the truck, inside the cab.

Austin continues, "Uh. You testified earlier that Gene was controlling." "Yes he was." "Did, did that extend to matters of a sexual nature?" "Yes it did." "Did you own a wig?" "Yes I did." "Why did you own a wig?" "Be... well Vernon had got it. And we had used to go to the auctions and apparently he had picked it up. And it was in a box with a lot of things we had gotten from an auction." (First she said they used it at the auctions, then claims he got it from the auction.) "And he decided that he wanted me to put it on, because he was wanting me to go have sex with somebody else. And he didn't want 'em to recognize me, in town, on a regular basis."

"Did this happen one time, or did this happen more than once?" "More than once." "On these occasions, well first off, did this happen... when in time did this behavior begin to occur?" "It was... it was way past 1993. I don't know exactly what year, but it was quite a while." "Was it still when you all were actually married to one another?" "Yes." "Okay, so it would've been sometime between '93?" "'93 and 2002." "Okay. So, how, how many times would you say this happened?" "About three, maybe four." "Okay. On the day that Patsy was last seen, did you walk up and down 231 wearing that wig?" "No I did not." "Had there, I mean... had, had you ever touched that wig at that point in time?" "No sir."

155

He continues, "Okay. So uh, tell... tell me about your relationship with Mildred Dunning." "She was my sister-in-law." "Did you and she have a good relationship?" "Yes we did." "Okay. Now, uh, did that ever change?" "Yes it did." "When did it change?" "Uh, about... a little over two months ago." "Do you have any idea what caused that?" "Yes I do, because uh, Vernon was cremated. And uh, his grandson could not tolerate his ashes being at his mother's home where he lived. So uh, Linda his daughter, asked me if I would keep 'em at my trailer and I said yes. And Mildred knew that they were there. And, a little over two months ago, uh, I met somebody, and I'd been seeing him for over two months. And I ran into Mildred. He was with me. We were at WalMart. Uh, run into Mildred and Billy. And uh, she was tellin me about some of the distant family that was kin to them that I know that was uh, really very ill, in Illinois. And then she asked me who he was and then I told her. And she looked at me and said, "Is he living with you?" And at first I didn't say anything and then, I just told her the truth. I said, "Yes he is." And after I said that, she wouldn't speak to me no more, so I just turned around and walked off, and went to the checkout, and paid for my stuff, and left." "So, this happened about two months ago?" "About two months ago, maybe a little over." "Okay." (This was two months prior to trial, so what bearing did that have on Mildred's witness testimony that she gave to police at that time? None. Her and Gene were already arrested and charged with the crimes.)

"We had a witness claim that you said that uh, you did whatever you did 'cause you had to. Do you remember that testimony?" "Yes sir I do." "Uh, do you remember saying that?" "No I do not." "Okay. Did you ever tell anybody about the situation with the uh, the wig and the sexual behaviors?" "No I did not. Nobody other than the detectives." "Okay. Uh, now you did tell the police at some point during the investigation?" "Yes I did." "Okay."

"Did you ever uh, tell Angie and Ricky about a... a letter in the back yard?" "I told them about something in the back yard. I at the time, I didn't know what it was." "Okay. Well, how'd you know that there was something back there?" "Because, one day I was in the house, and Vernon went... and was back in the back of the trailer and I went in the living room and he wasn't there. So I thought he had went out to the kennel to do something, so I walked up out there and he wasn't out there. So, I was lookin for him and I walked towards the back yard, and he was down in the edge of the woods, and I started walking down there and I got part of the way... where he was at, and when I got... stepped there, he looked at me and he gave me a look, used cuss words... and told me to get back in the house. I turned around, as I was coming out, there was the cinder block or concrete block, I don't know... whatever you want to call it. I hit my foot on it. I almost fell, as I was going back to the house. I went back in the house, and I stayed in there and I didn't come back out."

"What about that would cause you, when you got arrested, would you feel like that somehow had a relationship? There was some reason to bring it up now." "Okay. Well, because uh, after he'd done that, uh... I used to could go to the grocery by myself; go to town; pick up the mail; uh, go sit out on the porch; and visit with people... And, from after that time that he had

157

done that, uh, he never would let me go to town by myself. He'd always took me to town. Uh, if I was in the kitchen or the laundry room, he was settin in there, he would say, "Where you at? What are you doin?" If I went out on the porch to visit with Angie or anybody, uh, I wouldn't be out there maybe, luckily five minutes. "Where you at. What are you doin?" If somebody called me on the phone, "Who are you talkin to?" And he never let me call anybody. I could not call anybody. If they called me, he had to know who I was talkin to." "So, he became more suspicious is what it sounds like." "Yes, he kept me in his sight all the time. He would not leave me alone not... at all."

Defense attorney continues, "I, I, I, I still, I want to be clear... Why? Why did you draw a connection between these two things?" "Because, after I'd seen him out there with that, and then he made me stay with him, he'd go... like I said, he took me to town. He wanted to know where I was at all the time, in the house. Even if I got up and went to the bathroom, if I was gone too long, he wanted to know where I was at. I was not allowed outside by myself. If I walked out, he made me come back in the house. Uh, he would... used to have bad dreams. He would wake me up at night and he would tell me what they were about. And, after he'd done that, he got to where he was havin more dreams during the night and he would wake me up and I would say, "What's the matter?" He just say I had a bad dream, but he wouldn't tell me what it was about. And he always, when we went anywhere... he would keep looking in the mirror. And, instead of going directly to where I needed to go, he would turn off on another street, or go a different way. He would never go the same way we always used to go. Just like going to the grocery. He, instead of going straight from our house to the grocery, he'd like... down 69 and then 231. He would take a different route every time. He would never go the same way all the time... no matter where we went."

"Did you tell him to write a letter?" "No I did not." "Did you tell him to do anything having to do with that box?" "No I did not." The defense asked the judge if he could approach the witness and ask her to identify something. He was granted permission.

"Um, Miss Calloway, uh you testified that you were married to Gene Calloway?" "Yes." "And you'd known him for a number of years." "Yes." "Were you familiar with his handwriting?" "Yes I was." "Okay. Uh, I wanna show you what's been marked as, uh, Commonwealth's exhibit #28. No is, do you see writing on that?" "Yes I do." "Is, is... does that handwriting look consistent with what you knew Gene Calloway's handwriting to be?" "Yes it does." "Your honor, I'm also now going to show Miss Calloway what's been admitted as Commonwealth's exhibit #21. Do you see the handwriting on that document?" "Yes I do." "Is that handwriting, is it consistent with what you knew to be the handwriting of Gene Calloway?" "Yes it does." "Okay."

"Your honor, I'm gonna move at this point, what's been marked for identification purposes as, uh... well, it's Commonwealth's exhibit #20, for ID purposes only. The judge agreed after they'd discussed it. The prosecution objected. At sidebar, they discuss both versions of Gene's confession letter, redacted and un-redacted. Defense attorney argues that the entire document should be introduced in its' unaltered form. The prosecution withdrew his objection after the conference. The judge explained to the jury that the two versions of the confession letter were the same letter, but one was redacted and now, they're both fully admitted.

"Ma'am, I'm gonna show you what's now been introduced, what's known as Commonwealth's exhibit #20. I'm gonna ask you if you recognize that first of all. I say Commonwealth's. I guess it would be... no that's right." "I recognize it as his handwriting and I remember seein it at the jail when Detective Whittaker brought it down there and showed it to me." "What does it say?" "It says, "I kill Patsy. No one had nothing to do with it but me, not Debbie and not nobody, but go out to Andy Andersen's 2nd drive, go up to the cross, go to the right." I mean, that's all that I can see that I can read." "Okay."

"There's some, there's some other, what may be writing on it that you can't read?" "Yes." "Okay. Your honor, I'd like to publish this to the jury." "You may," instructs Judge Dortch.

"How has uh, do you know Ricky Calloway?" "Yes I do." "Ricky's not your son. He was your step-son at one time?" "Yes." "And then, did you also know Angie?" "Yes I do." "His then wife? Or..." "Yes." "Ex-wife now I guess? Um, how is your relationship with him?" "It was fairly well, not good all the time. It was pretty good with Ricky, but not with Angie all the time." "Okay. Did it uh, was there a defining moment where it got worse?" "Yes it did." "What happened?" "It was after I was released from jail. And I went back home and they had moved into my trailer, and were living there with me." "What, what happened?" "Well, uh, things that I would do... I would do the laundry, I would do the cookin, I would try to keep the house clean... and then when she would come in from school. She would go right behind me and repeatedly do what I had already done. Like I didn't do a good enough job to suit her in my own home. And, it seemed like everything I'd done, I tried to do their laundry and she would leave me a note on the refrigerator, "Do not touch mine and Ricky's laundry!" All I was trying to do was trying to help, because she was going to school. And, I was there trying to keep the house and help with the meals so she wouldn't have to come in from school, or he wouldn't have to deal with it when he come in from workin, after workin all night."

"At, at some point did, did Gene move back in with you?" "Yes he did." "Um, did you live with him until the end of his life then?" "Yes I did." "And uh, tell me, do you remember the last couple weeks of his life?" "Yes I do." "Were you able to have conversations with him?" "No you were not." "Um, was he able to verbally communicate? Things that he wanted?" "No he was not." "I'm sorry." "No he was not." "Okay." "Um, can you think of him... can you, can you recall a time, during that time period, where he completed a sentence?" "No. I cannot." "Okay." "Did you do anything to help get rid of anything relating to the disappearance of Patsy Calloway?" "No I did not." "That's all I've got of this witness your honor."

Chapter Twenty-Two:
Debra's Cross-Examination

The anticipation for Debbie's cross-examination is palpable. I believe everyone in the courtroom was awaiting this moment, to see what she had to say for herself. The judge advised that Miss Calloway was back in the box and the prosecutor could begin his cross...

Tim Coleman goes at her... "Mrs. Calloway, I do have a few questions for ya. When did you... you said that you had first got with Mr. Calloway back in the early 80's, is that correct?" "Yes." "And you lived together from...pretty close in that point, up until the end of his life for the most part, is that a fair statement?" "Yes." "And, you said that, uh, well I guess it would indicate that you were fairly close to his family?" "Yes." "And that included Ricky?" "Yes." "And you were his, for all intents and purposes up until you married, you're "sort-of" step-mom, and his step-mom actually, from after that point. Is that a fair statement?" "Yes." "And as a step-mom to Ricky and the other children I would assume that you took some great pride, in uh, their families and their children and so forth?" "Yes I do." "And it felt like they would be, you know the fact that there were births and things that go on in their lives, were significant to you." "Well, it meant a lot to me." "It meant a lot to you?" "Yes."

"Now, let's go back to that March 3rd day. Uh, that was the day that one of these grandchildren were born wasn't it?" "Yes it was." "And, that's a significant event?" "Yes it is." "And that's also the day being significant that Patsy died, or at least went missing?"

162

"Yes." "So that was a day that kind of sticks out in anyone's mind. You've got two very large events surrounding that day, fair statement?" "Yes." "Yet on, in discussing that, with the number of times you talked to Detective Whittaker, and now in front of this jury, you don't really remember, or can't tell them what you did that day. Isn't that true?" "I don't remember exactly that it's been over 21 years ago." "Well I understand that it's been 21 years and if I was bringing this up for the very first time you ever talked about it, that would be a different matter, and I'd certainly understand that. But you have had two major events... the birth of your uh, Ricky's child, and the disappearance of Patsy, which was of great speculation about you and Vernon from that day on, fair statement?" "I assume so." "You assume so. You don't know?"

Debra's mild demeanor immediately changes and her voice clearly gets loud towards the prosecutor. "Well, as of that day, I didn't know that it was." "But very soon thereafter right?" "Yes. Very soon thereafter." He goes right in on her. "So you have this very much suspicion, surround the events that you did, and the events that Vernon did, and the things that you found out happened that day. And you can't tell this jury you remembered what went on that day?" "I put... yes I remember, the best that I can remember. I know what went on that day."

Coleman continues, "Why is it... when you were talking to Detective Whittaker, at... you gave two different stories, whereas one you, went over with Gene or maybe you went over there with Mary, or maybe you didn't do that at all... you just went home and changed clothes? Which was it?!" "I don't understand what

163

you're trying to say." "You gave at least two or three different versions. Which one is true?" "I worked at, the best I can remember... I worked that day. We went to the hospital after I got off from work. I was in the lobby with his daughter and his grandchildren, while, uh... they were seeing the grandbaby. Then, I went home, changed clothes, and I don't know who it was that said that Patsy didn't come home from work. We got in the vehicle and we started going through town, and around through town and driving and seeing if we could see her anywhere." (The whole time Debbie's speaking, she's got her eyes closed and her face shows annoyance and defiance. I find it very interesting that she referred to the car as "the vehicle" just as Larry did. What vehicle? Patsy's car? She didn't say, "Our car or Gene's car... She said, "The vehicle.")

"So now you're certain. When just a few minutes ago, when you were talking with this jury you said, "I assume I did this, or I may have done that, or I really don't remember." Debbie lets out a heavy sigh and rolls her eyes at Tim Coleman's probing. "Well, exactly no, I don't remember exactly." "So." "But I am." "So when you just said, told them specifically what happened, you're just making that up?" "No, I'm not just making it up. That is the best that I can remember, that I think, that I did do... that I did go to the nursi... to, to the hospital, after I got off from work, because I did... the best I can remember, I did work that day. And..." "The best that you can remember, but you may not?" She's shaking her head, "Oh, I remember that I did work that day." The prosecutor interrupted, "And the best you can remember is that you went to the hospital at some point."

Both parties are talking or arguing at the same time. "Because Vernon came in, to the nursing home... after the baby was born, and I was on my hall, he seen me. He stopped me and he said Stacey and Ricky had had a little girl. He was going around to tell Mary, his ex-wife... well, at that time she was still his wife. I'm not exactly sure when their divorce was final. And he went to tell her. I went on about my work. And, where he went or when he left, I don't have the faintest idea."

"So you're certain about that little piece but what are you not certain of? You keep saying, "I assume or I think." "Well I think, I'" "If I... If, if this is your life..." "I know it is." "Here and this has been surrounded you forever, why is it so... I don't know?" Debbie responds, "I don't remember the exact time that, how long we stayed at the hospital, or if we went home first, and we helping look for Patsy and then we went to the hospital later... I don't know exactly which way it was done, but I know, I did go to the hospital, uh... I assume that I did go to the hospital, because he came and picked us up after work. He told us that the baby was born and then, when I went home and changed clothes out of my work clothes, I, the best I can remember. I don't know if it was his mother. His mother lived right there in, not in front of us, but the next trailer. And, somebody said that Patsy did not come home from work.

Coleman probes, "So he told you, that, when he came to pick you up that he had a granddaughter, is that what he said?" "He came and told us at the nursing home, that morning." "And then he came and picked you up later?" "Yes, at 3 o'clock." "And, you heard the testimony of Ricky who's this, who was a son to you right? And it was his grandbaby and you heard his testimony." "Yes it was." "And you heard his testimony." "Yes I did." "It said that you were there *midday*, not after work. "Right?" "Um, well." "Did you hear that testimony?" "Yes I did." It's clear that Debbie is a bit shaken. With her testimony, she shakes her head no or yes and her body language doesn't match her statements, while keeping her eyes closed.

"And, Ricky... that being a big day in his life should remember that day pretty well himself. Is that a fair statement?" Debbie doesn't respond and so he asks again... "Is that a fair statement ma'am?" "I would guess... yes I would say it would be, probably."

Clearly frustrated, Coleman continues with his questioning. "Alright, so... Let's talk about this arson a little bit. When did you first find out that your husband or boyfriend was involved in the burning of Larry and Patsy's house?" "When they came and charged him with the arson. Pressed charges." "First you heard of that?" "Yes... about fir... about it being arson, yes." "So why did you tell somebody at a later time that you let Gene off at the graveyard?" "I did not let Gene off at the graveyard." "You heard that testimony, didn't you?" "Uh well, they might have said that, but I did not let Gene off at no graveyard." "And that person has nothing to gain from saying that does she, when she said that, is that true?" "I don't know if they do or not." "You don't know?" Clearly Debbie is angry. "I don't know if they have any, anything to gain or not. But I did not let him off at a cemetery."

"Now do you remember seeing Larry and Shane when they found Patsy's car?" "No I do not." "So that's another bit that you... you said you went out lookin." "Yes we did, we were..." "You went out looking. You didn't see anybody?" "We drove around looking for Patsy and the vehicle." "So did you see?" "We didn't see anybody that I can remember." "Never came across Larry? Never came across Shane?" "Not while we were looking, no." "Didn't know the vehicle was found?" "I didn't. No. Not 'til way later that afternoon and they said they... after I went home they said that they'd found it at the community center."

"Now, you heard reports about this wig and you're walking down the road right?" "Yes I did." "Now up until your testimony, did you deny ever having a wig?" "No I did not." "When was the first time you told somebody you had a wig?" "When I talked to Mr. Coleman and to you and to Mr. Whittaker, when my attorney here at uh, uh, in a conference room." "After you were charged?" "Yes." "But every time before that you were asked about a wig, you denied it. Isn't that true?" "No. No I did not. I was never asked about it, that I ever remember."

Commentary: She wants the people to believe that she can't remember what happened the day her grandchild was born and her sister-in-law was murdered, but yet she clearly remembers speaking to detectives and the prosecutor about the wig for the first time, according to her. How telling. She's also denying the testimony of everyone on the prosecution's side of the case. She can't keep up with her lies.

"And this wig, wasn't it very similar to Patsy's?" "No it was not." Coleman approaches the witness with a large photo of Patsy Calloway. "No it was not," as she looks at the photo. She is very cold in her demeanor. "How was it different?" "It was like, down to here, and it was a reddish brown." She holds her hands on her shoulders, describing that the wig, according to her was much longer than Patsy's hair and a different color. "It was not that dark." "So why did somebody that saw it said that they looked alike?" "I don't know." She said with a smirk on her face. "You don't know?" "No I do not." "You just... everything is just befuddling you isn't it?" "No it's not."

"Did you ever tell anybody that Gene liked you to dress up with that wig, so you looked like Patsy?" "No I did not." "Why would he do that?" "Because he, he enjoyed doing that." "He didn't do it, but he enjoyed doing it, is that what you're telling this jury?" "No I'm not." "Well uh, you said that he didn't do it, then you just said that he enjoyed it?" "I don't understand what you're sayin. I don't understand." "I asked you did it happen, you said no." "But you asked..." It's difficult to hear the two of them arguing because they keep interrupting each other. "I asked you why would he ask you that and you said "he enjoyed it." He continues, "Asked me why that happened." Debbie, clearly shaken, responds, "What are you, I don't understand what you're talking about." "I think the jury heard the answer." "Well, I don't understand why, what you were asking" "Objection. Judge I think she's asking him to restate the question." Judge says, "Miss Calloway, just listen to the questions and try to answer them."

"I asked you, Did Gene ever have you dress up like Patsy? "Because he enjoyed it." Debbie replies, "No he did not have me dress up like Patsy." Coleman responds, "Then I said why would he do that, and you said, "because he enjoyed that." Debbie gives her excuse, "He had me dress up in the wig, because he enjoyed watching other men have sex."

"But, haven't you told Detective Whittaker on a number of occasions how jealous he was?" "Yes he was." "Didn't you tell Detective Whittaker that he wouldn't let you out of his sight, your whole time with him, because he was so jealous of you?" "Yes." "So now, after years of denying that you had a wig, when you finally come up with it..." "I" "It's because Gene wanted you to have sex with other men." "Yes." "Is that what you're telling this jury?" Debbie replies, "The wig did not come in... did not even have the wig or get the wig 'til way later in 19 and '93. And he had me to put it on, because he wanted me to go have sex with somebody. And the gentleman that he had picked out, he did not want them to recognize me when we were out in town, because they lived in the same town." Coleman goes at her, "So why, up until the time you were charged then, did you not have a wig?" "I did not uh, deny having a wig, because I didn't have one until late in 19 and '93." "You were asked on a number of occasions if you had a wig and you said no." Angrily she replies, "No I did not."

He continues, "And now you're saying at one hand he's jealous, but on the other hand he's making me have sex with..." Debbie says, "Yes he was jealous of me going, out by myself and talking to a male person. But, if it was his idea, to have sex, he got off on that. That's

169

what he liked. That was okay. But I was not allowed to speak to a man or a boy, unless he said it was okay."

"Do you remember the testimony this morning of Amy Hamilton today?" "Yes I do." "You heard her testify that she saw you out at some point right after the uh, Patsy's disappearance, and you had gotten stuck. Correct?" "Yes." "And you told this jury all about that happening. You went up to that house... all the details of it. Is that correct?" "Yes. I remember." "How you all were out looking for deer and so forth." "Yes."

The prosecutor approaches the defendant and asks her to read the first line of a page to herself. "Read that first line right there to yourself." He hands her papers, then gives her a few moments to read. "Have you read it ma'am?" "Yes I have." "Do you agree with that statement?" "No I do not." "Did you tell Detective Whittaker that?" "I do not know, but I do know that I did not give uh, his... Vicki Hoheimer anything." (To clarify, Vickie first told police and Darrell that Debra gave her the wig to dispose of, then she changed her statement to police and denied saying that.)

Coleman replies, "I'm not asking about that, I'm just asking this first sentence here, this report... Debra denies ever being stuck in a field at night out at Johnson School Road with Gene." "I was, as far as I..."

Defense attorney Austin, "Judge I'm gonna object to the hearsay. I think what we're getting is uh, I think we're getting a summary written by presumably Detective Whittaker, but some, some police operative. Uh, uh, and and and, that's being used as, and that's being used as means of cross. I think that's not the best evidence of that, and its hearsay." Prosecutor responds, "I can play it later judge, I just wanted to make sure we're clear that she's saying, that she didn't say that to Detective Whittaker." "Overruled." "So that's your testimony right? You never said it?" "As far as I can remember (as she shakes her head no) I never said it, no." (It's obvious that she's lying about denying being at Burton's farm when questioned by Detective Whittaker. There has to be a specific reason, like Patsy's remains or evidence, otherwise, why would she need to lie about being at Burton's farm?)

"Now did you also tell Detective Whittaker that, there was never any carpet taken out of that truck?" "No I did not." (Now, she's attempting to call Detective Whittaker a liar, even though she's not saying it and he recorded it in his notes and interviews.) "And now you're saying that your son-in-law was involved." (Coleman is referring to Tim Smith and the car wash "detail shop" incident.) "I didn't, did not know anything about the carpet being taken out of it." (There is a very long pause, where she's visibly swallowing and closing her eyes. It looks like she's going to vomit.)

Debbie thinks for a long time, then responds. "Until, they came and had the uh, came and took the truck and took it off." (Debra is struggling to find words with clear hesitation. Took what off Debbie? Patsy's body?) She continues, "Then they said then they said, uh... his son-in-law said, that they had been fishin, and that one of them had fell through the bed of the truck and it had a ho... a rusty spot in it. And that Gene had took it up there. They took the carpet out; fixed the hole; fixed everything else; and he said they had the old

171

carpet up to the carwash, where they took it out. And fixed, he fixed it for him."

"Okay. And that's what you're saying now but, isn't that something that you knew prior to this time?" "Yes I did. I knew that because Timmy had talked to me." "And the best person to have discussed that would've been your son-in-law correct?" "Yes." "Has your son-in-law been at the trial?" "What do you mean has he been at the trial?" "Is he here today?" "Yes he is." "So, even though he would've been your best witness with regard to that, you didn't have him named as a witness. You didn't exclude him. You didn't ask him to come up and testify to the jury did you?" "I didn't." "Yes or no!" "No I did not ask anybody..." He interrupts her, "Okay. That was my question."

Commentary: Here's the deal... I don't know if the police questioned Tim and Linda (Gene's daughter and son-in-law) about what occurred at the carwash/detail shop. If they chose to invoke their 5th amendment rights, this would prevent the prosecution from calling them as a witness. As Tim Coleman the prosecutor eluded to, Debbie never had Tim Smith or Linda Smith called as witnesses, so we will never know what they did in regard to Gene's truck. That said, Darrell has been told by informants that they cleaned out Gene's truck for him after Patsy had been murdered. He was told that Linda made the statement "This wasn't the first mess I had to clean up for my dad."

"Alright. So. When did you first believe that your husband, the man you married after the experience of Patsy... killed her?" "Not until, about two years ago."

"And how did you find out about it then?" "Because, he got to where, he would not let me go anywhere by myself. If I would go outside he would holler, "where you at? What are you doing?" If I'd go in the house, uh, like in the laundry room; or in the back of the trailer; he would be hollering for me to come in there. He'd say, "Where you at? What are you doing?" He just kept, had to know where I was at, at all times."

"And you said that had happened a month or two before you were charged?" "Uh, that or maybe a little longer." "A little longer? But up unto that point, now what exactly about him being... you, you were just telling the jury a few minutes ago how jealous he was... how, other than the fact that he was having you have sex with other men, he was so jealous and, and kept up with you but, that seemed to be more so then? Is that what you're saying?" "Yes." "And somehow, THAT told you, he killed Patsy Calloway." "No." "Explain that to the jury." "No. That didn't tell me that he'd killed Patsy, but that, there was something wrong, but I didn't know exactly what it was. But, I just thought, by him being so paranoid and staying with me, making me stay with him all the time that he knew something... or he had done something, but I didn't, I don't know what."

"So, that was 19 years after Patsy's disappearance. You knew at that time your husband was the last person to see her alive, right?" "No, I didn't know exactly, no." "Or at least that's what was said?" "That's, I just know what was said, to hearsay." "Well you saw it in the newspaper. You saw these articles. All this kind of thing and he'd get so angry about it right?" "I don't know, because I never did get the paper and read that stuff, that much." "Aw didn't the fact that you were living with the guy, was being thought of as a murderer was of no consequence to you. That's what you're telling this jury!" "No." "That it wasn't anything you wanted to talk about. That's what you're telling the jury." "I don't understand what you're trying to say."

"If, if I was..." "Alright!" She replies, "Sorry. I just can't understand your question. I ju... I do not understand exactly what you're trying to say." "Well, I'm not, I'm not trying to say anything ma'am. I'm just asking questions." "Well, well I don't understand your questions." He asked, "I was just wondering here you've got a, a man who: was the last to see a woman as she disappeared; who had issues with regard to this arson; who was charged with the arson... was he charged with the arson before you married him?" "I don't think so." "But, did you know it was coming at that time?" "Before I married him?" "Yeah." "No."

"So you've got this... the, all of these issues going on. You go ahead and marry him. Right?" "Yes. I married him." "Without taking any stock into the fact that he may very well be a murderer?" "I had no idea of that at the time." "No, no clue?" "No."

"And you're telling this jury, up until he got paranoid, two years ago, it never entered your mind, whatsoever, that he could've been involved in the uh, disappearance of Patsy Calloway? That's what you're telling this jury?" After a long hesitation, she finally whispers, "I still, I'm sorry." "I'm sorry... so you didn't understand that?" "No. I don't. Not really. No." "Well you just said, and I asked you a few minutes ago, and make sure I'm telling you straight here. I asked you a

174

few minutes ago, "When did you first get a clue, that your husband murdered Patsy Calloway?" "After he." "I understand." "Okay," she says with a heavy sigh. "And you said, "A couple of years ago, or a little bit more than that." Fair statement?" "Is that what you said ma'am?" "I don't know." "Well when was it then? Answer it again, let 'em hear you again."

"Well. Okay! When I had, the idea, that I thought, that he did do somethin, was the time that I went out there, and he made me turn around and go back in the house. And then, he would not let me out of his sight. That was after he was out in the edge of the yard, in the woods. I don't know what he was doing. I went down there. He, gave me a cussin. Told me to get back to the house. I went back in the house and after that, I was not allowed to go to town by myself. I was not allowed outside on the porch, without him hollerin at me and wantin to know where I was at. If I was in the house he wanted to know where I was at and what I was doin. I was not allowed... he was not allow me to be by myself. He was with me at all times."

The prosecutor and Debra are bantering back and forth. "I guess what I'm asking ma'am, and I, I, is why any of that, put in your mind... that that was involved with the death of Patsy Calloway?" "Because he did not want me out there anywhere. He did not want me to go out there and even try to see, figure out what he was doin out there. So he was trying to hide something from me and everybody else." "So. Well, I mean, he could've been hiding gold." "Well, I don't know that until..." "Well what could've given you the assumption that it had something to do with Patsy?" "Well, he asked..." "I mean, did you think he buried her

175

body back there, he'd been carrying it around all those years?" "No."

"Well then what was it?" "What was it that tied it to Patsy?" "I think there was something." "What was it then?" "I just thought he had something, that he didn't want me to know about, and that he had hid it. And he did not want me to go out there and bother it, whatsoever, or turn it in; if I did find it; whatever it was; he did, was afraid I would take it to the law." "Because you thought it could be some incr..." "Because he always, well, he started being paranoid. Every time we'd go to town, he would go a different way. He was a thinking somebody was... he would think the law... an unmarked car or somethin was following him all the time. He did, every time we'd do anything, he thought that someone was somebody followin us, or they'd bugged his vehicle. He wouldn't let me keep the same vehicle. He made me trade vehicles."

"So what'd you think was in... buried back there? Did you think it was the murder weapon?" "I didn't have the faintest idea what it was." Whittaker probes, "In your mind, just" "Only reason I think that..." "Nothing was... he didn't tell you anything at all that said "That has to do with Patsy?" "Well, the only reason uh, that it made me suspicious, is uh... he was talkin about gettin a lock box for his shells. He had high powered shells sittin in the bedroom, on a dresser. And he said, he was afraid with the grandkids comin around, some of 'em were young... that he didn't want anybody around pickin those shells up. So he said he wanted to get him a lock box, to put 'em in, so nobody could get 'em. So, Robbie had told him, that he had a old one that he could have. Well, I didn't think nothin about it. One

176

day, Robbie brought it over there and he said, "There. Papaw can have this." So he said, "Okay." He said, I said, "Okay, so, well, what are you gonna do with it?" "I'm gonna put those shells in it, that are in there on the dresser." Well, 2 or 3... a few days went by. And I went in there, but the shells were still there, but there was no sign of the lock box anywhere... that I seen."

"And?" "And that made me wonder what he'd done with it, when he did not put the shells in it. What did he do with it?" "And?" "So, I, and then when he went out there and I seen him out there, and he made me go back in the house, and wouldn't let me out there with what he was doin in the back yard, I just assumed that he had used it for somethin, and was keepin it hid from me. That's why... he wouldn't let me out of his sight... so I could get back there and try to see if I could find it." "And?" "And what?" "Well that's what I was wondering." "Cause I thought at some point..." "Well, well I..." "You was gonna say, he stood up and said, "I killed Patsy."

"What ties it to Patsy?" "Because he was so paranoid about the law following him, about the law comin to the house. Everything that, anything that pertained with them comin, and questioning him about Patsy, he kept gettin more nervous and more jittery." "Alright." "And, and stayin on top of me more, all the time." "I guess I, and I keep asking... I apologize for redundant." "I mean," Debbie interrupts. "But basically when it comes down to it, that's it. You don't have anything else... fair statement? No other reason that is tied to that box or that... him digging a hole, was tied to Patsy or to you or anybody else, other than he was paranoid?" "No, but..." "Is that your answer?" "No."

"Have you told them your whole answer? I want to make sure we got that done."

"I told you that, I told that, Detective Whittaker, when I called him from jail, that I had seen him out there doin that. I went out there. He made me go back in the house. He had somethin hid. He buried somethin but I didn't know what it was. And then after that time, when I was cleanin house, I noticed the SHELLS were still sitting there! And I had no such see, not seen the lock box anymore. So that made me wonder, where the lock box was, if he didn't put the shells in it. Where was it at? And then he was out there. Wouldn't let me out in the back yard." "And why does the lock box have anything to do with Patsy?" "Because... I didn't know that it had anything to do with Patsy, but I knew that he had hid somethin and he was stayin on me all the time. So... I knew there was somethin hid, that meant somethin, that he didn't want me to get aholt of."

"So at some point after you were arrested. And you're in jail... uh, you were in contact with Ricky and Angie. Fair statement?" "Yes I was." "And they were being good to you and you were telling them how much you loved them. Is that a fair statement?" "Yes I did. Yes." "And, uh, at some point, you wanted them to go out and find this box that, you've been telling them, said somehow, it had something to do with Patsy's murder. Correct?" "Yes, because somebody had uh, come and said, had told, that he was going to have somebody to go up there and find what he had buried in the back yard, and destroy it." "And how did you hear that?" "I don't remember who it was, but, but it was..." "Have you ever told anybody that before?" "I don't remember."

"Aw, okay, so..." "Well, I don't remember but it was while I was in jail. I'm not sure who it was, or when it was." "So... you made a call to Ricky and tried to get them..." "Yes I did." "You'd already, also written them a letter with a map." "Yes, I had called and I couldn't get ahold of 'em. So I wrote the letter and told them that he had buried something out there and I knew in the area of where it was at, because there was trees, where they had hung a deer and we had an old picnic table. And that was the only clear spot to go in, to where he was at." Coleman informs the judge, "As this time, I think I'm gonna play the call."

Chapter Twenty-Three:
Jailhouse Recordings

"You made this call to Ricky and Angie, is that correct?" "Yes I did." The recording begins. "Yes I'm here mom." "Okay. Have you all been talked?" The call was then interrupted until the payment verification could be made. Then, the tape was restarted. "Angie?" "Yes. I'm here mom." "Okay. Have you all been talked to him?" "To Gene?" "Yeah." "No. We haven't even been over there." "Okay, well I didn't know, but uh, I know everything went bad today. Just uh, give me some money so I could write you some letters." "So you can what now?" "I can, I can write you a letter. I can get me some writin paper; some envelopes; and a pen; and I can write and you can write me." "Oh. Okay."

"Did you get that letter today?"   "Uh yes."
"Okay, so I can write you.   I don't like callin 'cause I
know it's expensive, but you could get some money out
of his checking account, with his debit card, and you
can get some out of my checking account with my
Commonwealth card, if you can get it to work."   If you
can't, go in there and tell them that your debit card
won't work.

Angie Calloway asked, "Okay and that's the blue
one?"   "The blue one. Yeah."   "Yeah. Okay."   "The letter
explains everything."   She then began explaining to
Angie about deposits that needed to be made, into the
particular accounts, and what to do with the monies.
She gave them permission to use her and Gene's debit
cards, which is a little alarming to me, since they're no
longer married and it's illegal for them to use Gene's
card without his permission.

Angie asked, "Well, are you doin okay?"   "Well,
the best I can, I... lay here and watch, stare at the walls;
try to watch TV; and I can't hear it, and I can't read it.
I'm just doin the best I can."

The discussion changes.   "I can't believe he, that
they, I can't believe that they let him sit beside you!"
"Well they made him move, but they're tryin us both
together!"   Angie replied, "That's because he was sittin
there talkin to ya."   "Yeah, but that's because they took
us both up there together instead of separately.   We're
supposed to have the same lawyer!   Well what am I
gonna do? And how am I gonna talk to a lawyer and tell
them things? And..."

Angie said, "He said you all can't have the same lawyer." "Yes he did... he said unless we had a conflict of interest." "Well then, I would, would request a different lawyer." "Well, that's what I'm sayin! If I get to talk to her. Did you all go?" Angie answered, "You can get a court appointed attorney on your own." "I know it. That's what I said. I got a court appointed attorney," replied Debbie. "Oh."

Then, the conversation changes to what she wanted Angie to find. Debbie to Angie, "Did you all look for that? "Look for... what?" "That... that I was tellin Ricky about." "Yes. I want you to explain that to Rick 'cause we cannot find it." "Okay. There's the picnic table. "Alright." "There's the bushes and the trees and stuff. Just right there, there's a little openin as you're goin towards Daniels', just look behind them bushes and there's a concrete block and looks like a concrete block. Just take a rake or shovel or something, and just start tearin the ground up." "Well, here's, here's Ricky. I'm gonna let him, let you tell him okay?" "Cause there's somethin there. I can't... It's just... it's, it's in that area. I don't know just exactly where, but it is there."

Ricky Calloway got on the phone. "Okay. Tell me." Debbie said, "Okay, where the picnic table is, as you're going towards Daniel's, okay there's a tree... there's a tree there by the picnic table. Okay then, as you go along the front, it looks like a tree or bush. Anyway, right behind that, kindly in that... go down in there and there should be, it looks like a concrete block, like one of those cinder blocks... a gray one, and it's right in there, you'll see, find it... in it, in that area somewhere, just take a shovel or rake or something like that and rake the hell out it. There's something there! It's gotta be." (Note: Ricky said it was buried about an inch or just over, deep. If Debbie didn't know where or what was buried there, why did she suggest they take a rake to it, instead of a shovel?)

Ricky stated, "Okay. We looked everywhere, you, you, the other day. We couldn't find nothing." "Well, it's back behind them bushes close to that picnic table, I mean where there's a big, thick clump of bushes... it's kindly."

"Daniels" he relayed to Angie. "Down toward Daniels, from the picnic table?" he asked Debbie. "It's not, not... yeah, but just a little ways. It's up above where they cleaned that deer. It's up above it, not where Daniel's is, up above where they cleaned it." He stated, "Okay. Then that's, that's toward the pond part." She replied, "Okay well, it's up, it's between the picnic table, and where they cleaned that deer. It's in that, area close to a concrete block. I know it is." "Okay." She spoke with desperation, "Just try to find it buddy, because they have got us both with the same lawyer... we're gonna have. And he got mad at me today and we left... And they took him to the bathroom, and he come back out. You know how he give you that dirty look that he gets, and he was sayin somethin, but I couldn't understand what he was sayin."

"Right." "Cause he was tryin to talk to me and I said well, "Well we're not supposed to talk to you" and he got uh, sit down by uh, made me sit by him in court... and then the uh, the, they made him get up and move. He said they told me, I'm supposed to stay here with her

182

and they said "No. I don't care what they told you to do," and they made him move on the back row." "Right," Ricky acknowledged.

"Well uh, we're looki, we're going now. We're gonna try and find it again. And if I can't tonight, we'll try again tomorrow, but..." Debbie cried out, "Well it's there! There's a block there. It's stickin up like. But there is a block there. If you find that block, just go five or six foot around it. I mean, from that, down in that woods, it is there, in that area, some... where! But it's close to that block. It's not too far, but it is there."

"Is it buried?" **"Yes! Yes!** Two feet... three feet... but it is, it is there. Because I seen the fresh dirt. I know he dug something up down there and put somethin down there." "Okay." She continued, "I don't know. I don't know if it'll help you or not, but it, but I remember him doing that. I remember seein him. But see, he told me not to ever go down in the woods." "Right." "And I just did and I seen it one day. And I thought, I'm gonna find out what's goin on, and I sit down there and I seen the fresh dirt. Of course it was covered with leaves and stuff, now. But there is something there. Just dig, go ahead and dig a little bit, cause he just got it enough, of the thing it took, you know, wherever it is. But there is something there. There's got to be. Just keep lookin." (Again, how did she know that Gene just got it "enough?") "Okay." "Just try to keep lookin buddy, that's all I'm gonna tell ya. Keep lookin till you find it. There is something there. I know there is. There's gotta be, cause why would he, or why would he, or why would he just dig a hole up and put fresh dirt over it? You know what I'm sayin?" "Yeah."

"First of all they're setting this up... (inaudible)."
I couldn't understand what she was trying to tell Ricky
in that moment.

He interrupted her, "So listen, what... I've gotta
go make me a call for a second. I found your payment
book on the house." "Yeah." "Now that's due the 1st
right?" "That's due the 1st." "Okay now. Okay. Now,
but that's through uh..." She responded, "That's
through... take it out of Commonwealth." "That's Bank
of Ohio county right?" "It's just, yeah, the payment goes
to Bank of Ohio County, but you have to take it out of
Commonwealth Bank." They continue for a moment
discussing getting monies transferred and how to do it,
for paying their bills.

Ricky said, "Okay. Now. Tell me between where
they, where they cleaned that deer..." Debra replied,
"It's somewhere between where they cleaned that deer
and the picnic table... in that area, where there's a block.
It's between it." "No." She continued, "Where they
cleaned the deer and comin up to the picnic table. But
you might have to go..." Ricky responded, "Between the
deer, there's supposed to be a block down in the woods
a little bit, kinda like a concrete block?" "Yes. There
should be a concrete block, behind some of them
bushes and it's between them..."

Ricky is giving Angie directions at this point,
"Behind some of them bushes baby." "In-between,"
Debra relayed. "It's probably covered by leaves or
something." Debbie said, "Yeah, because it sticks up
and there's a pile I know, cause I kindly know that's

184

where I seen it at, you know. But it is there some...
where, and Robbie knows where they cleaned that deer
and it's in that area some... where, I don't know just
exactly where, but it is there some...where. I just have to
try." She's almost crying at this point.

"I know, know this is runnin up your all's phone
bill up, and then the call is like $10 on her card, but I
just had to call. Okay." "Oh that's fine." "He give me
hell today, and I don't know what he said, cause Angie
was, I was talkin to her a while ago and she said ..." He
interrupted Debra, "Listen." She goes on, "And I don't
know what he said. He got mad at me, but I don't know
how we're gonna do this with the same lawyer, because
Ricky if I do that, he's gonna know I done something, I
can't have the same lawyer!"

"Okay. So..." She kept going and wouldn't let
Ricky finish talking. "I should've told him, just what am
I gonna do now?" "Okay." "I told him that the other
night that things was goin on. (Wait, so Debbie was
allowed to talk to Gene in jail? What the hell!) And
they know how he's beat me and stuff. They already
know that!" "Right." "He just wanted to make sure I
wouldn't tell them nothing." (Her statement to Ricky, is
that Gene wanted to make sure she didn't tell them
anything. If she didn't know anything, why would Gene
be concerned at all? She's clearly lying about her
involvement.) Quickly she added, "But I told them all I
know! But he did, freaking did kill Patsy. If I knew, and
everything else, I'd a told... (There is a brief pause.)

Commentary: Right there, in her own words,
Debbie Calloway admits that she knew Gene killed

Patsy. Now in court, she's telling prosecutor Tim Coleman that she didn't suspect it until just a month or so before their arrest. Clearly she was lying in court.

She continues, "I would, I'da divorced him." (Debbie was talking really fast to desperately try and explain where this box was. At this point, I believe Debbie was trying to cover her slips on the call, because they were already divorced, and Gene was worried she'd say something to police. She caught herself admitting she already knew Gene killed Patsy. There divorce was in 2002, so she'd already divorced him at that point. This proves she'd known about Patsy's murder long before they were arrested.)

"Okay. Now, down this thing Debbie, between, between the picnic table and the tree. So it's basically, in that area right?" She responded, "It's in that area between the picnic table; there at the edge of where the woods are; it, it, from the picnic table in, to where they cleaned the deer. In that area behind some of them bushes. That's where, kindly a clear area. There's no bushes." Ricky asked, "Kind of in?" Debra replied, "Yeah, it's just in-between, kindly in a clear area. You know, right behind them bushes; behind them trees; as you go in the woods there. Between where they cleaned the deer and..."

"Okay. Is it, is it in-between, 'cause I'm not quite sure about the tree they cleaned the deer in? Is it where we buried your cat? Remember where we... cat?" "Huh?" "Remember where we buried your cat?" "My cat? No. It's way up... way past that, down towards Daniel's. It's way past that." "Aw." She continued, "It's past that. It's between where they cleaned the deer. Robbie should know where they cleaned that deer at, and the picnic table." "Honey we're we're, we're just tryin not to get the kids involved in it," Ricky explained.

This upset Debbie that he didn't want to bother his son or get him involved. She responded, "I know what you're thinkin! I know. But he could tell you where they cleaned the deer. But just go for the picnic... end of the picnic table, back to Daniels'. That's where to start from, down to where they cleaned that deer in there, in behind them woods right there. It's a clear spot there. And there should be a concrete block there." "Okay. I found the clear spot. It kind of leads into the woods."

Debbie continued, "There's a clear spot, kindly there by the picnic table, between the bushes and the woods... just a little spot right there, where I dropped straw and stuff, one time for the dogs." "Yeah I found some hay stuffed, it was stuffed in..." She interrupted, "It might be in that area down below it, or beside it, or something. But I dropped, I dropped a bunch of straw down there that once. I think it's in that area. Behind the bushes, there should be a concrete block; a half a concrete block; or block of some kind, stickin up. That's where I remember seein it, because I remember kindly where it's at." There is a long pause.

Desperately she stated, "You've got to find it! You've got to just keep lookin till you find it. But there is somethin there. I know there is, because that block's there and nobody goes down there. Cause I seen..." "Well I'm sure it's here. We'll find it." "Well it should be there, but still, because like I said... he kept me, I mean, he'd bring me to stay right with him all the time. So he has, and he hasn't been out. Because when he'd go down I could not see, I couldn't see... where he'd go? And he'd no longer been sittin on the lawn mower." (Clearly Debbie knows she's being recording and is pushing her agenda. This statement she makes about him on the mower, she knows is a lie, because I'd already published the article with Gene riding his mower and mowing his lawn. This was a month before he died, and we have the time-stamped pictures to prove it.)

"Honey come here!" he said to Angie. "Is it in a plastic bag Debbie?" Elated she screamed, "**Yes!**" Ricky replied, "I found a plastic bag underneath some bushes." Frustrated she stated, "No this is... it should... what all I remember is he got it there with... I seen him with a garbage bag, one thing. And all the only kind of bags I used was black." "Okay." "No. It's buried. I know that. It's buried, because I seen the dirt on top of it, cause of the fresh dirt. Of course it won't be fresh now." "She said... She said it's buried in the fresh dirt," he instructed Angie. "It's buried in some dirt there close to that walk, some... where. It's not too far from that block. If you find that block, he did bury it some... where. I, I..." (Clearly she's lying about knowing what it is and where it's buried, because it was in a taped-up, black, garbage bag. If she didn't know that, why would she say she saw him with a black bag? The whole thing was wrapped in tape.)

"Well, we can't find the rock. That's our problem." Angie can be heard talking in the background to Ricky, but you can't understand what her

188

question was. "It's something big honey. It is big," he says to Angie. Debbie continued..."There's a block there some... where. It's a concrete block. I remember that block because I..." Ricky is getting frustrated. "Here, well you talk to her. I can't do all this." "Okay because I..." "Here hon," as he handed the phone to Angie. "Okay hon." said Angie.

She gets on the phone. "Yeah. We're tryin to find it, but we don't see a block." Debbie said, "Well there is a block there. It's between the picnic table and the end facing Daniel's, not towards the pond. Get at the picnic table facing Daniel's, and go in the woods and go up; like where that, where they were doin that; where they cleaned that deer that time; when they went deer huntin; at deer season. Where we hung that deer up. It's in there and there's a..."

"Okay. Hold on! Hold on! Hold on! "What?" she asks Ricky. He tells Angie, "She found a little concrete cinder block." Angie relayed to Debbie, "She found a little concrete like cinder block." **"Yes. THAT'S IT! THAT'S IT!"** Debbie exclaimed. "That's it. That's it," relayed Angie to Ricky. Debbie is elated and again, it sounds like she's about to cry. "Somewhere in that area by the cinder block, is what we talked about. I think it is, but there is something there." "Yeah, but how big is it?" Ricky asked. "I don't know how big it is." "She don't know how big it is" relayed Angie to Ricky. "Somewhere around here?" "I don't know, but it's there some... where. And it can't be too bad 'cause he couldn't a dug that deep, but it's in there some... where, and there is something there. I don't know how far down; if it's a foot down or ten foot down, but it's in that area, within that area some... where."

Debra continued, "If you find the cinder block, go down about four or five foot, and over four or five foot, towards the, about five foot towards the, where they cleaned that deer, towards Daniels'." Angie asked, "It's not a big block, it's a small block. Right?" Debbie replied, "It's just a cinder block. I don't know how big it is, but just a cinder block, like a half." "A cinder block. A cinder block," Angie relayed to Ricky. "Yeah she's got... he, we found that." "There's a clear spot right there," said Ricky. "There's a clear spot right here behind the bush." **"Yes! Yes!"** yelled Debbie.

"Yes, this is it," Angie relayed. You can hear Ricky in the background agreeing, "Okay." Debbie goes on, "Okay, it might not be where that begins, but it's there close to there, some... where; down in front of it." Angie relayed to Ricky, she said, "It may not be right there next to it, but its right there close to it."

"It's close to there, where you're kindly down in front of it, and maybe over to Daniels'. I don't know just exactly where, but it is there. Because I know I seen him doin somethin, because I fell over the block when he was comin out. That's how come I remember where it was at." (She keeps telling them exactly where it is and describes the area perfectly, yet she claimed she doesn't know exactly what it is, or where it's buried. Right.) "Yeah, I laid the shovel down somewhere," Angie said to Ricky. Debbie replied, "Just take... if there's anything there like a stick or a hump, cause like I said." The call is interrupted by a message, telling them they have one minute left on the call.

Debbie said, "We got one minute left. Uh." "Do what?" "I just got one minute left." "Okay." "So I, I'll tell you what, uh..." Call was interrupted again. Debbie said, "Go out there and call me back tomorrow." Angie replied, "Yeah. It's alright. I'm gonna get your cigarettes and everything, I mean your money and everything." Debbie said, "What time can I call you tomorrow?" "Uh, I don't have school tomorrow, so anytime." "Okay. Well, I'll call and, and... focus on the letter and the yard. If you can't find anything, I'd keep lookin hard please. And I love you all." "We will." "I love you with all my heart." "I love you too." "I love you all. Give the kids a big hug and kiss for me and my babies too, tell 'em all that I love 'em." "I will." "I love you all, sweetheart. You, you..." "Love you too." "You don't know what this means to me." Debbie is clearly upset and starting to cry. "Sometimes, we'll always be there for ya." "I know what ya do and you are. And I seen you today. Just when I was over there and I seen ya'll today and (inaudible.)" "That's why I waved at you in the courtroom" said Angie. "That's why..." The phone hangs up. GOODBYE.

Chapter Twenty-Four: Called Into Question

Once the tape recording was finished, questioning continued. The prosecutor asks, "Is it a fair statement ma'am, from listening to that phone call, that, for somebody that doesn't know what's there, just some dirt, you were pretty anxious for them to find it weren't you?" Debbie's whole demeanor changed from what was on the phone call. At this point, she's loud and defensive with her arms crossed and a mean look on her face. "Yes, I was, because I knew he had went out there, with something! And, the shells were still on the dresser. The box was not in the house that I could see anywhere. And... he made me leave. Like I said, he made me leave and go back to the house, when I was comin up by that bush. I was... I hit my foot on that rock. That's how I remember which bush it was. There was a bush, 'cause I had dropped straw where I had cleaned the dog kennel out. And... he stayed, like I said, he stayed right on me all the time. So, I knew he had hid somethin that he didn't want me to get aholt of."

Coleman continued, "I'm. Just a couple of ques... and I'm, I'm about through with you finding this thing and uh. For whatever reason you thought that was important. But you said initially, that you went down, and you saw him, and he told you, "Get back to the house?" "Yes." "And you didn't get right up next to him. You were a distance from him?" "No. I was a little ways from him. I." "How far is a little ways?" "Probably a foot or two from the bush. I don't know how far down he was." "How close there, were you... to me? Ma'am, is this how far away you were?" He steps back about 8 feet from the defendant. "Or is it closer or further?" "From what?" she defiantly asked. "When you first... when he saw you and said that, you saw him..." Debbie interrupted, "I was up there by that, right in front of that bush and that rock that I hit when I turned around and come out." "How far where you away from him?" "He was like, from maybe from here to John or further." "Okay. And that's where you believe the uh, he was digging. You saw fresh dirt?" "Yes." "And... you turned around. And you ran over that cinder block?" "Yes I did."

"So why on this phone call, when they find that cinder block, you said, "Yes! Yes! That's Right!" he accuses. "You may not be right on top of it." Debbie interrupted again, "Because..." "But it could be right in that area." "Yes, because I knew it was in that area. I didn't know exactly where, but I..." "Well it certainly wasn't where your foot was when you stumbled over it, was it?" "The cinder block was, that's what I was talkin about... where the bush was, and the cinder block, when I come out. He was down, in the woods... a little ways there, and I seen him." "The jury heard the call." They're talking over one another at this point, bantering back and forth. She replied, "I don't know exactly where at."

Coleman challenged, "It's a fair statement on that call you said, when they found that and you got all excited... It's right there! It may not be right there next, on top of it, but right in that vicinity around that block?" "No." "And that's contrary to what you just told me. Is that a fair statement?" "No." "Alright."

"But, you know, that even though you surmised from his paranoia, that this had to do with Patsy, it did in fact have to do with Patsy, didn't it?" "Yes it did." "And you seen that. And, the first thing he says is "I kill Patsy." "And that's Vernon's handwriting, right?" "Yes it is." "So you don't have any doubt in your mind right now, that Vernon, your husband, killed Patsy Calloway. Fair statement?" "Yes." "You don't?" "I don't what?" "Do you think he killed, your husband killed Patsy, your husband killed Patsy?" "Yes I do." "Okay." "So after all those years, and all those rumors, and all those statements, now... you believe he killed her? Fair statement?" "Yes I do." "Alright."

Prying further, "Isn't it true ma'am, that on that day, you were with your husband during the middle of the day, just as Ricky Calloway said to this jury? Isn't that true?" "I'm not sure." "You're not sure?" "No I'm not. I'm not gonna answer a question that I'm not sure of." (So now she's not sure if she was at work or not?) "Okay." "I mean, I'm not as sure..." At this point, he grilled her, "As much as that should be in your mind, you're not sure if that was the truth or not?" She attempted to give him an explanation, "I'm not sure exactly as to time... the time it was." "And so then, if you were with him, as Ricky said, in the middle of the day, there was very little time from that 10:30 time that Patsy left, 'til when Ricky saw you at the hospital with your husband. Fair statement?" "Yeah."

"So then, that was well before you were seen by Mildred, walking on 231. Isn't that correct?" "So that would've been midday to 2:30 till 3:00 o'clock. Right?" "I guess so." (Missed opportunity, but Debbie just admitted in open court that she was wearing the wig and walking that day! She didn't say no or attempt to deny it in the moment.)

"So if you were with Gene that day, as Ricky said, rather than at work, and he killed Patsy... tell this jury, you were there. Weren't you." "No I was not." "How were you with him, and him killing Patsy?" "I wasn't with him, I was with him that afternoon." Debbie is really defensive at this point, still with arms crossed, yet she just admitted to being with Gene, midday.

194

"I was..." The prosecutor puts her through the wringer, "You just said it was quite possible that Ricky's correct and you were with him in the middle of the day. And he said around noon. You just said that." "I was with him..." "And if that's the case, you..." Debbie interrupted, "Later that day..." "Let me finish first ma'am." She goes on, "That day but I don't exis, that day but I don't know the exact time." He queried, "That's not what Ricky said, is it?" "No. That's not what Ricky said, no," she replied sarcastically. "But you just said, Ricky could've been telling what was correct." "Ricky could've been mistaken about the time, that, I don't remem..." "That's not what you said ma'am." "I know that's..." "You said he could be correct and you, you thought he could be. And then when, you look at the times, if Ricky's correct, you're with Vernon right after Patsy leaves the nursing home. Fair statement?" "No," she whispers.

"Well, isn't that what... Isn't that fair? She leaves 10:30. You're at the nursing home with Gene at noon? (He meant to say hospital.) And if that's the case, you were with him the rest of the day." "No." "Was there ever any time, after you were with him in that middle of the day, that he left and you weren't with him?" "I wasn't with him during the middle of the day." Debbie looks like she's going to throw up again. She looks as though she knows she's caught.

"So from the time that you got with him, that day... was there ever any time that you weren't with him for the remainder of the day?" Debbie sits there for a long time without an answer and the prosecutor grilled

195

her, demanding an answer. "Yes or no?" Still, she sits there in silence for a moment, trying to find an answer. She coughs and crosses her arms tighter, looks down, then finally says, "I know I was at home that afternoon, after I went to the hospital. I'm not for sure, where he was at all the time. I wasn't with him all the time." (Previously, she testified that he never let her out of his sight.)

Seeking her reply, "So now, he's left you!" "He was, he took... is the best I can remember, that day, I was at work. He took me to work. If, and... that afternoon, he picked me up. And that was 7, 8 hours. He came in, some... time." "That's the best you remember?" Debbie said, "Yes it is. That he came in..."

Tim Coleman knows he's got her now. "And that testimony is just as truthful as your testimony, that you didn't know what was in that box." "No I did not know what was in that box." "Is that testimony you just gave, just as truthful as you not knowing what was in that box?" "Yes it is, because I did not..." She's shaking her head with her head down. "No further questions." "Have anything to do with it," she added.

"Re-direct" instructs the judge. There is a very long pause from the defense attorney. In a very stern voice he replies, "No sir." You could see his demeanor was taken aback, like he was now questioning his client's reliability, and that it was in her best interest to shut the hell up. "Thank you Miss Calloway. You may step down," instructed Judge Dortch. "I'd like to confer with my client for just a brief second judge." "Sure," he replied. "That'd be fine."

They sit at the defense table with their heads down, quietly discussing their next strategy. He stands up with a softer demeanor and states, "We'll rest." The judge then discussed with the prosecutor, if he has any rebuttal witnesses. He said if he does, they could do that in the morning. The judge instructed the jury about the possibility of rebuttal witnesses. He then admonished the courtroom, under the usual instructions not to read anything about this or watch anything, or discuss the case until it's over. He then released the jury and the court members. Debbie didn't look at the jury as they exited, rather stared down at the floor, like she knew she'd been caught. Her demeanor is very sullen now. The court will reconvene at 9:00 a.m.

Chapter Twenty-Five: Rebuttal

The judge asked the prosecutor if he had any rebuttal witnesses before the jury came into the courtroom, to which he replied "Two, and it shouldn't take more than about ten minutes." They sorted out instructions from the judge regarding the charges, prior to the first rebuttal witness being called. The jury and defendant entered the courtroom.

The prosecutor recalled Sergeant Whittaker to the stand. "A couple of quick questions Sergeant Whittaker. Did you have the opportunity to interview this defendant at or on February 29th, 2012?" "I did" he replied. "During that interview did you ask her any questions with regard to the, uh, whether or not carpet was removed from uh, their, her and Mr. Calloway's vehicle, in around the death of Patsy Calloway?" "I did." "And at this point, I'd like to play a short clip of that interview."

Interview recording begins:

On the tape recording, Whittaker asked Debra, "Um, would there be any reason why anybody would tell me they... Do you remember that Blazer that Gene used to have? I think it might have been black, back then." "I don't think so. I know we've had several vehicles." Again, Debra and Detective Whittaker are talking at the same time, so it's difficult to hear at times. "I'm just curious. That was a long time ago." "Yeah." "Was there any reason why he would uh, or do you know why he would pull the carpet out of that vehicle? And the seat covers, and or do you ever remember that happening?" "No I don't." "Okay." "Absolutely not," said Debbie. "Would there be any reason why somebody would tell me that they saw you go in there and do that?" "No. I don't know why they would, because I would never... as far as I know, we never done anything like that." The prosecutor stopped the tape.

"Alright, Detective Whittaker, during that interview, did you also discuss with the defendant um, anytime she was caught or, or... stuck in the mud?" "Yes sir. I did." Whittaker replied. "If I can key this up, I will play this next clip. Recall her testimony, yesterday, of her being very specific about an instance of that." The next tape recording began. Whittaker asked Debra, "Do you know of a time, it'd have been like the day after, maybe two days after Patsy went missing, that you and

Gene got hung up... out here on Johnson school road?" She said something about a field and he responds about the field, but it's difficult to understand. Then he said, "'Cause you were out there dumping trash?" She responded, "No I don't." They then stopped the tape recording. Prosecutor said, "No further questions your honor."

Defense attorney John Austin asked Detective Whittaker, "That was in 2012?" "And uh, was that before or after she was charged in this case?" "That was approximately nine months earlier, that same year." "Okay. Prior to that time do you know when she was last interviewed by the police about that case?" "Hmmm. It was probably the first interview, she's probably ever had with me. Um... I don't know. I'd have to refer to my notes a while." "Okay." "I don't have anything else of this witness," said Austin. "No further questions your honor," replied Coleman. "Alright thank you Sergeant Whittaker. You can step down."

Judge asked, "Any other rebuttal witnesses for the Commonwealth?" "No your honor." "Any rebuttal by the defense?" "No sir." "Good enough. Folks, that's all of the witnesses that are going to testify. We'll give you all another short break. Get everything ready so we can begin with instructions on closing arguments." The judge gave the standard admonishing, from discussing the case. He said that if anyone wants to smoke, that would probably be the last chance they get for a while. The court and members were released on break.

I don't know if the prosecutor forgot, but I wish he'd have played Debbie's denial of ever having or owning a wig. I think it was a missed opportunity by the prosecutor, but clearly the rebuttal, proved Debra Calloway was lying on the stand. Her testimony offered a variety of stories, everything except the truth.

Chapter Twenty-Six
Defense Closing Arguments

Before the jury returned, the defense came forth and requested a direct ruling, citing that he didn't believe that enough evidence was presented against the defendant, in regard to the three remaining counts she was charged with. The prosecution argued that he believed there is enough evidence for the case to be presented to the jury. The judge overruled the defense. The judge then asked if the defense has any objections to the jury instructions to which he didn't object. However, he did request further review of the charge "Retaliation against a witness in the participation of the legal process." The judge discussed it with them and noted that the court is unaware of the appropriate ruling at this time and if the defense found cause, those charges would be reviewed and subsequently dropped and/or relieved, and any such conviction relating to that charge would be vacated.

The court once again came to order. Jury instructions were passed out and reviewed with the jurors. The instructions were given to the floor person, in regard to their deliberations and the rest of the jurors. The judge thanked the jurors for their service and explained the difficulties in the jury system and how important their service is. He explained to the jurors that they can write and request an explanation pertaining to the case. He continued with the remaining instructions regarding the deliberations, unanimous verdicts, and charges.

Defense attorney John Austin began his closing. "You just got a lot of instructions and uh, I know that as jurors, you're gonna take your job seriously. And you're gonna attempt to, uh, decide based on the instructions you got, uh, what you think happened here today, or rather what happened in 1993. A key word that runs throughout these instructions, and it's come up in regard to the allegations against Debra, is the word complicity. You're not given a specific definition of the word complicity, but again and again, throughout the instructions, you find in conjunction with the instructions about complicity, the uh words, aided and abetted. That she some way aided or assisted uh, in the commission of the crimes."

"Well let's start by deciding what it is that happened. What happened? Was there a murder? I mean let's get right to it. There's several other charges, but was there a murder? There's no body. We heard from Detective Ballard who has, who lived with that case the longest of any investigator, uh and, and he admitted on the witness stand, that during the time that he had the case, during the time that he conducted his investigation, they never did attempt to, to, to charge anybody in connection with this case, because quite frankly, they didn't feel like they could prove there was a death."

"In fact, Detective Ballard said, that it appeared as if she might have just, that Patsy might have done, just what it was that she had threatened to do. What was that? Remember, we had a discussion from several witnesses about the fact that, that a Patsy was upset, because her ex-husband and current boyfriend, maybe, uh Larry was uh, in her mind, apparently cheating on her with his girlfriend, who is now his long-time wife, Shirley. And on the morning that she was last seen, we heard witness testimony that she was told by Gene Calloway, that uh, Larry had gotten a marriage license and he was going to get married to Shirley. That same morning, excuse me... the same witnesses told you, remember Detective Ballard specifically telling you that, uh, during his investigation he had uncovered the fact that on, on, on several occasions, Patsy had been known to tell people that if this situation didn't get better with Larry and Shirley, she was just gonna up and leave and nobody would ever see her again." (*This lawyer's testimony just goes to show how attorneys sometimes twist the truth. He doesn't mention at the time, that there's an eye-witness, who saw her in the back of Gene and Debra's Chevy Blazer. I know he's got a job to do, but that's really disgusting.*)

"So, is there a murder? Well, when do we first have somebody, anybody, we heard, I'm gonna say at least 15 or 16 witnesses by the Commonwealth. When's the first witness, who's the first person who claims to have actually seen any physical evidence that there was uh, a, a death? It was Jimmy Calloway. When did Jimmy Calloway tell that? When Jimmy Calloway wanted to stay out of jail, in 2008. (*This testimony is really angering for Darrell and me, because we know different. We now know the truth.*)

202

"Remember, this supposedly happened in 1993." (**There was no supposed to it**.) "For 15 years, he walks around and keeps this under his hat. Kind of an important thing, right? I mean, sort of a traumatizing event in your life, to see your, your now former sister-in-law, uh, in a trash bag and you see an eye that you know is hers and you see a throat that's cut. That's a big deal. That's something you tell somebody." (**Well, Jimmy said he told Officer Dan McEnroe right away, but they ignored him. Yet the defense attorney skips over that**.)

"That's not something you hold under your hat for the day where, it keeps you out of jail. Did it keep him out of jail by the way? Remember the testimony? The testimony was that he pled guilty with a recommended sentence of twelve years in the penitentiary. And that was in 2008. And you know when he's been sentenced? He hasn't been sentenced. You know what he's done every night since then? Slept in his own bed."

"He hasn't been in the penitentiary. Apparently he knew the right words to say. That's the first person, that's the only person who claims to have seen physical evidence that Patsy passed away." (**I'm sure this attorney knows that most people don't have many eye-witnesses to murder! Most murders aren't committed under the watchful eyes of the public, rather they're done in secret**.)

"You also have some other evidence that could point in that direction. You have a letter, which was apparently was written by Gene Calloway. Remember the letter? You saw a couple of different versions of it yesterday. Uh, in both versions it said, that uh, it said "I killed Patsy." The 2nd version you got to see when you became aware of the whole picture, remember when we talked about the grand jury and we talked about the fact that they don't get to see both sides of the coin? You get to see both sides of the coin. The full picture of that note said that, that Debra didn't do it. Said Larry didn't do it. Gene claimed to have done it."

"So again, what happened? Is she dead? You're gonna have to decide. That's, that's part of your job. But if you don't think she's dead, then, you have to find Debra Calloway not guilty. Cause, you can't, shhh, I mean it's obvious. If you do think she's guilty, uhhh, if you do think she's dead... if you think that Patsy is no longer with us, then the question becomes, how was Debra complicit? What did Debra do? Well let's talk about this for a minute. What evidence did you hear about Debra Calloway doing anything to bring about the death of Patsy Calloway? You heard a lot of evidence about whether she had a wig; and when she wore the wig.

And, remember Mildred Dunning, the older lady that came in here in the wheelchair and she testified on the first day of the trial? Remember Mildred came in and she said that she very clearly remembered on March 3rd, 1993, that driving down 231. And she looks over and she sees a woman that at first she thought could be Patsy, and then she told you but no, I can tell that it was Debra. Now, upon some further questioning, she also acknowledged that actually, she just knew it was Debra. She didn't see the face. She was coming from behind this person walking down 231, at about 2:30 in the

204

afternoon. And uh, she saw her from behind, and she kind of saw her from the side as she drove past. Didn't really see the face, but she knows its Debra. Upon even further questioning, Miss Dunning said that, "Well, you know, when they brought me down here in December, and had asked me about it, I said I didn't remember anything about it, but you know what, I lied that day." "I, I lied that day." Some days she tells the truth. Some days she lies apparently."

"As we delved into that even further, Mildred said that, or Mildred acknowledged that uh, she's kind of upset with Debra. She, she feels like Debra is dishonoring her now deceased brother Gene, by the fact that she's moved on, and that she's got a boyfriend that lives with her. She thinks that that's shameful and she thinks that uh, that's, that's not being faithful to the memory of Gene Calloway. And she expressed that anger. And you saw that anger. That's part of why in trials, we bring in the witnesses and you get to sit there, and you get to look at 'em and you can read things from their, their mannerisms, and take that into account as well as the words that they speak. And plainly that woman, she was so moved... she was so angry, that she started directly addressing Debra Calloway. And, she expressed that anger. And she acknowledged to you that she doesn't always tell the truth. So, she's a big part of the Commonwealth's uh, proof if you want to call it that. That, Debra was in some way involved with, with this, this so-called, this alleged killing of Patsy. And they want you to believe what she said because today, she's telling the truth. You're the trier of fact. You're the ones who decide."

"And then, they bring in Jimmy Calloway. I hit on Jimmy a minute ago, but, you know, Jimmy is, is, you'd have to say based on the evidence that was presented that Jimmy's statement is the lynchpin, is the thing that causes this case to accelerate, go forward, and bring charges, and bring us all here today. You can't possibly find Jimmy Calloway's word trustworthy. The man, the man is a convicted felon. The man said, you know... the man knew the tune to play, in order to get the Commonwealth to dance. And he played it."

"Debra acknowledged to you when she testified, that she had a wig. She told you why she wore it. Gene was abusive toward her. And Gene was manipulative. And Gene got sexual gratification from forcing her to dress up and to have sexual relations with other men, while he watched. (*Wait, what? I don't EVER recall Debra testifying that Gene FORCED her to have sex with other men. She just said he "got off on it." I listened to her testify about how he'd hit her on occasions, but not ONCE did she say that he FORCED her to have sex with other men. I'm pretty sure he just violated the rules of conduct as an attorney. I could be wrong.*) So yeah. She had the wig. What does any of that have to do with whether or not Patsy died? And how she died. In what way, is ownership of that wig proof that Debra did something to cause the death of Patsy?"

"Remember the testimony we had early in the trial from several people who were employees at the nursing home that Patsy worked at? Those witnesses all came in and they talked about, they remembered seeing Patsy that morning, the last day that she was seen around here. They said, uh, you know, she's at work.

206

She had had an argument early in her shift, with another co-worker. Uh, she talked to several people. She carried out her job duties. She took her lunch break. She has an argument with Gene Calloway. And then she's seen, after she checks out of work. She leaves early. She's seen leaving the facility with Gene Calloway. Not at a gunpoint, not at knifepoint, he's not shoving her. He's not carrying her over his shoulder. She's seen leaving. In fact, one witness said, "I think she's having some car problems." Did any of them say that they saw Debra anywhere with the two of them, that morning? No." (*The attorney needs to go back and listen to the first tape recording played in court, because of Debbie's Freudian slip. She says, "Nursi... hospital. She told on herself sir. Also, Ricky said that she was at the hospital with Gene, midday, but none of the co-workers saw Debbie that day and he avoided that statement like the plague. He could've cross-examined every one of the prosecution's witnesses, to whether or not Debbie was at work that day, but he didn't.*)

"Commonwealth wants to make a big deal about uh, discrepancies in times. They wanna say, "Well, you know, uh was, was Debra at the hospital seeing her grandchild around the noon hour, or was it later in the afternoon. Uh, she'd indicated that she wasn't sure if she'd gone home to change clothes first after work. Or, or, she couldn't remember which order things happened." We're talking about something that happened 21 years ago. They show, they wanna, they make a lot out of these tapes and the audio, the video tape was saw this morning. And uh, do you remember, I asked Detective Whittaker this morning, I said, when was that? When did you have that conversation? And then he said that that was uh, several months, I think he said 9 months, but he said it was several months before Debra was charged, sometime around 2012."

"Now, at that point, it had been many, many years, uh that uh, the allegations had been out there. There had been some, some talk... some, some investigation back then by Detective Whittaker's predecessor Detective Ballard. And Detective Whittaker had been involved in the case, but I said, "When was the last time that Debra was questioned about this situation?" And he said, "Well, you know...it had been a long time." You're talking about asking people, you know, you, you might as well say, you know... what movie did you see in 1993? What did you have for lunch? I'm not trying to equate the two. I'm not trying to say that what you had for lunch, is as serious as a missing family member. That's not my point. But my point is, if you're asked to get into the minutia of a single day 21 years ago, or at that time, 19 years ago... are, are you gonna be able to tell what you did at every second of that day?" Are you gonna be able to recall every detail?" (*Like he eluded to, it was out there they were suspected of involvement for many years. You know Debra thought about it over the years.*)

"Now more likely than not, the Commonwealth's gonna try to tell you, "Well, you know... doesn't it kind of seem like her recollection sort of fades in and out. You know, some days she doesn't remember as well and then here we're at the trial and she's telling you what happened, you know. And this is the farthest point in history from that day." (*Any point after and current, is the farthest point in history from a specific moment.*) Well, you gotta also remember that since that point in time, she's been living with this. She's been under

208

indictment for this. (*So if she's been living with this, then why doesn't she remember it clearly? Well, because she's lying.*) If people tell you, if, if I say to you what did you have for lunch on March 3rd, 1993, and you sit there and say, "Oh gosh I'm not too sure. I don't know. I mean I know some places I used to like to eat around that time." And then, we go on for about two years, and I provide you with a ton of evidence that, that demonstrates that uh, a lot of people saw you around uh, MacDonald's on that day, you're probably gonna think, well hey... you know, that does sound about right. I believe that could be. That's probably right. That's how human nature works. People do refresh their recollections back, based on information that they're provided." (*Well if you're talking about something as arbitrary as drinking coffee or having lunch, of course that's not the same thing as having a missing family member, that you claimed to search for; or the same as having been accused! You'd remember those events of the day.*)

"Does it make sense though? Does it, does it pass the smell test, to follow the Commonwealth's timeline?" Does it make sense that somehow Debra went to work that morning. She, she, mysteriously and, and, and not while being seen by any of her co-workers, slips away and helps Gene abduct, completely free of detection, uh, Patsy... kills Patsy, or helps him kill Patsy... and then goes around lunchtime to the hospital to see their grandchild being born? (*Note: In that moment, he acknowledges that Debra wasn't seen by her co-workers.*) And then later in the day, goes out and helps trying look for it? Does that, is that how it works... I mean the level of ruthlessness that would indicate is, is, is not... there's no evidence that that was present. There's no evidence... you have no reason, to believe that that's what occurred."

Now, they want to place a lot of weight behind, "Well wouldn't it have been an important day for Ricky?" Remember Ricky is the, is Gene's son. He was during the marriage, Debra's stepson. He was the father of the child that was born that day. Ricky said, "Well, it was around lunchtime that she was there. You've, you've probably come to realize there was a big family. A lot of people, related to these folks, living in Ohio County. It's the day his child is born. It's a big day. That was a point made by Mr. Coleman yesterday wasn't it? Wouldn't that have been a big day for him? Wouldn't he remember that? Yeah, sure... you're gonna remember that your child was born. Or you're gonna remember everybody that came to the hospital and what time they came there to the hospital? Or you gonna be more involved in how, what's the health of your child? How's your wife doing? Yeah... you know. You may remember yeah, my dad held him up. Okay. I give you that. But are you going to remember everybody that came to the hospital? And are you gonna remember what time they were there and how long they stayed? (*The old hat trick... we're not concerned so much with Ricky remembering who and what time, but Debbie. Ricky's not accused of murder.*)

"I'm back to, what did she do? How did she assist in this? Now, the Commonwealth also put on evidence from Jimmy Calloway, our fiddler, that uh, somehow you know, he saw Debra help him to pull out the carpet out of the, uh, out of the SUV. He saw her that day. That he comes over to the house. They're there. Uh, Patsy's dead body is in these bags. He stealth-fully sneaks around and sees that it's there. They don't know he's there. He sees them pulling the carpet out and settin it out. Uh, and then he goes away. And they don't, they don't ever know about it. And he doesn't say a word for 15 years. (*Again, Jimmy testified that he told Officer Dan McEnroe from the beginning when Patsy went missing, a fact that this attorney wants to lie about or glaze over. He also testified that he discussed it with Gene later.*)

That's their, that's that and our, our wig testimony... these are the things that the Commonwealth wants you to hang your hat on to say, "Well somethings fishy." "Somethings not right and you know, um... she must have been in it with him. She must have been in cahoots with Gene." "She must have been helping him some way." And that's good enough. Well, is that good enough? Is that proof beyond a reasonable doubt that this woman committed a murder? Or that she helped somebody to commit a murder? Or that she tampered with physical evidence?"

"Do you remember uh, when Larry testified, you know, cause we also have this charge of retaliating against a potential witness, uh, and, and, what the Commonwealth is trying to convince you of is that uh, that Gene wanted to silence Patsy. Wanted to keep her quiet. And uh that, the way he chose to do that... she's threatening I'm gonna, I'm gonna tell everybody about uh, about how you and, and Larry uh, burned down her house a couple years ago. You know uh, what, what they want you to believe is that, that, that that threat is the thing that motivated uh, the killing of Patsy, by Gene with the assistance of Debra. Larry, is the only person ever convicted of ca, of, of setting that fire. Gene

211

faced the same gauntlet Debra faces today. Gene sat in, in here in this building and had a jury trial, in which twelve Ohio Countians found him not guilty. Furthermore, Larry said that he wasn't even sure if uh, if Patsy ever knew that it was Gene that set the fire. That was his testimony." (*Note: Austin doesn't state what Gene was found "Not Guilty" of, and it was arson, not murder. He died before his murder charges ever went to trial, but this seemed like a lawyer trick to make it look like Gene had been tried and exonerated.*)

"You've heard a lot of witnesses. And obviously though, you're gonna have to assign credibility to these witnesses. You're gonna have to decide who you believe, and whether or not, based on what you believe uh, you're satisfied there's been proof beyond a reasonable doubt, that Debra Calloway committed any of these acts. When you look at the evidence; when you look at all the discrepancies; when you taking into account what's not there; like proof that she did anything that aided or assisted in the commission of any of these crimes, you're not gonna have a choice but to find her not guilty on all counts. Thank you for your service."

Chapter Twenty-Seven:
Prosecution Closing Arguments

Judge Dortch instructs, "Mr. Coleman, you may give a closing on behalf of the Commonwealth." Tim Coleman began. "If it please the court and Mr. Austin, ladies and gentlemen of the jury, I want to join the court in thanking you for your service. And I want to do that on behalf of the Commonwealth and of, for the family of Patsy Calloway. They've waited a lot of years for this. Over twenty years, to be able to get a case presented to a panel of jurors just like you, and I want to thank you for being here."

"I said at the beginning of this case that you are the fact finder. And you are going to base your evi... uh, decisions, solely upon the evidence that you've heard on this jury; out of this witness stand; and on the documents that you received. And we'll go over those facts here in a second and I'll tell you how they play in the scheme of things and why this defendant is guilty on all counts. But I said as jurors, as fact-finders, you would apply those facts to the law that was set forth in these instructions that you have, and that the court will give you to take back with you."

"And there's a couple of points I want to make about this, before we talk about the evidence that you've heard in this case. You basically have three sets of charges. You have murder, which may be simple enough. That's the killing of another person. You've got tampering with physical evidence. That is trying to alter, or destroy, or conceal evidence that may be used in a legal proceeding. And you've got retaliation. That's an additional charge in this case, because why she was murdered by Gene Calloway and this defendant was, because she was going to, or had indicated she may give information in a legal proceeding. So because of that fact, that's an additional charge."

"Now you see as the ju... court read 'em to you, these additional instructions to you, that we've got, on each one of those charges, there's kind of two different facets. You've got complicity and you've got facilitation. And you may be thinking, "Well, what's the difference in those, because I heard it... all those instructions based on her aiding and assisting." And the real difference is, is her intent. Her intent, if the complicity is, if she intended... if she aided and assisted Vernon Calloway in doing any of those acts, and it was her intent for that to happen, if she intended for him to murder her, then that is complicity... part of the trunk crime. If she just aided and assisted without that intent, just disregarded, well, he says he's gonna... I'll help ya, you're gonna kill her but I don't really care if you do that or not, that's facilitation. So the difference is in her intent. Did she care whether he killed her? Or did she intend for him to kill her? And I'll state to you, that as we go through these facts, you will see beyond a reasonable doubt, that her intent was the same as his... to murder her, and to see that she isn't there to testify against them."

"Fact: Patsy Calloway was murdered. Um, Mr. Austin argued that, how do we know that? Well you can listen to the evidence that we've got here. You've got family! You've heard from two of her children. Had close relationships with their mom. Does anyone really believe that she would just walk off for over twenty years and not contact her children; find out about her grandchildren? Her other family, her brothers or sisters, does anyone really think that Patsy, who had a close relationships with them, would just walk off, with no contact? How was she able to do that... no vehicle, no car, no clothes? It's been twenty years. But, proper has it more so... Vernon Calloway said he did it. There's no

214

doubt what happened. He told his sister. And you heard Miss Dunning get up here and she didn't even want to talk about that part. She said, "Oh I don't want to talk about my brother." But when I'd asked her, "What did he tell ya?" She said, "He told me he killed her, and he told me he buried her." That wasn't easy for her to talk about. That wasn't easy for her to be able to admit, that her brother was a murderer. But she did that. She wanted to tell the truth before, before she went on. So is there any real doubt at all that Patsy Calloway's dead? Is there any real doubt that she died back in 1993? None whatsoever."

"Remember this note left by Mr. Calloway. And do you really believe not only, I mean he, this was identified to be his handwriting, by the defendant. And do you really believe her story that she just knew that he'd dug some hole, back in the backyard? And that somehow convinced her that he had killed Patsy Calloway, when there's no connection to Patsy or any discussion whatsoever? Frankly, she couldn't tell you the straight story. Why, because she was too involved. Too much a part of it. She was too much a part of "I kill Patsy," to even be able to tell you, even after he's gone what happened. If she didn't have a part in that, she'd have said, "Well I thought he did it, or instead of, well I thought he did something and something led me to believe that; or there's a note; or he told me he'd write a note and tell." But she didn't do that. She went into this malarkey, about him somehow digging a hole and catching him, and somehow, that had something to do with this case. And she was so frantic and you heard that frantic on the phone, "Find it! Find it! Find it!" "I don't know what's there, just saw some dirt." But when they find a plastic bag she said, "That's it!" How does

215

she have any belief that it was in a plastic bag? Turned out it was. It hadn't even been dug up at that point, but somehow, she knew. Why? Cause she's not telling you the truth. She's not givin ya what really happened. And the reason somebody doesn't tell you the truth is because the truth inculpates them. It makes them a part of the crime. If she wasn't a part of the crime, she would've said it. She would've just told you the truth. But rather she didn't."

"Why was Patsy Calloway murdered? Well Larry Calloway told ya. And he's the one that kind of sicked himself... sicked the authorities on himself back then. He told Phillip Ballard about this arson. And he said that he and Vernon and Debbie were involved. And they conspired to do the... to burn this house for the insurance money. And Patsy wasn't even in the state at the time. After the fire, she and her husband were divorced, because of his relationship with Shirley Phelps, but they didn't completely divide. They still stayed together. Even though they were still living together though, Larry was still seeing Shirley. And he knew that could be a problem. On February 25th, 1993, the newspaper recorded, and you'll see a copy of that newspaper, it was part of the exhibits that you got. That was be received, from Vernon Calloway. And one thing I find very significant of that, it's got the, you'll see that the notice of the marriage license is in there, but look at that date. This wasn't the day that it happened. This didn't just come up on March 3rd, 1993. This came out almost a week before. And why is that significant? What does that tell us? Vernon Calloway had this paper. He knew, "Uh oh. It is about to hit the fan!" It wasn't something that just came up at the last moment.

This is about... something's gonna happen. And we gotta do something about it, he and Debbie."

"Why Debbie? Well we know Patsy wasn't aware of it until he came up. And we know that they were concerned, because she was telling people, "If my husband doesn't straighten up, I'm going to the authorities." You heard her brother say at least a week before that, "That's what I intend to do." But that's not the only person that he told. That he told... you heard from Mike Hertzog and we'll get that out in a minute. So it was out there. What I'm gonna do? So they needed a plan. Vernon needed a plan. This defendant needed a plan. If Patsy told the authorities, both of them could've been sent to prison, not just Vernon.

Remember the testimony of Shirley Calloway? She said, the defendant told her, told her that she had dropped off Vernon on the day of the fire, to commit the arson. And came back and got him. And what does that mean? She is an accomplice. And as an accomplice, she could've been a, held as guilty of that fire, as Vernon. She had as much skin in the game as he did. She could be as much trouble as he was. Patsy was a threat, not only to her, or to him, but to her as well. And they knew about it a week going in. So Patsy, as a result of their plan, was murdered by both Vernon Calloway, and his girlfriend/soon-to-be wife, Debra Calloway."

"The murder, the cover, and the plan were completed by them. And why, how do we know that? We gotta really look at the timing here. They had a week to think about what they needed to do. This is, uh, Misty Gorby. She was a girlfriend to her son (He points to Debra Calloway.) Not connected to the Calloways, but her son, about that time. And she told her, when she mentioned Patsy's disappearance, "I, whatever I done, I was forced to do."

"So when they developed this plan, there was a couple of things they had to address. They needed to get Patsy alone during working hours. And why do I say that? And why, from the evidence do we know that? How quickly did they find out that Patty, that Patsy was gone? Pretty fast. Pretty immediate. She didn't come home from work. People would've been there, cause she'd... if they'd come to her home. People would know where she's at. So they had to get her some time, somewhere, where she wouldn't be missed for a while. Where she could walk off without being seen. So they needed to get her away from work. And how did they do that? Well we know, that they, they, also needed a diversion. Once the problem of work and getting her to leave was done well, people know where you work... went there. So they needed somebody to say, "I saw Patsy later on; walking down the road; at other locations. They knew from Larry and from others, and from their own information that when Patsy got mad sometimes, she would just walk for a while. But she always came back. This time she didn't."

"Remember Detective Ballard said, in his questioning of Vernon Calloway, that he kept coming back to that walking off. That was his... he was really kind of forceful in discussing that. You heard this defendant's own statement, when she was talking about how much in defense she was of that... about talking about how much she walked off. This was even after she tells us later she did, had decided he was the killer. She

218

was still pushing that line, after she told you, "I thought he killed her," after that box was buried, because that was the story they wanted to push. And how did they push it? Vernon brought the newspaper. After holding it a week, brought it to the nursing home. He confronted Patsy. And we remember from the testimony of the, the co-workers... how she was normal that day. How she didn't know anything was going on, until he got there, until he confronted her."

"And remember Mike Herzog. The victim told Vernon, that she was gonna turn them in. He heard that. Showed her intent. In Vernon's eyes, there's no real working with her at that point. It was gonna hit the fan, cause he already knew this marriage license was out there. He heard Gene Calloway threaten Patsy, keep your mouth shut. Cynthia Likens saw the victim walking home? NO, out the nursing home, with Vernon Calloway... opened the passenger door and she left with him, never to be seen again."

"Let's go to that testimony heard about where this defendant was. She said sometimes, "I was at work." That's only her testimony. Is there anyone else that you've heard, that said she was at work that day? You heard from Ricky Calloway. Gene's son. Her stepson, for years... the years she lived with him before, then after they married. What did he say? That same day his child was born, he remembers it very well. The defendant and Vernon Calloway arrived together, and they left together. And they left... were there during the mid-part of the day. The defendant wasn't working. She was with Vernon."

"And Mr. Austin was saying, "Well, that would be awful cold." Yeah. To be able to uh, uh, get ahold of somebody, and then go to the hospital. It was cold. That's exactly what happened. It was cold for Vernon to do it. And it was cold for this defendant to do it. But they needed to, because they needed an alibi. He also, Ricky Calloway Gene's son said, they left well before someone was seen walking down highway 231, the second part of their plan. Cause not only have they taken care of Patsy this time by getting her out of the nursing home, they needed to cause that diversion. Mildred Dunning said, "I saw somebody walking down the road. She was dressed like Patsy. Thought it was Patsy. Goes to pull over. Got closer. Saw that it was this defendant. Mr. Austin will say, you know, "She changed her story in December to now, but remember, this is what she said back in 1993... before her brother passed away... before this defendant got a new boyfriend. That's what she said then, and we heard that from Detective Ballard. She had nothing... she loved her brother. But she told the truth then, and she told the truth now. This defendant was walking down the road; wearing a wig; dressed like... in order to her walking theory. Why else would she have done it?"

"She says she was with her husband all day, from the time they left the hospital. Could that have been the truth and her not be a part of this? If that was the truth, how was he able to get rid of the body without her knowing? Or, do the other things it took, with regard to the murder of Patsy Calloway? Cause we know he did it. We seen he did it. It couldn't have been done without her... without her help, her assistance. And part of that was walking down the road, trying to divert attention, to what they had done. And that wasn't just something

220

they could set up in a minute. They had a waddle around with a wig in their back. See. That was a plan. And if it was planned, she's just as guilty as he is."

"There's a lot of discussion about this wig, because as you heard from your... uh, from the testimony of Detective Whittaker, Sergeant Whittaker now, she had always denied this wig... until enough people came forward that she had to finally figure out a different story. She came up with the story about him making her have sex, with some other guy. Even though, she said how many times he was jealous of her."

"But Misty Gorby, again, no connection... I mean she's the mother of her grandchild. Not connected to the Calloway's, but through her and her son (*As he points to the defendant.*) Her son alone. She said she saw this wig and this and out the... what she described as a trench coat, in the bedroom. And the defendant told her... I mean, this is significant. This is her mother of her grandchild, said, this defendant told her, "She walked down the road with a coat and a wig, to appear as though Patsy had been seen somewhere, other than seen leaving work that day." This is someone who lives in Indiana. Not a part of all this. No axe to grind. You didn't hear her (*as he points to Debra*) say she would, or been any reason other than it was the truth, to have said that. Why did they do that? Because in order to kill Patsy, they had to establish an alibi. They had to say that she was seen somewhere other than the nursing home. Just as she told Misty Gorby. Angie Calloway testified that Debbie's told her, that she had a wig like Patsy's, and Gene liked her to wear it."

"So after that point, after they had diverted attention; murdered Patsy Calloway; they had to get rid of the body. And how'd they do that? According to the note from Gene, Vernon Calloway, they buried it. And he drew this little map out. And you'll see that. According to what he told his sister, he buried the body. Now we heard from Jimmy Calloway. And Mr. Austin brought up a number of things of why you shouldn't believe James Calloway. And I have a problem myself with someone who holds that information for that long. But we've got to remember, this is a brother. A brother who's a murderer. Can you believe what he tells us? Well, remember when Sergeant Whittaker heard that, if it was just standing on its own, maybe we'd be having a tough time here. But the thing was, he was able to tell things, he shouldn't have known, that we had already surmised, in the investigation, or we'd heard from different people."

"He talked about when he walked up there and saw these black garbage bags. He saw Patsy's dead body. They were tearing the carpet out of that vehicle that she had denied. But what, during the search of the vehicle did they find? The carpet had been removed. How would he have known that? Or why, how would he have known that... a number of years later, that that was significant in this investigation? He wouldn't. But when you put that together, it was supported by the evidence. What he also, did he say, they did with it? He said they buried it. Again, as I said, she denied it initially, but she changed her story when she got on the witness stand."

"Then Amy Hamilton saw the defendant and Mr. Calloway out in a field, late at night. The defendant says

222

to get rid of trash, the same way they referred to that body, to James Calloway. Why would they be out, late, late at night, burying trash? Seems like a lot of effort, for something she said that they had some trash bag, cans at the end of their property. Why would you go out after midnight, with a shovel, and bury trash? Unless it was really something you didn't want to be found, like a body. And who was there? Vernon Calloway, and by her own admission, this defendant. For the first time, she changed her story again on this witness stand. Can you believe what she says? Not a chance."

"Then we have this whole letter situation. She claims to not know anything about this letter. That it just, occurred to her, that this confession of the guy that she has lived with for going on twenty to thirty years. She can't even be straight with us about that. Why? Cause the truth does not set her free. The truth is, she was involved from the beginning. Not only with the arson, with the murder; with the tampering; and with the retaliation. Those are the facts. That's what we've heard from these witnesses on this stand. By her own testimony, she was with the defendant at noon, on the day Patsy Calloway disappeared. She was with him before that time, cause she came to the hospital with him. What happened in that short hour/hour and a half? Patsy Calloway went missing. And by Vernon Calloway's own note, or his own confession to his sister, she was murdered. Where else could've the defendant been, but by his side."

"I'm gonna ask you to look at that evidence, and see that there is no other explanation for those simple facts. She had to be involved. Cause there wasn't

223

enough time for anything else to happen. She had to be involved in the murder. She had to be involved in getting rid of the body. Because, even after that point, she was supposed to be with him, from that point on. She doesn't tell us, and she had all the opportunity in the world to tell us, "He was out on his own doing things." She chose not to tell us the truth. Now it's time for you to decide, and hold her accountable after all these years... for what she did. And that was being involved in the murder; being involved in the retaliation against Patsy Calloway; and being involved in the tampering and the disposal of her body, which remains out in some field somewhere. Thank you."

At that time, the judge asked for two alternate, jurors names' to be called. After they drew the names, he released those two jurors and the remaining jurors were sent to deliberations.

Chapter Twenty-Eight: The Verdicts

Judge Dortch admonished the courtroom gallery that he'd tolerate no outbursts... nothing, no gestures or anything from them. "Failure to adhere to this warning will be a risk of contempt." The jury is brought back into the courtroom.

"Be seated please. All twelve members of the jury are present and present are the parties and counsel.

Has the jury reached a... who is the floor person? (Floor person stands up.) Has the jury reached verdicts?" "Yes." "On all counts?" "Yes." "And, have you signed off on the verdicts?" "Yes." "Alright. Would you hand them to the bailiff please?" The verdict sheets are handed to the bailiff, then to the judge. The judge briefly reads over the verdicts to himself.

The judge then began to give the instructions. "Alright. Instruction number one: We the jury find the defendant not guilty of complicity to murder on instruction number one. Was that the verdict of all twelve of you?" "Yes."

"Instruction number two: We the jury, find the defendant Debra Calloway **guilty** of Facilitation to Murder, on instruction number two. Is that the verdict of all twelve of you? "Yes."

"And instruction number three: We the jury find the defendant **guilty** of complicity to tampering with physical evidence, on instruction number three. That of course is signed by the floor person. Is that the verdict of all twelve of you? "Yes."

"Instruction number five: We the jury find the defendant not guilty of complicity to retaliating against a witness from the legal process, on instruction number five, signed by the floor person. Is that the verdict of all twelve of you? "Yes."

"And, jury form number six: We the jury find the defendant Debra Calloway, **guilty** of facilitation to retaliation, retaliating against the participant in the legal process, on instruction number six. Is that... it is signed by the floor person. "Yes." Is that the verdict of all twelve of you? "Yes."

"Thank you folks. If you all would retire to the jury room, we'll get ready for the second phase of the trial where you all will fix punishment." He handed Mr. Austin a copy of the jury verdicts. Then, he called for Debra Calloway to approach the bench. He says, "Miss Calloway, will you come up here?" "I'll show you the verdict forms."

Debbie Calloway walked up in front of the judge's bench. She wasn't crying. She wasn't showing any sign of emotion. She stood firm at the bench. "Alright Mrs. Calloway. You've been convicted of Facilitation of Murder; Facilitation of Retaliating against a Witness; and Complicity. Your bond is hereby revoked, and you'll be taken into custody. So do not leave the courtroom without my permission." Debra whispered, "Yes sir" as she nodded her head in acknowledgement.

"Now, we're getting ready to do the second part of the trial. That includes setting the sentence for you, on those three charges. I will tell you that, I will set this matter down for a pre-sentence hearing on September the 4th. You'll be brought back at that time. We'll have the Department of Probation and Parole to do a pre-sentence report. You'll get an opportunity to read over it and to discuss it with Mr. Austin, your attorney. And, sentence will be pronounced on you at that time. I will also tell you that you have the right to appeal this verdict, and there are certain time limitations involving that right of appeal, thirty days. You've gotta file the notice of appeal within thirty days, after I sign the formal sentencing order. So be sure, that if you can't afford an attorney, that Mr. Austin know, and one will be appointed to represent you. Do you understand what I have said?" "Yeah." "Okay. You all may have a seat." Debra and her attorney walked back to the defense table.

"The court will be in recess for a few minutes. While we're getting the instructions ready, you all may remain here, or you may step outside. The court's in recess."

The court once again reconvened and the prosecutor called Joel Elliot, from Probation and Parole to the stand. Mr. Elliot explained that the sentence for Facilitation of Murder carries one to five years. He testified that the Tampering with Physical Evidence charge carries the same punishment. Retaliation charge carried a one year sentence. For the facilitation charge, it was possible for her to be paroled after only serving 20% of her sentence, and 15% of the time for the other two charges. Given that she'd already spent time in the county facility, this means that, depending on the sentences given, Debra Calloway could walk out of the courthouse with time served. If her sentences run concurrently, meaning at the same time, she would serve less time than if they run consecutively. If the sentences run consecutively, she has to complete each punishment, in the order in which they are fixed. It was up to the jury to fix punishment and the judge to sign off on it.

Debra Calloway was once again called to the stand by Judge Dortch, to plead her case on her own behalf. The defense attorney Austin, began questioning. "Please state your name." "Debra Calloway." "Miss Calloway, uh, where do you live?" "1775 Vine Hill Road, Beaver Dam." "Uh, Miss Calloway, how old are you?" "Sixty." "Okay. And, in your sixty years, how many felonies have you been convicted of?" "Zero." "When was the last time you were charged with doing anything contrary to the law outside of this case?" "Just uh, one speeding ticket years ago." "Okay. How's your health?" "Not good." "Can you explain?" "I have hip problems. I've had back surgery twiced. I have anxiety, depression. And, where I've had my hysterectomy, my bladder is not right." "Okay." "I have problems with it." "I'm sorry to set you out here in public to talk about your bladder, but I think it's relevant. What uh, what kind of uh, in what way do you suffer as a result of that problem?" "My bladder has dropped and my bladder leaks. Sometimes all the time and sometimes it don't, it just... I never know."

"Are you under a doctor's care for any of the problems you talked about?" "Yes I am." "And uh, you mentioned earlier, some problems that are more of a psychiatric nature. Um, during your testimony, during the case in chief, you testified that Mr. Calloway, Gene Calloway..." "Yes." "Had uh, hit you." "Yes." "What uh... how would he hit you?" "Hit me in the head or in the face... in the head or sometimes he would hit me in my body." "Would he use an open hand or a fist?" "Sometimes he'd use an open hand. Sometimes he'd use his fist." "Ever use any weapons, any bats or sticks?" "One time he pulled a rifle on me and another time he pulled a knife on me." "Kick ya?" "No. He's never kicked me. He's always used his hands."

"When, assuming you outlive a sentence that you receive in this case, what are your plans when you're released from custody?" "Just to try to continue my life and go back to church, like I've been doing." "Are you employed?" "No sir." "Uh, you testified during the trial that at one point in time, over twenty years ago, you had worked in a nursing home." "Yes." "Um, what other kind of work had you done?" "I was a waitress for 5½ years and I worked as a certified nursing assistant for about 15 years, until I tore my back out at the nursing home." "How long have you been out of work?" "It'll be twelve years in October." "Are you on disability?" "Yes sir." "And uh, how much do you receive in disability benefits each month?" "$911." "Do you have any other source of income?" "$217.50/Month from Workman's comp." "Is that a result of the incidents with the back?" "Yes." "Okay. So... a little over $1100/month?" "Yes." "And, are there any other sources of income?" "No."

"Um, do you have family here in Ohio County?" "No I don't. Well, I have two sons, sorry." (**WOW! She forgot her own sons!**) "And, do they live here in Ohio County?" "Yes." "Okay. Any other family here?" "No." "Okay. Would it be your intention upon your release to reside in Ohio County or?" "I'm not sure." "Okay. Alright. Um, I think that's all I've got of this witness."

Prosecutor Coleman challenged the now convict. "Mrs. Calloway, you allege to this jury that um, you were abused. How many times did you report that to the police?" "I never reported it to the police." "Not one!"

"It was so bad that you've never reported it to the police. Correct?" Debbie immediately got defensive and began to argue, "No. Uh, No I did not." "Just answer the questions. Did you report it?" "No I did not." "How many times did you go to the hospital because of abuse?" "I never went to the hospital." "Okay. So they're supposed to take your testimony as you give it. Is that a fair statement?" "Yes." "Okay. Now, you have income right? You were working at one point and then you were drawing?" "Pardon?" "You had income of your own right?" "Yes. I was working at the nursing home." He charges, "So you couldn't move out?! If you were being abused, you could've moved, because you had income or allowed to live on your own. Fair statement?" "No."

"In the twenty years that Patsy Calloway's been missing, how many times have you consoled or told the family that you were sorry?" "I've not associated with her family." "You couldn't reach out? Are they around?" "They don't... they didn't want anything to do with me." "I don't blame 'em for that a bit! How many times did YOU make an effort?" "I don't." "Zero, right?!" "Zero 'cause I don't go around them." "For twenty-something years, they've wondered where the body of Patsy Calloway is! Have you ever told them where the body is?" "I do not know where the body is," Debbie states coldly and defiantly as she closes her eyes." "Have you ever made any effort whatsoever, to help that family get past their grief?" Debbie doesn't answer. "You haven't right?" "I have not spoke to them, anyone." "No further questions!"

Defense attorney Austin re-directed, "During the remainder of Gene's life, did you all live together?"

230

"Yes." "I mean, in other words, I'm speaking of the period from March 3rd, 1993 – to his death last year?" "Yes." "Okay. And uh, how would you describe your uh, opportunity to, to go and freely move about the community?" "Not very good." "Why do you say, "not very good?" "Well, because if he told me if I ever tried to leave, that..." Objection. Judge sustains. Defense states, "I think it would be a statement against interest." Again, Dortch sustained the objection. "You can rephrase that."

"What concern did you have, if any, if you were to go freely about the community and do what you wanted?" "That he would find where I was at and that he would take a high-powered, and be at a distance and he would kill me with it." "Did he own a high-powered rifle..." "Yes he did." "To the best of your knowledge?" "Yes he did." "Was he someone who shot that weapon when and, and, and practiced with it?" "Yes." "Did you, um... why didn't you report the abuse to the authorities?" "Cause he told me if I did that he'd kill me. And I did try to leave one time and he hunted me down." "What happened on that occasion?" "He hunted me down and drug me back in the car and drug me back home." "I don't want you to use hyperbole here. Did he literally drag you or..." "Yes. He grabbed me by the hair of the head and dragged me in the car, and then knocked me down after I got out of the car at home, and pulled me into the house." "Do you remember approximately when that was?" "No sir, not just exactly, I don't." Was there further abuse following that occasion?" "Yes there was." "More than once?" "Yes." "That's all I've got of this witness."

Time Coleman accusingly picked her brain, "But this abuse was never reported right?" "No it wasn't." "And you knew this, who this man was 'cause you lived with him all those years. Right?" "Yes I did." "And even, in fact, after he was charged and you were charged, you came to this court and asked to have him move back in your home. Isn't that correct?" "I done it for his daughter." "Is that correct?" "Yes it is." "You had to actually get permission because he wasn't supposed to be around you, but you came here, 'cause you wanted him back in your home. Fair statement?" "No." "Is that what happened?" "I done it because of his health and for his daughter, because she did not know how to take care of him." "And you did." "Yes I did, because I had fifteen years of CNA training, to take care of a sick person." "No further questions!" Defense attorney Austin stated, "Nothing else of this witness." "Alright," replied the judge. "Thank you Miss Calloway. You may step down. Any other witnesses?"

Defense called Sergeant Whittaker. The judge instructs Whittaker to have a seat and he's still under oath. "Sergeant, uh state you name." "Brian Whittaker." "Okay. And you're still employed with Kentucky State Police?" "I am." "Okay. Earlier in the case, you testified. And during that testimony you had indicated that you had been there for some period of time. Right? In that employment?" "Yes." "How long has that been?" "Nineteen years." "Okay. And have you received uh, training in police work, uh, generally during that time?" "Yes." "And you had an extensive training program at the outset of your employment too, right?" "Yes." "Okay. And have you been a, I, I, I don't want to use the wrong term, but a, a field trooper? Someone who is out on the road?" "Yes sir." "Uh, how much of your career

232

have you spent doing that?" "A little over eight years I think, almost nine."

"Okay. And in that time, and in that time, uh... have you been assigned to respond to any calls involving domestic violence?" "Of course." Prosecution objects, "I would object to this line of questioning unless it has anything specifically to do with Gene Calloway or gist of him." The judge orders, "Make it relevant quickly please." "Well sir, what I want to know is, in your experience, is it uncommon for uh, acts of domestic abuse to go unreported?" "Objection." "Overruled." Whittaker responds, "Um... of course it has happened. Um, but to the rate that she's referring to, you know, all she had to do is make a call. Um, it's ridiculous to think that the police are not gonna respond, that they're not gonna help. I think that's the point I'm trying to make here. Um, she calls... he's gonna go to jail. You know, it's that simple. Um, and the fact that she took him back in, I think it's a big issue here. So."

"Did you observe Gene Calloway in the latter part of his life?" "Last time I talked to Gene was at the Sheriff's office before he was let out of jail. That's the first... last time I ever saw him. Okay. Um, did you see him during the period immediately from the time he was out of jail – to the end of his life?" "No. Again... he was still in jail the last time I personally laid eyes on Gene." "Okay. Alright." "That's all I've got of this witness." "No questions," said Coleman. "Thank you Brian. You can step down. Any other witnesses?" Austin responded, "No sir."

The judge requested for the instructions from the prosecution and ordered both attorneys to approach the bench. They discussed a correction made and the jury instructions for the fixation of punishment were given to the jury, as read by Judge Dortch. After the instructions were read out, defense attorney Austin spoke to the jury. "It's been a long process and we're getting really close to the end. Uh, I think some of you served on a jury a couple of weeks ago and you kind of know how this process works and you may have served at some other time in your life. But I would have to tell you that, there's... I would not want to be in your shoes. It's a tough job and it's, it's, it's particularly difficult when it's come to this phase in the case. Cause now, not only are you asked to listen to the evidence and decide what you think happened, but furthermore, you're put in the position of having to say what's gonna happen to someone's life, for what may possibly be the remainder of her life. We're talking about a sixty-year-old woman who's not in the best of shape. A ten year sentence, may in fact be a life sentence.

"You heard testimony from Mr. Elliot from the Department of Probation and Parole. And uh, he was asked about a, parole eligibility. There's kind of a popular perception out there in society that uh, you know, our court system is all about catch 'em and release... that people come in, and they're just, uh, you know. They go to jail and they're just pushed right back out on the street, and they're free to go about committing new acts. On cross-examination, Mr. Elliot had to admit that, while it is the case that Miss, uh that Miss Calloway may be eligible for parole consideration at some point during her sentence, which is going to vary depending on the length of the sentence... there's no way to say that she will ever be released, until the completion of the full term. You're never gonna know. To go back there and make a decision based on some kind of a belief, "well, you know... gosh, I don't think we ought to give her a one year sentence, or a three year sentence, because uh, she'll just be right back out on the street in a few months. And that's just not enough." That's not how this works. That's not a, a reliable indicator. Her eligibility, if we're gonna talk about her eligibility, it could happen, that a court could grant her probation in sentencing in this. In which event, the, the number of years would be somewhat less relevant. Now, that's unlikely. But my point to you is, whatever sentence you give her, the only thing we can safely assume is that that's the, that's the worst event. So, a five year sentence; a four year sentence; a three year sentence; she very well could serve all of that and that could be a life term.

There's a reason that the General Assembly in its wisdom, granted you all the ability to choose from a range of punishments. This isn't the Old Testament. We're not gonna take her out and stone her. You've got the ability to decide what an appropriate punishment should be. The easiest thing in the world would be to just go out and say, "Well, give her the maximum." Do you remember during jury selection that was something that was kind of broached? And, and you all indicated that you were able to consider the full range of punishment, and, and decided what was the best and most appropriate punishment based on the evidence. In doing that, you take into account all of the facts."

"Apparently, Gene Calloway was a mean, nasty guy. He was an abusive husband, and he had control

235

over this lady.   You heard witnesses for the Commonwealth, who got up there and said, said over a period of years, that, that Debra had said to them that whatever she had done... she had done, because she felt she had to. You heard about from Detective Ballard, you heard about Gene Calloway over a period of time making threats to people in various situations. In fact, for that matter, you heard facts about Gene Calloway making a threat to Patsy the day that, the day that she was last seen. You have the ability to take all of this into account, and I'm sure you're going to. And, I'm not gonna stand here and tell you "Give her one year; two years; four years." I don't have the ability to do that. I'm gone. I'm not in your shoes. But, when you go back there, take into account everything you've heard. And, and I'm sure you're gonna render an appropriate uh, punishment. Thanks."

Tim Coleman stood up to address the jury. "To please the court, Mr. Austin. First I want to thank you for your verdict. I know this is not an easy job, but I want to thank you on behalf of the Commonwealth, and on behalf of the Calloway family as well. At the beginning of the trial on voir dire, we talked about the differences in phases, and the first phase is the guilt phase, which you have done admirably. It's the fact finder, and we talked about you being fact finders. At this point, in this part of the proceeding, you're no longer a fact finder. You're in essence, a conscience. Looking at the range of penalties, what is the appropriate, given all the facts that you've heard in this case?"

"Now, Miss Calloway wants mercy. But, she has shown no mercy. She's shown no mercy to Patsy
236

Calloway. And she has allowed, her family, to wonder... to grieve without knowing for twenty years. And she shows no remorse! Did you see any remorse on this stand, either in the guilt phase or this part? Nothing. She doesn't care. It's all about her! She wants to say, "I was abused." With no proof. She could've done something! She had the chance, possibly to stop him back in 1993 and Patsy would still be here... to be with her kids; her grandkids; her family. But no! Not only does she not stop him, she doesn't tell anybody; she participates; and then allows the family to wonder. Can only imagine knowing the pain that must be, to go years... knowing that something had happened to your mom; to your grandmother; to your sister. And she does nothing, but now she wants your mercy. I wish you could give her a year for every year that family has suffered... for every Christmas that they'd missed... every birthday, but we can't do that."

"The most you can give this woman (*as he points at Debra Calloway*) for allowing that to go on, is ten years. Don't discount that. Don't discount the grief. Don't discount what that family has gone through. She could've stopped it a long time ago. She chose not to. What are we going to say to her? Could anything less than the maximum, be the appropriate sentence in this case? Thank you."

"Alright, if the jury would... please retire to the jury room. If you reach a verdict, knock on the door and we'll bring you into open court." The judge states that if they want a break before they start deliberations, that'd be fine. The court will be in recess until the jury returns."

Chapter Twenty-Nine: Sentencing

Judge Dortch, "Be seated please. Now that all twelve members of the jury have returned, present are the Commonwealth attorney and the defendant with counsel. Has the jury reached verdicts on sentencing?" "Yes." As he nods his head, the judge asked, "And you filled out the verdict forms and signed them?" He shakes his head in acknowledgment that they did. "Would you pass them to the bailiff please?" The bailiff handed off the forms to the judge. He briefly looked at them.

"On the charge, on the verdict... on instruction number two, the Facilitation of Murder, sentences as follows: We the jury fix the defendant's punishment for the Facilitation of the Murder at five years in the custody of the state Department of Corrections. Signed by the floor person? "Yes." "Is that the verdict of all twelve of you?" "Yes."

"And under instruction number three... verdict is as follows: We the jury fix the defendant's punishment for the offense of Tampering with Physical Evidence at five years, signed by the floor person. Was that the verdict of all twelve of you? "Yes."

"And under instruction number four... We the jury fix the defendant's punishment on the charge of Retaliating Against a Witness as a Participant in a legal process, set a fine of $500 and confinement in the Ohio

County jail at 365 days. Signed by the floor person. Was that the verdict of all twelve of you? "Yes."

"Instruction number five, on the multiple sentencing recommendations, you have recommended that these sentences should run consecutively. That would make it a total of ten years. Signed by the floor person. Is that the verdict of all twelve of you? "Yes." He hands the verdicts off to the defense attorney.

"Alright. Mr. Austin, Miss Calloway, come around please. "I, I, I don't need to see it," says Austin. "Come on around Miss Calloway please." "I'm gonna do this one more time on the record. Of course your bond is hereby revoked. You're remanded to jail. Sentencing will be on September the 4th. I've informed you that Probation and Parole will interview you. They'll prepare that report. You'll get a copy of it. I will sign that formal sentencing order on that date. You'll have after that to file the notice of appeal. If you cannot afford an attorney, let me know and I will appoint one to represent you. With that, you are remanded to the sheriff with transportation to jail. Thank you. Just have a seat over there."

"The members of the jury, thank you all for your service. I appreciate that so much. Personally, this is a personal, not a legal opinion. I would have reached the exact same verdict that you all did. So I want you all to go home, not that that makes a difference to you, but you all did your job, and you did it right. And for that, we can thank you."

"Alright. Brian?" "Uh huh." "Bill. Robbie. And is Max still here?" "Escort the jury out and make sure they get to their cars please. As everyone remains seated, the jury may leave. Now if any of you need a work excuse, just wait in there. You all can have a seat and John (Defense counsel) you are free to go." "I'm gonna hang out for just a second judge." "We're off the record."

Throughout this entire trial, Debra Calloway didn't shed a tear. She sat there stone-faced and cold. When the defense was questioning her, she tried to appear demure and fragile, but when the prosecutor went at her, she was angry and defiant. She crossed her arms defensively and had a nasty tone and look on her face. She spoke throughout her testimony with him, in a manner of distain and sarcasm. Any fool could've seen through her lies.

While this may not be popular opinion, I concur with the judge, that what the jury decided, were the correct verdicts, with what they were presented. However, Darrell and I have more information prior to, and since the trial that the jury has never seen. For example: The jury never got to hear that Debra Calloway, not Gene or Larry, but Debra... threatened to kill me on the phone.

When I called to speak to Gene Calloway back in 2012, it was Debra Calloway who answered the phone. I said, "Is this Debra Calloway?" "Yes." "I introduced myself and explained I was writing an article on the missing person case of Patsy Calloway and asked to speak to her and Gene. Immediately, she hung up the phone. Later that day, I got a call back. It was the same number I'd dialed earlier, Debbie and Gene's phone number, and so I hit the record button on my tape recorder. I heard "Fuck off! Leave this investigation alone or you could be next!" Then the phone was hung up. Within minutes, I got another call, same number. This is what I recorded: "You fucking bitch! You stay the fuck away from this case or I'll fucking kill you, you fucking bitch! Stay away from it or you're next... fucking bitch!" Then, they hung up.

Immediately, I knew they'd done something to Patsy, before they were ever charged, because a person doesn't bite so defensive and aggressively if they're completely innocent. She told me everything I needed to know about her in that moment. Darrell said that Debbie and Gene also threatened to kill him on numerous occasions. They'd call and threaten him and hang up. This wasn't a shock to me after hearing Debra, but I never did get that opportunity to speak to Gene Calloway. Still, I have no doubt he's serving his punishment in the hereafter.

Trial Discussion: Darrell and I would like to delve further into a few of the submissions and testimonies given at Debra's trial. So many unanswered questions remain.

1. Initially when questioned, Debbie told defense attorney Austin, that she remembered the events of the day on March 3rd, 1993. We know she remembered the events, but we all heard at trial, how she flip-flopped and tried to come up with excuses. On cross, she said she couldn't remember anything, only what she "though she did do that day." She claimed she couldn't remember the circumstances around the birth of her step-granddaughter or Patsy's disappearance. The employees at the Hartford Professional Care Center all remembered what happened that day, twenty-one years prior, but Debbie suddenly and conveniently got amnesia in court

2. Debra testified that Gene came to work that morning and informed her and Mary Calloway that the baby girl was born, Gene's granddaughter. This would've been before 10:36 a.m. if it was true. Why didn't anyone question Mary Calloway, because this is simply a lie from Debbie in court! Mary told Darrell, according to his notes from '93, Debbie didn't work that day. We believe they later planned saying this, to bolster the impression that Gene or Debra Calloway had nothing to do with Patsy's murder, and that Patsy just left on her own. They had to give a reason, other than to kidnap Patsy, for him to be at the nursing home that morning.

Ricky, Gene's own son, testified that Gene and Debra were at the hospital midday, right after 1:00p.m. He said that Gene was the first one to hold up his new granddaughter. He said it was "after lunch" when this happened. The fact is, if the baby was born in the morning or after lunch, it proves that *Debra wasn't at work that morning* like she claimed, because she would've been at the hospital with Gene, as *SHE* testified to in court. If the baby was born that evening, it skews the timeline a bit, but *still,* contradicts Debra's testimony that *"Gene came to the nursing home that morning to inform them that the baby was born."* If the baby wasn't born until that afternoon, how could Gene

242

go to the nursing home and tell Debra and Mary, that Stacie just gave birth to their granddaughter? It's *NOT* possible!

Either way, she's obviously lying. Again, she wasn't at work that day, but was with Gene when Patsy was killed. Ricky already testified that his dad and Debra were there at the hospital when his daughter was born. He confirmed that their daughter was born on March 3rd, 1993. You have to be a pretty cold, heartless creature to go to the hospital to hold your granddaughter as an alibi, after you'd just committed cold-blooded, first-degree murder. This happened within hours of Patsy's murder! Debbie tried to convince the jury that Gene came to the nursing home first and they went to the hospital later that day, together. Well that did happen, but not in the timeframe she'd like you to believe. That would've been plausible, but Darrell found out the truth.

Darrell Kessinger asked Stacie, the baby's mother, many questions regarding Debra's so-called timeline. Stacie said, she knows for a fact they didn't come to the hospital until after noon. Darrell asked, "What time was she born?" Her response via text was that she had the baby before noon. She said, "I thought they were (Debra and Gene) at the hospital by 1:00 o'clock. I always thought it was earlier (than they said) in all the reports. I know that Gene tried to get Ricky to lie and say they were at the hospital the whole time but Ricky, "I swear they didn't get there till after 1:00," and I told him (Ricky) if he lied for him, I would leave him."

So there you have it folks... straight from the mother's mouth. Therefore, it's obvious that Debra lied in court, which Ricky's testimony was now corroborated by the mother of his child, Stacy. Even though Gene tried to get Ricky to lie, Ricky told the told the truth in court. There's no possible way for Gene to have come to the nursing home that morning for the purpose of informing them that the baby had been born, because she wasn't born until mid-morning, just before noon! Ricky also testified that they left shortly after his daughter's birth and before his mother Mary got there, giving time for Debbie to dress up like Patsy and walk through town. They left before Mary ever got to the hospital.

My question is, "Why didn't the prosecutor summon Stacy to testify in court?" She would remember the events of the day, plus, she'd have the birth certificate to clear it all up. Your guess is as good as mine.

Darrell further asked Stacy how she felt about Gene murdering Patsy, then coming to the hospital to hold her newborn daughter and try to use it as an alibi. Stacy said it was nauseating and made her sick to her stomach. How else could she feel? They stole that new precious moment from her and her daughter as well, and turned it into something despicable and ugly. She couldn't remember the exact time of her daughter's birth, but she *knows* it was just before noon and said she will check the birth certificate.

Note: After a baby is born, unless something is wrong, the mother is given a few moments of skin to skin contact so they can bond. Then the baby is taken

244

for their Apgar score; to be weighed and measured; and then to be bathed, while the mother is delivering the placenta and being attended to. After the initial examination and bathing of the neonate, which takes about an hour, the baby is then reunited with family upon their request. So, it stands to reason that the newborn was reunited with mom and family approximately an hour to an hour and a half, after she was born. This would put Debra and Gene arriving at the hospital between 12:45 – 1:30 p.m. Stacie said it was by 1:00 p.m. That gives Gene and Debra a two hour window after Patsy was kidnapped. We'll discuss this window and our projected timeline.

3. Debra told Sergeant Whittaker that she believed Patsy was still alive, but then changed her story in court, to later believing Gene murdered Patsy. Yet even though proclaiming her innocence, she petitioned the court after their shocking release from jail, that Gene would be allowed to return home with her. She said he wasn't in good health and wasn't expected to make it, and said she would take care of him.

In court, she also brought up that Gene could no longer ride a lawnmower. Why would she bring that up? The reason is, she knew we have a picture of him on a riding mower just two months before he died. This shows that he was still active prior to his death. I'd written the article, protesting his release from jail. Debbie stating this, contradicts the testimony of James Johnson and Debbie in court, saying Gene was basically in a vegetative state at that time. The picture was published before trial, so why wasn't it used? Darrell was watching Gene and trying to capture pictures for evidence and the news articles, up until a month before he died.

Gene Calloway on riding mower
April 30th, 2013.

Gene Calloway died on July 11th, 2013, just two months after this photo was taken. Darrell was told by the prosecutor, they released Gene from jail, because the county couldn't afford his medical costs. He was sick, granted... but there's no excuse in our eyes for releasing this murderer back to his own home. He died in hospice care, surrounded by family. They stole those comforts from Patsy Calloway. He should've died in prison, alone. After all, Patsy didn't even get a proper burial.

4. Let's talk about Gene's bite mark. Debra lived with Gene and eventually married him, but was never questioned in court about the bite mark on Gene's hand by the prosecutor. Shirley saw it. Larry saw it. They testified to it in court. Hell, even Darrell and Detective Ballard saw it, but they weren't questioned about the bite mark? What the hell? Why wasn't Debbie questioned about it in court? Yet she wants people to believe that she didn't know Gene had done something

246

to Patsy Calloway's murder. She was living with Gene! Of course she saw the bite mark!

5. Debra stated that she was with Gene for 7 or 8 years before her and Gene got married. We know she was also having an affair with Gene while he was still married to Mary Calloway, not that it matters. It does confirm her lack of character. According to her own testimony and the timeline, she's an adulteress. We also wonder if Gene was prostituting Debra out. Debra claimed on the stand, that Gene would have her go out and have sex with other men. She said Gene liked watching other men have sex with her and that's why she used the wig. Her defense attorney claimed she was forced to do that, even though she never testified to that at trial.

6. Why didn't anyone question Mary Calloway to whether or not Gene drove her and Debra to work on March 3rd, 1993? She was never called as a witness by either side. Darrell asked Mary in 1993, and she said it never happened and that Debbie wasn't at work that day. In fact, Darrell and Wanda Winkler checked Debra's time card. Patsy wasn't even scheduled to work that day because they were short-handed and she got called in to work because she was needed. That's one reason why she was able to leave early, because it was not her scheduled day to work.

7. Debra claimed that when she gets out, she was going to start attending church. That's laughable considering she claimed that she and Gene were already going to church. We believe them going was a smoke screen. Her testimony regarding post jail release, was just a charade to try and get a lighter sentence. If she believed in God or Christ, son of God, she would've told the truth and told the family where they buried Patsy. She's had ample opportunity to come clean, or at the very least, give up Patsy's remains. Gene's deceased now, so he's no longer a threat, if he ever was.

8. Jimmy was asked, "Do you know Debra Calloway?" He replied, "Yep. After he divorced his first wife, and married her." We believe they did this for spousal privilege if this case ever went to trial. They got married August 17th, 1993, just months after Patsy's murder. We don't believe they knew that there wouldn't be spousal privilege in this case, especially since Debra showed so much concern for having separate attorneys. She couldn't reveal things to an attorney shared with Gene, because he would know the truth... per her own recorded statements. Gene was dead, so she was trying to shift all the blame onto him.

9. Jimmy testified, and it was concurred in court that he gave his statement to Detective Whittaker in 2008. He also testified to telling Dan McEnroe, another officer, of Patsy's murder, right after she left with Gene. Why didn't the police investigate it that day, or for 10 days after? Officer Dan McEnroe is deceased, so he's not here to answer questions regarding Jimmy's statements, but we believe Jimmy is telling the truth, about seeing Patsy's body and going to the police.

The police want Darrell to believe that they just agreed initially, that Patsy walked away from her life with Larry. They said that's the story the Calloway's were "pushing." While that's true, rumors had been floating around for years that the police there were corrupt and doing all sorts of illegal activities, like human trafficking and pornography. It was told to us by several individuals that the Calloway brothers were in cahoots with the local law enforcement, so it was unlikely that Patsy's case would ever go to trial. We find it fascinating that the only person prosecuted for Patsy's murder was Debra Calloway.

Jimmy Calloway's sentencing was delayed over thirty times, while waiting for this case to go to trial. Gene ended up dying in hospice care at home. Even Detective Whittaker admitted on the stand, he didn't think it would ever go to trial. Why not? Why did it take so long for this to go to court? Why so long for the arrests and trial, and why didn't anyone listen to Jimmy's eyewitness accounts from the beginning? Whittaker was the only officer who would take his statement. We understand that Whittaker was pursuing justice, but what about those before him?

10. At trial, Larry testified that Ballard was the one who showed him the paper with the wedding announcement on the day Patsy went missing, but Ballard didn't get the case until, according to him, March 18th, 1993. How is that possible? It's not, unless again, Ballard knows more than he "remembers." His memory was kind of fuzzy in court too. This isn't rocket science and it clearly shows impropriety. Larry is clearly lying, but was Ballard as well? I guess we'll never know.

11. The hood of Patsy's car was up. We believe this "loose" battery cable was used as a device to get Patsy to leave with Gene. Patsy couldn't stand Gene Calloway, so why would she ask *him* of all people, to work on her car, unless Larry set it up? Larry worked on cars in his garage back then according to his own children, so it doesn't make sense that she wouldn't just ask Larry, if he was still living with Patsy.

It is our belief that Debra Calloway got off easy. Had they known the information Darrell and I now know, the jury may have come to different verdicts and handed out much harsher sentences for Debra Calloway. Still we wonder why Larry was never charged with Patsy's murder and why Debra won't roll over on him now that Gene's dead.

Chapter Thirty: Bombshells

BOMBSHELL #1: Maryann Phelps, Shirley Calloway's sister, told me in a recorded interview in 2014, that she didn't know Larry was using her as an alibi, until *AFTER* Debra's trial, and she read it in the first book I wrote. She said she *NEVER saw Larry* the day Patsy disappeared, and later admits to lying about it to Darrell in 1993, because she wanted to protect her sister Shirley, from Larry and Gene.

Maryann said she didn't know what Larry was capable of. Patsy was already gone and presumed dead, and she feared for Shirley's life. She was terrified that Gene and Larry would also kill Shirley and that's why she lied to Darrell. So Larry was never informed about Patsy leaving the nursing home with Gene that day by Maryann Phelps, at Shirley's house. She clearly states that Larry was *never* at Shirley's house when she was there at any time that day. Larry Calloway lied under oath at Debra's trial. **He has no alibi!** With everything I've got going in my life, I guess I forgot about this detail, until I learned that Debbie was getting out of prison soon. Whoops. I did however, turn the recordings of Maryann over to police, right after I obtained them in 2014. So my butt's covered. Perhaps they failed to listen to it. One can only guess. Maybe the recordings got damaged in the mail. Who knows? Either way, Debra had to serve some time, even if it wasn't enough. I still have the recordings saved, just in case.

Maryann said she heard Patsy left work with Gene, so she immediately clocked out at work to go to her sister's house. Maryanne Phelps first told Darrell this in 1993 that she went over to her sister Shirley's house to protect Shirley because she was pregnant. After the trial and the book came out, Maryanne admitted that she lied about Shirley being pregnant, but said that she really wanted to protect Shirley from Larry and Gene, and *that's* why she left the facility, to find out what was going on. She said she knew it wasn't good. Shirley wasn't pregnant and she was much bigger than Patsy in stature. Why would she go over to Shirley's house at the very time Patsy is about to disappear? I can't answer that, but perhaps *SHE* knew the shit was going to hit the fan!

Maryanne said she stayed with Shirley and her kids that *whole* afternoon and she didn't go back to work. She said they'd had lunch together and she spent that time with Shirley, playing with the babies. I asked her if Larry was in the bedroom or shower, or perhaps she didn't see him in the bedroom. She said, "No." He wasn't there at all. She said she knew Shirley was lying about it and she didn't understand why Shirley was still protecting Larry.

Note: Let's go back to Patsy's own words that were heard by the maintenance man. "My son-of-a-bitch husband <u>brought</u> this young girl and he wants her and me to have a threesome arrangement." Was Maryanne supposed to go over there on her lunch hour to give them an alibi, or to babysit, or both? I don't think Maryann realized she was about to be used. She said that she followed Patsy's leaving work, shortly thereafter and her timecard showed that.

Darrell confirmed this because the supervisor checked all the Calloway's and Maryann's time card in 1993, when she left the facility. This has left Darrell questioning whether or not Shirley Calloway was also involved on that day. The maintenance man testified to Patsy's own words. "Brought" doesn't have to mean into the relationship. He could've brought Shirley to the nursing facility. Or he could've told *PATSY* that he had Shirley out at her trailer. The latter is what we suspect. It has always been Darrell's contention that Patsy wouldn't leave work, just because of some marriage announcement and Mr. Herzog's testimony confirmed that much.

At the time of the interview, Maryann also told me that originally, their mother, Barbara Phelps was having a sorted affair with Larry Calloway, while he was married to Patsy. She said they'd been seeing each other for a couple of years by then, and everyone knew it, except for Patsy. She said that Barbara found out Shirley was pregnant with Larry's child and it infuriated her. There wasn't much she could do, but to confront Larry and break it off with him, while supporting her own teenaged daughter. Maryann believes that her mother didn't know the full extent of Larry and Shirley's relationship in 1990, when she and Sharon Mattingly beat up Patsy. She said all Barbara knew was that she had to protect Shirley, because she was a pregnant teen. So to put it bluntly, Larry Calloway was messing with his lover's teenage daughter. Oh how history repeats!

Commentary: After learning all of this in 2014, it was easy to see that Larry had also groomed Shirley at a young age and he was clearly, at the very least, a hebephiliac. I suspected he was also a pedophile.

BOMBSHELL #2: After Larry Calloway's testimony, he exited the courtroom and was immediately put in handcuffs. On August 6th, 2014, Larry Ray Calloway was charged with nine counts of Sexual Assault on a minor (victim under 12 years of age); Incest, victim under 12 years of age; Rape 1st degree, victim under 12 years of age; and two counts of Sodomy, victim under 12 years of age. His trial began on 12/11/14. He allowed one witness to testify and heard what she had to say. When the court was on a break, he took a plea bargain agreement, which ultimately mean he would only serve 5 years flat in the penitentiary. He had four victims that we know of, but we are not at liberty to discuss their names or circumstances. Out of respect for the victim's, we will not discuss their suffering. That said, we have to wonder how he made a deal for so little amount of time. He should've been locked away for life. Again, we're left scratching our heads. Darrell informed me that one of the victims told him, that they could only give him the amount of time that the statutes dictated at the time of the crimes. His plea bargain did not include the rape or sodomy charges.

BOMBSHELL #3: For years, it had gone around town that Larkin Johnson was Gene Calloway's real, biological father. Everyone said Gene looked just like him. While we have no proof of that, J.T. Boling reported to Darrell back in '93 to '96, that Larkin Johnson was paying for Gene's trial attorney for the arson. He said that Johnson always gave him money. Boling told Darrell that he tried to talk Larkin Johnson out of getting involved and doing that for Gene, because he thought Gene was using him, but Larkin wouldn't listen and continued to give Gene Calloway money. It was also confirmed by Larry Calloway, that he and Gene worked on Larkin Johnson's farm as laborers as well as Ballard's. Who is Larkin Johnson you ask? Well, he was a retired parole officer in Ohio County. He worked very closely with all of the officers in the city and county police departments. He was also the supervisor for the Ohio County Highway Department. He passed in July 2008, right around the time Jimmy Calloway came forward with his testimony to Detective Whittaker. One has to wonder, even if Gene isn't Larkin Johnson's biological son, why in the world would he pay for Gene's attorney at the arson trial and constantly give him money?

BOMBSHELL #4: Darrell Kessinger has written to Debra in the penitentiary, asking her and pleading with her to tell him where they buried his sister's remains. He told her he'd make a deal with her and agreed he wouldn't testify against her at the parole hearings, *if* she would just tell him what they did with his sister. He asked her to come clean about Larry and the others involved. I have the original 5 page letter of Debra's response...

Page 1. Debra wrote: "Darrell, I was the one that call the number you had on the bottom of your letters you sent to me, that you wrote when I was at W.K.C.C. In 2014, I was just wanting to make sure it was you, and that the address I have is still yours. Before I wrote this letter. I'm assuming that it is by you or who ever answered then hung up. It would have to let you know who was calling. I don't know how to start this being that I never responded to your letter in the past. There was something that happened this morning, is the reason I am writing this now. As of now, I'm an inmate at Ross Cash Center (W.K.C.C.) I don't know if you remember this person Rebecca Farmer Calloway. She is an inmate here, she came to me this morning requiring (verbatim) if I was from Ohio County. She was married to Gene's nephew. We sat and talked for a while. She told me things that I didn't know. But while talking with her, I was able to put the pieces together. More about what happened. I just wanted to let you know,

Page 2: that I am so sorry for your loss. I didn't have anything to do with what happened in 1993. But I found out today, I was set up, all over the years, from the time it happened. According to what was said, it was planned 3 months at the least ahead of time. And I was the hold card, the one to take the fall when things turned out the way it did when they reopened the case. They set it up. And I was left in the dark. All I can say is if I had have known then maybe I could have done some thing. I don't understand why things turned out the way they did, But God has a reason for every thing, I do believe that. As bad as feel about being in prison, now that I know things that I did not. Maybe it was God's way to keep me safe. I don't know what to say. I just wish and I have prayed over and over again that I wish things would have been different. I started to try

Page 3: and write and explain about what I was told Today and how the pieces fit together. I don't really know what to do. If you want I will write it all out and tell you. Or I don't know if you can get a way to come here, and I could talk to you face To face. I just want you to Know that I had nothing to do with your sister's disappearance. All I can say, is when I heard those things this morning, it tore my heart out, and I broke down. I can't understand how they could do what they did. God will be their judge in the end. for the ones that are not here now. I had nothing against her. She was a friend to me, and I though highly of her. She showed the ropes when I started at the nursing home, we never had a cross word. There's not enough words to say how sorry I am, for you and your family for what happened. I don't know what you want to do. But I can't say what to do. All I can do. Is

Page 4: write and try To tell you, what I have figured out. Today. Or for you to get some way to come and talk if you can get in the prison. I can't say anymore. God as my witness right now and here. I swear I didn't know what happened told To me today. Darrell all I can ask is that you realize that I could not do to anyone what they did to her. All I can say again is I am so sorry, very sorry. And that the one that did help him will be brought to justice and pay for what they did by taking Patsy away from her family. I would appreciate if you let me know you got this and what more I can do. I guess all I can say. I'm Sorry, But I think I am paying for some thing that I didn't do, except

Not turn that in Knowing he buried that. But that would not and can bring (over)

Page 5: her back. God I pray, for you and your family will find peace. God works in mysterious ways, even in things we don't under stand. He has helped me a lot since I've been in here. So it was some thing I guess he Knew I needed for me, myself, and for my own protection. All I can ask is for forgiveness for what you think I did. Sorry I should have turn him in the day I caught him out in the back yard when he buried that box. Rebecca Farmer Calloway said you tried to talk to her on face book. Thank you. Debra Calloway

The letter listed her inmate number and address of the facility.

Commentary: From the letter dated, 7/25/17, (Tues.) you can surmise that Debra is still not owning any part of Patsy's kidnapping and murder. Darrell did get a chance to talk to Rebecca Farmer Calloway. She told Darrell that all Debbie ever talked about in jail was how she didn't do anything and they did it to Patsy, not her. She said that Debbie cried all the time about how she was stuck in prison and she was afraid to say anything, because one was left out there alive. From what we can deduce, that only one is Larry Ray Calloway. Charlie Calloway died the same day as Gene. Curtis Calloway is also deceased and died prior to her letter as well. Unless she's talking about a law enforcement member, the other suspect is incarcerated.

BOMBSHELL #5: I do have to point out to the fact that Debbie testified Gene's daughter Linda and her husband Tim removed the carpets out of Gene's black

Chevy Blazer in 1993. Prosecutor Tim Coleman even questioned and attacked Debbie in court on that note. He said something to the effect of, "Now you're pointing the finger at your daughter-in-law and her husband Tim."

I find it fascinating that Darrell was told by an informant in 2012, that on the day Patsy was killed, they took the truck to the detailing shop and car wash to clean it out. The carpets and interior were replaced. This was shortly after Patsy was killed. No blood was ever found in Gene's Blazer, except a drop that didn't belong to Patsy. This explains a lot. Here in 2019, Stacie also reports she was told that Gene had the truck at the detailing shop after he killed Patsy. Darrell asked Stacie, "Did you hear about Gene's truck and what they did with it?" Her report was that it was taken to the detailing shop. How would she have known that if it didn't happen?

BOMBSHELL #6: Debra Calloway was convicted of Facilitation of Murder. Debra was also seen, along with Gene, cleaning the blood out of Gene's truck, for which she was convicted of Tampering with Physical Evidence. She was convicted of Retaliation against a Witness in a legal proceeding, because of Patsy's firm plan to inform police of the arson. After her appeal was filed, that conviction was later overturned. I will not go into the full details of the court ruling, except to read their initial decision.

Court Ruling: The trial court erred in denying the Appellant's motion for directed verdict as it related to the facilitation to retaliation against a participant in the legal process charge. Therefore, Debra's conviction was vacated and she would serve one less year on her sentence and would not have to pay the $500 fine.

Although Debra Calloway was convicted, she showed absolutely no remorse for her part in Patsy's murder, and has refused to tell anyone where Patsy was buried, or what actually happened on that fateful day. To date, we have not located her remains, although we have a pretty good idea of where they are currently resting, near a tree marked with a **cross**, on Andy Anderson's farm.

Going back to the beginning of Darrell's investigation, after a while he knew that Larry was lying to him, so he decided to test him on it, but at a much later date. In 2012 he asked Larry to take a drive with him. He said they took a drive up on "Hoopie Hill Road," which was right down the road from Patsy and Larry's shared trailer, on the way into town. It was a back road that ran into 1414 near their trailer. He said it was an old bootleg route that everyone knew about, but Larry pretended he was oblivious to the road, even though he'd traveled it all the time. Andy Anderson's farm gate is located on Hoopie Hill Road. When he pulled up to the gate, Darrell told him, "This is where Patsy is supposed to be buried at." Larry replied, "I've never heard of it." Along the way, Darrell kept insisting to Larry that he had to know about Hoopie Hill, because it was a back way to his trailer on 1414. Larry continued to deny it. Larry kept insisting that he'd had a stroke and had lost his memory.

From Hoopie Hill Road, they proceeded back in to Hartford to Church Street, which was formerly known as Snow Hill. As they drove up the street,

Darrell asked himself to test Larry's memory. He began to act like he didn't know who and where people lived so he could see Larry's true reaction. He asked Larry, "There used to be a house there but I can't remember." He said Larry would tell him who lived in each house. He said that Larry pretended like he'd never heard of it, but once they got up there, he told Darrell all of the people's names that grew up in whichever house they were looking at. He said that those houses no longer existed but Larry could remember every one of them in detail. That's how Darrell knew he was lying. Darrell said that Larry played dumb and forgetful a lot, and always at his convenience. At the time the initial searches began for Patsy though, Darrell didn't suspect him of foul play at first.

Timeline of Events:

May 1990, After Patsy learns that her husband Larry is cheating on her, she's confronts Shirley Phelps. She's physically assaulted by Barbara Phelps and Sharon Mattingly for confronting Shirley who was pregnant. This fact establishes the affair between Larry Calloway and Shirley Phelps.

November 1990, Nicholas was born to Shirley Phelps and Larry Calloway. This was the first child the two had together, despite the fact he was married to and living with his wife Patsy.

July 1991, Gary Fendel (Tanya's boyfriend) stated he overheard an argument between Patsy and Larry, in which Patsy tells Larry not to burn down her house.

August 1st, 1991, The brothers, along with Debra Calloway, committed the arson plot and Vernon Gene Calloway, burned down Patsy's house, according to their pre-arranged plan, while she was visiting with her mother in Arkansas.

August 1991, Patsy begins threatening Larry over the arson to keep him from leaving her for the other woman/girl, Shirley.

March 3rd, 1992, Fed up with his cheating, Patsy filed for divorce from Larry Ray Calloway. The same day she filed for divorce, he deeded the remainder of their property over to Patsy, which was a probable payoff to keep silent about the arson.

April 20th, 1992, The divorce between Larry and Patsy Kessinger Calloway was finalized.

October 1st, 1992, Ruby Renee Calloway was born. At this time, Patsy and Larry were still living together although he was seeing the young girl, Shirley, who'd had two of his children. Patsy was unaware of the delivery of Ruby Renee.

February 1993, Patsy learns of the 2nd pregnancy of Shirley Phelps. Unbeknownst to her, the child, Ruby was already born. This is when she decides to turn the brother's in for the arson.

February 22nd, 1993, Larry and Shirley file for a marriage license in Davies County, KY. The plot had already been planned by this time to kill Patsy, though I can't speak to everyone's involvement.

February 26, 1993, Darrell speaks with Patsy and she tells him of her plans to turn over the arson to police and be done with Larry for good. A neighbor of Patsy's overheard Larry Calloway making threats to her.

February 28th – March 6th, 1993, Marriage announcement for Larry Ray Calloway and Shirley Phelps runs in the Messenger Inquirer. He was still living with Patsy at the time, but we're not sure if she threw him out of her house or not.

March 3rd, 1993, Vernon "Gene" Calloway shows up at the nursing home in Hartford where Patsy Calloway worked. He showed Patsy a newspaper, The Messenger Inquirer, which contained a marriage license announcement for Larry Calloway and Shirley Phelps. She and Gene got into a confrontation. Patsy disappears after she was last seen leaving work with Gene Calloway, her ex-husband's older brother at 10:38a.m, according to witness Cindy Likens and others. Patsy was murdered and had her throat cut by Gene Calloway in her own home. Around 2:30pm Debra Deese Calloway, Gene's girlfriend at the time, was seen walking toward Beaver Dam, KY. She was disguised as Patsy according to Mildred Calloway Dunning. She did this in order to facilitate Patsy's kidnapping and murder.

March 3rd, 1993, Just after Patsy left the nursing home, Maryann Phelps left as well, to tell Larry and Shirley that Patsy left work with Gene. She told Darrell she did this, because she thought Patsy was going to beat up Shirley Phelps, her pregnant sister. As it turns out, the pregnancy was a lie that was fabricated. Shirley had already given birth to the 2nd child with Larry. In fact, Maryann now admits that she never saw Larry at her sister's apartment that day.

March 3rd, 1993, 12:15 p.m. Larry shows up at the police station to report Patsy Calloway missing. We don't know how he was aware of her disappearance unless he was involved. According to police, this did occur. What would make Larry go straight to police? She wasn't even gone for two hours yet.

March 3rd, 1993, Sometime that day, Larry spoke with Mildred and Jimmy, his siblings, and discussed Patsy's murder and the wig.

March 3rd, 1993, Larry goes to police three times that day, for his "missing" ex-wife Patsy. Soon after, he makes up a missing poster that is directly deceitful. Larry already knew that Patsy was seen leaving work with Gene according to his own testimony, yet the 2nd missing poster reflects her walking down route 231 from Hartford to Beaver Dam.

March 3rd, 1993, Around 5:30 p.m., Larry mysteriously finds the keys, or "it" under the floorboard, after the 2nd time he visited Patsy's car. He and son Shane then take Patsy's car over to the police station.

March 13th, 1993, Darrell Kessinger heads to Kentucky for answers and discovers that much of an investigation hadn't even begun in his sister's disappearance. We and others believe that this may have be intentional to some degree. The official missing person's report was filed on March 13th, 1993, the day that Darrell Kessinger arrived in Hartford, KY. It was later changed to reflect the actual day of her disappearance and murder. Darrell has a copy of the original report.

June 10th, 1993, Larry and Gene Calloway were indicted for the August 1st, 1991, arson. The grand jury had convened the week prior, after Larry had turned himself in to police for the arson.

June 1994, Tanya Cotrell notices awful smell in the trailer by the bathroom and back door, because of the heat. Tanya's ex-husband, Gary Fendel, said he noticed the rancid smell when they first moved in, **December 1993 or January, 1994**.

July 2012, Trailer is searched with cadaver dog and the dog Bear, makes a positive hit. Blood spatter is discovered about the trailer by a forensics instructor.

September 2012, Darrell Kessinger meets with Larry and Jimmy Calloway in front of the Harford Community Center, where Jimmy describes seeing Patsy's deceased body in the back of Gene Calloway's truck. He gives a rough description of Patsy's remains, located on the farm of property owner Andy Anderson.

September 27th, 2012, I wrote my first news article regarding Patsy, for MissingPersonsNews.com. It was titled, **"An Arson, A Wig, and A Murder."**

October 16th, 2012, Grand Jury handed down indictments for the kidnapping and murder of Patricia Calloway, among other charges.

October 17th, 2012, Debra and Vernon Gene Calloway were arrested for the kidnapping and murder of Patsy Calloway, along with other formal charges.

May 2nd, 2013, Debra Calloway was released from jail on a $30 clerk filing fee. Gene Calloway, confessed murderer, was released from jail on $5000 cash or property bond, due to physical illness. Both were still awaiting trial.

July 11th, 2013, Confessed murderer, Vernon Gene Calloway, passed away in his home, while receiving hospice care.

On **August 6th, 2014**, Debra Calloway, "Gene" Calloway's widow, was convicted of Facilitation of Murder; Tampering with Physical Evidence; and Retaliation against a Participant in a Legal Process. She was ultimately sentenced to 11 years in prison for her crimes. After an appeal, one of her convictions was overturned. Her conviction for Retaliating Against a Witness in the Participation of a Legal Process was thrown out. They'd discussed that after she was convicted in the murder trial, so Darrell expected that, but it was still a disappointment. She should've gotten life without parole.

Chapter Thirty-One: Our Theories

Let's get to the meat of Patsy's whole case. First of all, according to Debra's own letter to Darrell, she admits she was told a story that involved at least one Calloway brother that was still a threat to her. If she had nothing to do with Patsy's murder and didn't know anything, how could any of them be a threat to her? Through the process of elimination, the only brother that could be is Larry Calloway. She revealed that she was the pawn and the fall guy for their murder scheme and claims she was set up. She states that she has details of Patsy's murder, but refuses to tell Darrell the details. I believe Debra was using her letter to taunt Darrell, not to give details, because she gave him no information other than what I just revealed.

Darrell fears the only way he'll find Patsy's remains is if Larry is charged for her murder. So let's discuss Larry's possible involvement and our theoretic timeline, along with some facts of the case. After speaking with Maryann, Shirley's sister, Larry Calloway has no alibi. All of the statements made by Maryann were after Debra's trial and were recorded and sent to Kentucky State Police. She stated that Larry was never at Shirley's apartment that morning that she saw. I asked her if he could've been in the bedroom or bathroom where she didn't see and she said, "No. There is no way." So where was Larry Calloway when Patsy disappeared with Gene? Darrell believes that Patsy first saw Larry at the nursing home, because of the statement Michael Hertzog said. He testified that Patsy said, "My S.O.B. husband brought this girl in and wants me to have a threesome." Just because someone wasn't seen at the facility by others doesn't mean he wasn't there.

Darrell is adamant about Patsy needing another reason besides the marriage announcement, to lure her out of the facility with Gene. He said that knowing Patsy, she'd be extremely upset and livid if she found out Larry was out at the trailer with Shirley or if he was at the nursing facility with Shirley. Darrell believes that Larry, at some time in the morning hours, had to come to the facility near the time Gene showed up, in order to upset Patsy enough to leave. He believes he did this by asking Patsy if she wanted to have a threesome with him and Shirley, or that Gene had told him that's what Larry wanted. He also believes it was Larry that tampered

265

with Patsy's vehicle, because clearly she'd made it to work that morning just fine. Did he plan to meet up with Patsy and Gene at the facility under the ruse of fixing her battery cable? Maybe.

Let's assume for one moment that Darrell's theory is true, that Larry did come into the nursing home to bait Patsy. Darrell said, "That would make it more understandable for then Gene, to come in after with the marriage announcement and Patsy leave with him." Perhaps even Gene may have said something to Patsy in the nature of "Larry is with Shirley at your house." Darrell said knowing Patsy, she wouldn't just leave over something in the paper. It's his belief that Larry and Gene said or did something else to set her off. He said it would definitely take more than Gene waving a paper around to light her fuse. Also noting that Patsy's car was running that morning because it got her to work. So why wouldn't she just drive her own car? They needed to get Patsy under the control of Gene, so her car needed to "not run." Otherwise, she'd have been able to possibly get away from him if she was driving her own car.

We know that Patsy left with Gene that day and he ultimately killed her. Her murder was in fact facilitated by his then girlfriend Debra Calloway. We also know that there were others involved. We believe that Larry was the mastermind behind Patsy's disappearance and murder. After all, she wasn't supposed to be at work that morning, but was called in. If Larry wasn't at Shirley's apartment that morning like he claimed, how in the hell did he know that Gene left the facility with Patsy? He never saw Maryann and according to her he was never there. So he'd have had to have seen Gene and Patsy somewhere else, or he knew of the plan to kill her in advance.

In the first novel **An Arson, A Wig, and A Murder**, I discuss with Larry about Jimmy's statement that he saw Patsy's deceased body in the back of Gene's truck. He, not in so many words, told Jimmy that day at Hunter's trailer court, not to confront Gene about seeing Patsy's body. In court, Jimmy said, "I didn't want to end up dead too." Jimmy was never asked if he'd seen Larry on the day Patsy was murdered. Also, Larry stated after he'd learned that Patsy left the facility with Gene, that he went by her work; didn't see her car; and went over to his mother's house. Why then, did he not see Gene with his truck parked nearby and Patsy's remains in the back? Their mom only lived a couple of doors away. We believe he did see them and knew exactly why they were there. Why would he tell Jimmy not to confront Gene if he didn't know about Patsy's murder? Why did he not go over to Gene's house and ask Gene what happened to Patsy? Why would he generate false missing person posters regarding Patsy's disappearance?

My theories are as follows: On the morning of March 3rd, 1993, Patsy called into work to see if they needed help, which they did, according to Wanda Winkler. She then went to work around 5:30 a.m. Darrell and I believe that this threw a monkey wrench into the murder plans of those involved, because she was supposed to be off that day. Through one interview I did with Marla, Shane's then girlfriend, I learned that Larry Calloway borrowed her white car that morning. Why would he do that? It's my belief that Larry needed a car to transport Patsy's body that wouldn't be suspected by law enforcement. So, up to this point,

267

Patsy's remains were never found and it's never been disclosed as to who disposed of her, or buried her, and where her remains are in fact located.

We know that she left the facility with Gene Calloway at approximately 10:38 a.m. because of her punch card. We believe that Patsy was then taken to her home or trailer out on 1414 because of all the blood spatter that was found in 2012. Within moments after arriving at her home, Patsy goes in and we believe Gene followed her into the home where he then murdered her. I believe Debbie and Larry showed up and were waiting outside until the deed was done. A murder in Gene's truck in the middle of town is highly unlikely with so many other homes around. With the blood evidence in Patsy's trailer, it makes more sense.

Jimmy stated that Patsy's body was in black trash bags, coincidently the type that Debra claimed was all she used, when she discussed the locked box on the witness stand. Someone had to help clean up the mess at Patsy's trailer and get her into the trash bags, without dragging evidence everywhere in that house. We believe that Debra and Larry were there to clean up the mess. Then, while Larry was cleaning up the trailer, Debra and Gene put Patsy's body in the back of the truck and headed home to clean the truck and get themselves cleaned up. This is where Jimmy testified that he'd seen her body. All of this would've taken them about an hour and a half from the time Patsy left the nursing facility with Gene. That would put them at Hunter's trailer court around noon, which is consistent with Jimmy's testimony as to when he claimed to have seen her body.

At this point, we already know that they're cleaning out the truck. Larry is already headed to the police station to report Patsy missing. Initially I was told that he was there at 12:15 p.m. by Larry himself and law enforcement. In Larry's first interview, he said after he'd reported Patsy missing to police, he went over to his mom's house at Hunter's trailer court to stop an argument if one was going to occur. First of all, how did he know Patsy was missing if he wasn't at Shirley's apartment that morning? Secondly, why wouldn't he just go over to his brother Gene's, if he really believed that? He wouldn't, because he knew Patsy was already dead. Did Larry see Jimmy snooping around the back of Gene's truck and then tell him not to confront Gene? Probably, because he was already aware. The reason Larry went to police wasn't to report Patsy missing, but to establish an alibi.

Again, someone had to bury Patsy or dispose of her remains. We believe it was Larry, and somehow their Brother Charlie's name was brought into this by Debra and Rebecca Farmer. We believe that while Debra and Gene were getting ready to go to the hospital to see the baby and establish their alibi, Larry and possibly Charlie were out disposing of Patsy's remains. Why else would there be a cross carved into that tree? Certainly, Gene didn't give a damn about Patsy and he wasn't going to carve a cross. Larry however, was married to her for twenty years. He would have more motive to carve a cross than Gene ever would. He also had more motive to have Patsy killed than Gene, not only because of the arson, but because of the statutory rape.

269

So, Gene's truck needed to be cleaned, which Jimmy testified that he'd seen Debra and Gene taking the carpets out of the front of the truck and Debbie wiping it down with something like Purell. From there, it was told to Darrell that the truck was taken to the detail shop for Tim and Linda to clean up her dad's mess. The carpeting was already torn out. Debbie came up with the bullshit story in court about how someone fell through a hole in the bed of the truck and that's why the truck was taken there to repair all the carpet. It makes sense that Patsy's body had to be transferred into another vehicle at Hunter's trailer court or placed somewhere on that property. This is where Larry and Marla's borrowed car come into play.

Back in 2012, a mysterious caller, called Darrell and asked him to meet them at the car wash in Beaver Dam, KY. I advised Darrell not to go there alone, but he said he was armed and he'd be fine. He went to the meeting and the man informed him not to come around the other side of the wall. He then told Darrell, "Don't be afraid, I'm a friend." He told him that after Gene killed Patsy, he went to Larry and told Larry, "I done the dirty work, now you take care of it." At that time, the man told Darrell that Larry was in fact, the mastermind behind Patsy's murder. He said that Gene and Debra took the truck to the detail shop, while Larry got rid of Patsy's body. He said that Tim and Linda cleaned out Gene's truck. With that, he left and didn't say another word to Darrell. I asked Darrell if he'd recognized the man's voice, but he didn't. This mysterious witness is the lynchpin, because obviously he knew exactly where Larry Calloway was that morning and witnessed the conversation between Gene and Larry. It certainly wasn't at Shirley Calloway's apartment. I've always wondered if this mysterious man was a member of local law enforcement.

The biggest question now is how did they transfer Patsy's body? Who drove Patsy's car? Where was her car from 10:38 a.m. until 5:00 p.m. that evening? One theory is, that Patsy's remains were taken out to Andy Anderson's farm in the back of Marla's car, by Larry Ray Calloway. Obviously, someone had to drive Gene's truck and we believe Gene drove his truck to the detail shop and dropped it off, while Debra picked him up in Patsy's car. We then believe that they drove to the hospital together, in Patsy's car. They went in to see the baby, thus establishing their alibi. How disgusting!

According to Ricky, Gene's son, and Stacy his ex-wife, they only stayed at the hospital for about an hour. Also, Gene had asked Ricky to lie about the time they were at the hospital, according to his ex-wife. Matter of fact, Stacy threatened to divorce Ricky over it if he lied for Gene. The real time they were at the hospital was most likely between 1:00 - 2:00 p.m. Debra was seen walking near the school on Rt. 231 by Mildred Calloway Dunning around 2:30 p.m. Therefore, we'd deduced that Gene drove Debra in Patsy's own car to town, then let her out so she could do her walking, dressed up as Patsy. Then, we believe he later picked her up in Patsy's car around the corner, as testified to in court by Misty Gorby. Misty stated that Debra had told her that Gene picked her up that day by the IGA. Amy testified that she saw a woman that looked like Patsy walking that same route that day, right around that same time. Who knew their plan would backfire on Debra? Now, Debra wants everyone to believe that she's innocent in all of this and just "set up" as the fall guy.

Consider this... Shane said that he learned of his mother's disappearance by Gene, another no-conscience moment. He testified in court that Gene showed up at his mom's house, looking for Larry and that's when Gene told him his mom was missing. Shane said he'd just gotten home from work. We can deduce that he didn't go into his mom's trailer with no one home. He then left to go into town to start looking for his mom.

At some point, Gene and Debra had to go back out to the detail shop to get Gene's truck back and then get Patsy's car back to town. Gene had apparently already picked up the Chevy Blazer from the shop by the time he showed up at Patsy's house again and saw Shane. Even Debra stated that after they left the hospital, she and Gene went "looking" for Patsy, but she said she couldn't recall how she'd heard that Patsy was missing. Right! Shane never reported seeing Debra at Patsy's house, only Gene. So Debra was probably out somewhere driving around in Patsy's car at this point, perhaps Beaver Dam.

During this time frame, nobody seems to know where Larry is, or at the very least, they're not saying where he is/was all day. Shirley was never asked that question in court. Again, we believe he was out somewhere burying Patsy. That's why we believe the cross was cut into the tree on Andy Anderson's farm. How does that tie into the map that Gene supposedly was forced to draw out, according to Gene's statement to detective Whittaker? Well, back before the trial, Darrell was told of a witness who'd seen Gene out on Andy Anderson's farm, digging a hole. So Gene knew where they'd planned to bury Patsy in advance. That doesn't mean Larry took her there. He may have carved that cross to throw off law enforcement and buried Patsy somewhere else that HE knew of.

Remember, the witness thought Gene was digging for worms, but said the hole was the size of a grave. Just because there was already a hole dug out on the property doesn't mean Larry actually buried Patsy there. He could've put his ex-wife in an intimate space that was only known to him, somewhere that they'd never find her. Larry is smarter than Gene, obviously. He probably considered that someone would find Patsy's body on that farm and may have decided to put her elsewhere, which explains why after so much digging, and so many different searches with all means and tools, law enforcement have not found her remains, even with the map. For all we know, they may have left Patsy's body in the pond behind Gene and Debra's house on Hunter's trailer court, or buried her somewhere on Gene and Debra's property.

There was also testimony that Gene and Debra got stuck in the Mud College Bottoms otherwise known then as Frank Burton's farm, down by the river. We believe that Gene and Debra were disposing of the carpets and other belongings that were Patsy's, down on that specific property. After all, it makes the most sense. They're not going to wait around for days with Patsy's remains in the back of Gene's truck and him just driving it all over town with her deceased body in the back. They also couldn't throw away bloody carpets on routine trash day, especially with Patsy missing.

Larry Calloway testified that he ran into his son Shane in town, then later went back out to Patsy's trailer and waited there the rest of the night making phone calls. I've not heard from one person that says he called them, that is until Darrell and Patsy's family came to town. Tanya found out from her brother Shane. Later that evening, Larry claims he also went to the library and made up the missing person's posters that were directly deceitful, according to his own statements. Darrell believes the posters were made up in advance as well, to go along with the narrative they were all pushing. After all, he'd already testified that he knew she'd left the nursing home with Gene, so why then make up a poster that says she was walking down Rt. 231? Larry Calloway is caught in his own web of lies at this point.

Darrell Kessinger has tried to do everything in his power to get the court to barter with the defendants for his sister's remains, to no avail. All he wants now is to give Patsy a proper burial. He knows in his heart what he believes happened to Patsy and I concur with him. Two of the co-conspiracy suspects are now deceased. One is incarcerated on sexual assault charges and one walks free. The other suspects, after the murder, were never called into court to answer for their alleged actions.

Judge Judy always said, "If it doesn't make sense, it didn't happen." Well, I think we've laid out the scenario that makes the most sense. Everything we suspect, fits with the timeline of events as they were laid out in court. The question now becomes, "Will Larry Calloway ever be charged in the murder of his ex-wife Patsy?" We're hopeful. Darrell believes this is the only way he'll get the chance to put his sister to rest emotionally. He tells of nightmares that show him scenes of what happened to Patsy. It's the wondering that's the worst and it is relentless on him, which is the reason he refuses to give up and continues to fight for justice.

With all of the interviews and testimony Larry gave, it's clear to see he's lying about his involvement. However, many of the witnesses in her case are now deceased and many refuse to cooperate with authorities. Regardless, we know that Patsy is in heaven and one day, maybe not long from now, those people will have to stand for their own judgement by God Almighty. Until that day, we keep praying that Patsy will one day be properly laid to rest.

Personally, I'd like to add a few thoughts I have on the matter. From the beginning of Patsy's case to date, I continuously wonder about the initial lack of investigation in Patsy's disappearance and murder. With so many ties to Gene and law enforcement, it's easy to see why some people in that town don't trust the cops. Corinna Mullen was murdered by officers in the next county over. Heather Teague, whose name was mentioned among Gene's belongings and other information, was murdered on a beach where an officer just happened to sit at the other end, under very suspicious circumstances. Her mother still doesn't have all the answers. According to Jimmy's testimony, local police ignored his information from the very beginning that Patsy's body was in the back of Gene's truck on the very same day she disappeared. Any normal person is shocked by this. Are the local police there corrupt? You decide.

A few years back it came out in the local news that Judge Dortch had some sort of sexual contact with a defendant and that supposedly, that contact didn't affect the outcome of her trial. Yet they never revealed who the defendant was or what trial it was. We were wondering if it was Debbie Calloway. Debbie testified that Gene used to have her dress up in the wig and tell her to go have sex with other prominent men. She said he got off on watching. Was Gene her pimp? She told others that she "did what she had to do," in regard to Patsy's murder and in regard to having sex with those that Gene chose for her. One could deduce that he was pimping her out, perhaps even for "legal favors." It's not an established fact, just a possibility. The bottom line is, with so much corruption around that area and the lack of investigation in Patsy's case, Darrell is still left wondering with many more unanswered questions.

Darrell and I believe that if it weren't for Sergeant Whittaker and Prosecutor Tim Coleman, no justice would've ever been seen for Patsy. He is very grateful to them and Alan Lacey and also Judge Renona Browning. Darrell had no power to take anyone to court, regardless of what knowledge and information he'd obtained. So for their role in this tragic story, they emerge as the true heroes that deserve recognition. It took them twenty-one years to get a case before a jury, but they did it. That takes courage and perseverance... something they have in common with Darrell Kessinger.

Chapter Thirty-Two: Darrell's Chapter

While Darrell and I put our theories out there for the world to read, please keep in mind that we base those theories on information, statements, and testimony that has been given to us over the past 26 years. Much of the information we had, Darrell had inquired about back in 1993, when his sister first went missing. It took some time to confirm actual dates and such, but the information hadn't changed much in those 26 years. It has always been out in the public that Gene killed Patsy and had cut her throat. He'd basically dared the police to catch him. What has changed, is Larry's story and the narrative that she just walked away from her life, from him. That and the fact that he has no alibi and that he committed perjury in court. I still have the tapes, and Darrell still has the original missing person posters, but we're not the prosecutor.

Throughout the years, it has been very difficult for Patsy and Larry's children, as well as the rest of Patsy's family. The hardest part for Darrell to accept is that his sister is still out there somewhere and every time the police had a chance to barter for her remains, they dropped the ball, or the court system dropped the ball. That said, Darrell will never give up hope, until his sister is found, or until he takes his last breath.

Growing up around the town of Hartford was no country picnic for Darrell and his siblings. He said he could've easily ended up in a life of crime instead of having a military career and family. He chose his path.

Darrell wants to express what he went through growing up in Hartford, KY, in that he too, was molested. He revealed to me that not only was he molested by Curtis Calloway and Charlie Calloway, but his two cousins as well. When I asked Darrell about including this information in this novel, Darrell said "I'm not ashamed of it. That's their shame, not mine, and I dare anyone to say it didn't happen!"

When you're being molested at the ages of 4, 5, 6, and so on, you're confused and you don't really understand what's going on or what's happening to you. You only know that it doesn't feel right and you're terrified to say anything. Darrell said that what people need to understand is that, it was normal back then for children to be molested in that town, fifty plus years ago. There was nobody that the kids could report the molestation to. There was nobody to confide in for Darrell, except his sister Patsy. He said even if you did try to confide in adults, "Who would believe you?" He said that when he was molested by those adults, he was threatened with death. They said they would kill him if he ever told on them. He said that molestation in that town was a very common thing, especially in the area referred to as "Snow Hill." He said it wasn't only common with the Calloway's but many families in that town. He said that many people were more concerned about bootlegging and drinking or getting drunk, than taking care of their children.

He wants people to know, that as soon as he learned Patsy was missing, he knew it had something to do with the Calloway's, namely Larry, Patsy's ex-husband and his brother Gene. He said that this wasn't just about Patsy as a victim, but that his family has been victimized by the Calloway's, specifically, many times. Even his father Willis Kessinger had been beaten by the Calloway family, multiple times. He said his dad had all his teeth kicked out by the Calloway brothers and sisters. He said he witnessed it firsthand, where there would be 8 or 9 of the Calloway's on his dad, all at once. He said he told the detective of many molestation victims, of that generation of Calloway family, that have since been confirmed incidents, though we are not at liberty to tell their stories. He said that he knows there are more victims of this generation out there and he wishes they had the courage to come forward, and say it out loud. Darrell said when he was growing up on Snow Hill, child molestation was sadly, a common thing to happen.

Darrell wasn't going to let what happened to him as a child, dictate his future. I think that takes a lot of courage. Some other victims have begun to speak out and tell their story. May God give them the strength to follow through with justice. As a grown man, Darrell joined the Army and got out of Hartford, KY. Sadly, Patsy Ann Kessinger-Calloway never did. Darrell still believes that her remains are somewhere near that cross on the tree, up on Andy Anderson's farm. He said that in 1993, he pulled in to that farm driveway and immediately Larry acted like he'd never been there before and was sort of panicked by being there. In the future, Darrell and some search and rescue workers are hoping to search again for Patsy with ground penetrating radar and other equipment.

We do believe the Calloway brothers threw Debra under the bus, to be the only one to take the fall for Patsy's kidnapping and murder, but we also believe that's her fault. If she would come clean and told the truth about the whole events, she'd have probably gotten out of it. Darrell would certainly be able to forgive her and move on. We know Debra Calloway has the details of Patsy's murder and could possibly turn state's evidence against Larry Calloway, but to date, she has chosen to remain silent. Darrell has offered her several times, to go to the parole board and speak on her behalf, if she'd just give up Patsy's remains. She still remained silent. He's made several attempts to contact her and visit her in prison before and after her offers to talk, even in the county jail, but she refused his visits.

As of July 6th, 2019, Debra Calloway was released from prison. She walked out of jail without ever revealing the details she'd promised to give to Darrell. Now, she's on parole, but still is walking free and Patsy is still out there somewhere in the woods. In Debra's letter to Darrell, she made the statement that there is still a brother out there that could hurt her. Gene, and Charlie Calloway have passed on. The only two left who are involved that we know of, are Larry and Jimmy. Jimmy turned state's evidence and was a witness for the Commonwealth, so when I spoke of the process of elimination, the last person to magnify is Larry. He is currently incarcerated, so I don't see how he could be a threat to her. If she's referring another brother or to law enforcement? Those initial Hartford officers are deceased as well. What is she so afraid of? I guess she's the only one who can answer that.

Let's discuss the statements made by James Johnson to Darrell Kessinger after the trial. He told Darrell in emails that Debra Calloway told him exactly what to say on the witness stand, regarding Gene Calloway's mental status and ability to communicate, before his death. He admitted to Darrell that he lied on the stand. Darrell went to police with the emails sent to him by James Johnson, but hasn't heard another word about it. No charges were ever filed against Debra Calloway or James Johnson in regard to this matter. Again, we're not the prosecutors.

In her letter to Darrell, Debra talked about her faith in God. So Debbie, if you read this, I'm leaving this hear for you. **Luke 8:17 For there is nothing hidden that will not be revealed and nothing concealed that will not be illuminated.** May God the Father have mercy on your soul and give you the conscience to do what is right.

Larry Calloway is currently serving two concurrent 5-year sentences, for two counts of sexual assault, in which he plead guilty in 2017. More charges could be pending, but his plea agreement with the lesser amount of time to serve, reflected what he'd have been found guilty of at the time. Many of the charges against him were dropped or the witnesses backed out of testifying. He's never been charged in connection with Patsy's murder. He's set to be released from prison in January, 2022.

It was never our intention to make the police departments and those who took on this case seriously, to look like fools. There are specific officers who are

281

very dedicated to getting justice for Patsy. As in many departments, there are good cops and a few bad cops. Darrell and I have gotten a lot of flak from certain individuals who aren't interested in attaining justice. There are those people who couldn't care less if individuals got away with murder. I'm sure it is difficult to work in any police department, where certain individuals are not in compliance with the law, or in fact, criminals themselves. That would have to be a scary place to work, especially if those individuals were your superior officers. I'm not saying that's what happened in Patsy's case, just in general. Working under those circumstances has to be extremely stressful and scary. It takes a lot of courage to do the right thing. So again readers, you be the judge.

Darrell would like to send out a special thank you for those who helped in bringing Patsy's case to trial, especially Tim Coleman and Brian Whittaker. "It's not an easy path to do the right thing, but for those who spoke up and told the truth, thank you from the bottom of my heart. May God bless you!" – Darrell Kessinger

**Top Row: Willis (Dad), Phyllis Kessinger (stepmom)
Bottom: Patsy (Lt.) and Darrell (Rt.)**

Made in United States
Orlando, FL
31 March 2022

16363828R00157